The Bakassi Dispute and the International Court of Justice

On 10 October 2002 the International Court of Justice delivered the Bakassi Decision, which, among other things, excised the resource rich land and maritime territory of Bakassi from Nigeria and transferred its legal title to Cameroon. These two countries under the auspices of the United Nations established the mechanism of the Cameroon–Nigeria Mixed Commission to honour and implement their obligations under the ICJ decision. Over a decade later this volume brings together academics and practitioners to assess the impact of this decision and the challenges and issues that have been raised in the course of its implementation. Hailed by some as a model of preventive diplomacy and a blueprint for the future, this timely assessment illuminates the difficulties in imposing such controversial decisions and considers whether this type of Mixed Commission is an adequate mechanism for implementing them.

Edwin E. Egede is Senior Lecturer in Law and International Relations at Cardiff University, UK. His research interests are in the areas of: Public International Law; Law of the Sea; African Blue Economy; International Organisations, especially the United Nations; Human Rights and Civil Liberties; and International Relations. He has authored a number of books and journal articles on international law, the law of the sea and various international issues. In addition, he is a barrister and solicitor of the Supreme Court of Nigeria with extensive practice experience.

Mark Osa Igiehon is President, Oil and Mining for Good Global Forum (a centre of global expertise on the strategic utilisation of petroleum and mining resources to produce much good), and a Teaching Fellow, University of Aberdeen, UK. He has variously worked as a legal advisor within the oil industry. His research interests are in the areas of Oil, Gas and Environmental Law. He is the author of a number of articles in these and related areas.

The Bakassi Dispute and the International Court of Justice

Continuing Challenges

Edited by Edwin E. Egede and Mark Osa Igiehon

Routledge
Taylor & Francis Group
LONDON AND NEW YORK

First published 2018
by Routledge

2 Park Square, Milton Park, Abingdon, Oxfordshire OX14 4RN
52 Vanderbilt Avenue, New York, NY 10017

Routledge is an imprint of the Taylor & Francis Group, an informa business

First issued in paperback 2019

British Library Cataloguing in Publication Data
A catalogue record for this book is available from the British Library

Library of Congress Cataloging in Publication Data
Names: Egede, Edwin, editor author. | Igiehon, Mark (Mark Osa), editor author.
Title: The Bakassi dispute and the International Court of Justice : continuing challenges / edited by Egede Edwin and Mark Igiehon.
Description: New York, NY : Routledge, 2017. | Includes bibliographical references and index.
Identifiers: LCCN 2017030542| ISBN 9781472470621 (hardback) |
ISBN 9781317040750 (adobe reader) | ISBN 9781317040743 (epub) |
ISBN 9781317040736 (mobipocket)
Subjects: LCSH: Bakasi Peninsula (Cameroon)–International status. | Cameroon–Boundaries–Nigeria. | Nigeria–Boundaries–Cameroon. | Nigeria–Claims vs. Cameroon. | International Court of Justice
Classification: LCC KZ4565 .B35 2017 | DDC 341.4/2–dc23
LC record available at https://lccn.loc.gov/2017030542

ISBN: 978-1-4724-7062-1 (hbk)
ISBN: 978-0-367-88138-2 (pbk)

Typeset in Galliard
by Wearset Ltd, Boldon, Tyne and Wear

Contents

Contributors

Edwin E. Egede is Senior Lecturer in International Law and International Relations at the Cardiff University School of Law and Politics, and obtained his PhD in International Law of the Sea from Cardiff University Law School in 2005. He has authored a number of books and journal articles on the law of the sea and various international issues, including *Africa and the Deep Seabed Regime: Politics and International Law of the Common Heritage of Mankind* (New York: Springer, 2011) and (with Peter Sutch) *Politics of International Law and Justice* (Edinburgh: Edinburgh University Press, 2013). Recently, he was appointed as the United Nations Economic Commission for Africa (UNECA)/African Mineral Development Centre (AMDC) Consultant on the African Blue Economy. Furthermore, he has been appointed as an independent expert member of the African Union Commission Ad Hoc Experts Group, established to develop annexes to the African Charter on Maritime Security, Safety and Development in Africa (the Lome Charter) 2016. In addition, he is a barrister and solicitor of the Supreme Court of Nigeria with over 25 years' extensive practice experience. Currently, he is a member of the International Bar Association (IBA) Public Law Committee.

Mark Osa Igiehon is President, Oil and Minerals for Good Global Forum; Fellow, Aberdeen University Centre for Energy Law, and Principal, Aberdeen Commercial Energy Solutions. He is an international lawyer, commercial negotiator, corporate executive and adviser to governments and multinational corporations. Mark was in law practice before joining Shell in 1996. Mark left Shell International in 2013 after over 17 years' extensive international executive, strategic, legal and commercial leadership experience working across many jurisdictions while located in the United Kingdom and the North Sea area, Kazakhstan, Nigeria and the Shell Group HQ in the Netherlands. From 2007 to 2010, Mark was Managing Counsel for Shell companies in Kazakhstan and transaction counsel and co-negotiator for Shell in the two-year renegotiation of the Kashagan Field contracts and venture arrangements. He is an alumni of the Leadership Programme of the IMD Business School, Lausanne, Switzerland, and holds a doctorate awarded by Southampton Solent University and degrees from London Metropolitan University, the Nigerian Law School (BL, 1987) and Bendel State University. Mark for many years served as Shell Group's nominee on the distinguished faculty of Prague's CEELI/ABA Institute programme for judges and jurists from the former Communist republics. He has authored books and articles.

Tim Daniel is a solicitor practising in the City of London. He has represented the Federal Government of Nigeria in international litigation matters since the days of the 'Cement Armada' (1976) when 400 vessels loaded with cement for building military barracks across Nigeria threatened to overwhelm the port of Lagos. He is now a consultant with Cooley (UK) LLP, the successors in title to Hedleys and DJ Freeman, the firms in which he represented Nigeria over the years. He has acted in a number of African boundary matters and negotiated Nigeria's maritime boundaries with Equatorial Guinea, Sao Tome and Principe and Benin. Much of his practice is now centred around recovery of assets stolen by Heads of State and high-ranking officials. He is co-author of *Corruption and Misuse of Public Office*, published by Oxford University Press, the third edition of which is due to appear in the autumn of 2017.

Emeka Duruigbo is a professor of law and co-director of the Institute for International and Immigration Law at Thurgood Marshall School of Law, Texas Southern University in Houston. He is also an adjunct professor of law at the University of Ibadan, Centre for Petroleum, Energy Economics and Law (CPEEL), Nigeria. Prior to joining the legal academy, he was a senior legal counsel at Natural Heritage Institute, a resource development associate at LawFinance Group, Inc., and a Research Fellow at the Program on Energy and Sustainable Development, Center for Environmental Science and Policy, at Stanford University. He serves on the advisory board of the Institute for Energy Law and on the Education Advisory Board of the Association of International Petroleum Negotiators (AIPN). Professor Duruigbo received his Bachelor's, Master's and Doctoral degrees in Law and held academic fellowships at the University of Benin, University of Alberta, Golden Gate University and Stanford University.

Bayo Ojo, a Senior Advocate of Nigeria (SAN), was called to the Nigerian Bar in 1978. He later was admitted as a solicitor of the Supreme Court of England and Wales. He was Attorney General of the Federation and Minister of Justice of Nigeria when Nigeria formally handed Bakassi to Cameroon. He was until recently a member of the United Nations International Law Commission (ILC) Geneva, Switzerland, and Council member of the Section on Energy and Natural Resources Law of the International Bar Association, a member of the ICSID Panel of Arbitrators, Washington, DC, a member of the Panel of the Permanent Court of Arbitration, The Hague, Netherlands. He is currently a member of the Board of Trustees of the Chartered Institute of Arbitrators, London, President of the African Users' Council of the London Court of International Arbitration (LCIA) and Alternate Chairperson of the UNESCO Appeals Board in Paris. He holds an LLB degree in Law from the University of Lagos, Nigeria, an LLM degree in Law from the London School of Economics, University of London, and a Diploma in International Commercial Arbitration from the Chartered Institute of Arbitrators, London. He is a Fellow of the Chartered Institute of Arbitrators and a Chartered Arbitrator.

Nkwelle Ekaney attended Carleton University Ottawa–Ontario Canada from 1970 to 1974, and holds a BA (Political Science), a Bachelor of Journalism (Hons) and an MA in International Affairs from that institution. Ekaney has held senior positions in his country's diplomatic service, including Counsellor at Cameroon's Permanent Mission to the UN in New York (1978–1987); Director of Intergovernmental Political Organisations, Ministry of External Relations (1991–1997); Consul General in Paris, France (1997–2006); and Cameroon's High Commissioner to the United Kingdom since 2008. He has represented Cameroon in many bilateral and international conferences. His research interests include development issues and the law of the sea. He has published many articles on development issues, the Cameroonian media and African affairs, and has presented papers at United Nations organised seminars on the law of the sea. Ekaney is author of an ethnographic study, *Nninong Drums: The Search for Identity of Elum'Ekambode* (Yaoundé: Buma Kor Publishers, 2004) and is currently completing research for a forthcoming publication, *The Law of the Sea: The Perspectives of Cameroon.*

Hephzibah Egede is Senior Lecturer in Law at the University of Buckingham, UK. She is a dual-qualified lawyer with admissions in England and Wales and Nigeria. In Nigeria, she worked as a commercial lawyer in Chris Ogunbanjo and Co., and also with Mobil Producing Nigeria Unlimited (an ExxonMobil upstream subsidiary). In the UK, and prior to moving to the University of Buckingham, she taught International Banking Law and International Oil and Gas Law at the Cardiff Law School as well as teaching Environmental Law at the Schools of Engineering, Earth Sciences and City and Regional Planning at Cardiff University. She also previously worked with the ESRC Centre for Business Relationships, Accountability, Sustainability and Society (BRASS) and acted as lead researcher in Law and Your Environment, a project funded by the United Kingdom Environmental Law Association (UKELA) with Professor R.G. Lee (co-director, BRASS) as principal investigator. The project led to the establishment of the Lord Nathan Memorial Fund for the Environment.

Yoshifumi Tanaka is Professor of International Law with Specific Focus on the Law of the Sea at the Faculty of Law, University of Copenhagen, Denmark. He holds a DES and a PhD from the Graduate Institute of International Studies, Geneva (currently the Graduate Institute of International and Development Studies, Geneva) and an LLM from Hitotsubashi University, Tokyo. He is the single author of four books: *Predictability and Flexibility in the Law of Maritime Delimitation* (Oxford: Hart Publishing, 2006), *A Dual Approach to Ocean Governance: The Cases of Zonal and Integrated Management in International Law of the Sea* (Farnham, UK: Ashgate, 2008), *The International Law of the Sea* (Cambridge: Cambridge University Press, 2012; second edition, 2015) and *The Peaceful Settlement of International Disputes* (Cambridge: Cambridge University Press, forthcoming 2017). He has published widely in the fields of the law of the sea, international environmental law and peaceful settlement of international disputes.

Eddy Lenusira Wifa graduated from Rivers State University and was subsequently called to the Nigerian Bar in 2012. He then proceeded to the University of Aberdeen where he completed a Master's in Oil and Gas Law with Distinction. He is currently a Doctoral Researcher at the University of Aberdeen where he is completing his PhD on 'Risk governance in UK offshore wind energy: lessons from its offshore oil and gas industry'. He is also a Senior Partner at AccendoJuris, a Nigerian-based law firm. With awards and published articles, Eddy Wifa has proven to be an exceptional legal researcher and critical analyst. He is an astute contracts specialist with far-reaching proficiency in oil and gas law contracts. He is also an environmental law activist and an advocate for best global environmental standards and social corporate responsibility.

Mark Amakoromo is a qualified legal practitioner and was called to the Nigerian Bar as a barrister and solicitor in 2010. He holds a Master of Laws (LLM) degree in Oil and Gas Law (with distinction) from the University of Aberdeen and a Bachelor of Laws (LLB) degree from Rivers State University in Nigeria. Mark has practical experience in advising on different aspects of oil and gas law and has published peer-reviewed articles in different international journals. He currently works as a Law Lecturer at Niger Delta

University in Bayelsa State, Nigeria. Mark is also a member of the Nigerian Bar Association and the Nigerian Association of Law Teachers.

Ibiateli Johnson-Ogbo hails from Rivers State, Nigeria. She holds a first degree in law from Rivers State University, Nigeria, and was called to the Nigerian Bar as a solicitor and advocate of the Supreme Court in 2012. She is a member of the UK Chartered Institute of Arbitrators and holds a Master's degree in International Maritime and Commercial Law from the University of Swansea, United Kingdom. She is currently based in Rivers State, Nigeria, where she works as corporate lawyer for the law firm of Amachree and Wonodi.

Introduction

Edwin E. Egede and Mark Osa Igiehon

On 10 October 2002 the International Court of Justice (ICJ) delivered its decision on the merits in the Land and Maritime Boundary between Cameroon and Nigeria (*Cameroon v. Nigeria: Equatorial Guinea intervening*) case (hereinafter referred to as the Bakassi case). The decision, among other things, excised the resource-rich land and maritime territory of Bakassi from Nigeria and handed its legal title over to Cameroon. Prior to the decision, the Bakassi dispute was the source of long-standing conflict between Nigeria and Cameroon, which from time to time degenerated to violent armed conflict.[1] The factual circumstances underlying the dispute are representative of a number of simmering land and maritime boundary disputes across parts of Africa. Many of the border disputes across Africa are the legacies of the re-structuring of pre-colonial African structures by European colonial powers, which was done in most cases without proper regard to culture and physical boundaries of African Kingdoms and City-States pre-colonialism. The division of Africa appears to have been solely for ease of administration by colonial powers and access to the resources of peoples. The Bakassi dispute before the ICJ thus involved a close consideration of the role and treatment of pre-colonial treaties: in particular, what weight should be given to the treaties entered into by the European powers with pre-colonial African States and Sovereigns? The ICJ Bakassi Decision has generated much debate, particularly among African scholars, as it appears to discountenance the treaties entered into between the European colonial powers and the pre-colonial African States and Sovereigns. This remains an unresolved issue, which the ICJ decision did not settle but rather made more intractable.[2]

The decision and its aftermath are in some ways rather unique, for instance as shown in the exceptional mechanism of post-decision implementation, the Cameroon–Nigeria Mixed Commission, which engages the two countries and was established in November 2002 under the auspices of the United Nations. The Mixed Commission has, among other things, the following mandate: demarcating of the land border and delimitation of the maritime boundaries between the two countries; withdrawal of the civil administration, the military forces and police force, and transfer of authority in the zones concerned located along the border in the peninsula of Bakassi; demilitarisation of the peninsula of Bakassi; protection of the rights of the populations concerned; development of projects aiming at promoting the economic joint ventures between the two countries and cross-border cooperation. Since its establishment, the Mixed Commission has held several meetings and made progress in the implementation of the ICJ judgment. Further, on 12 June 2006 after intense negotiations the Presidents of both countries signed the so-called Greentree Agreement to establish the methods of withdrawal and transfer of authority of the peninsula of Bakassi. The African Union has hailed the implementation of this ICJ decision as 'a major event in the area of peaceful resolution of conflicts', showcasing it as a model for preventive diplomacy for safeguarding peace in Africa and pointing to it as 'a source of inspiration for all African actors involved in conflicts'.[3] Therefore, unresolved boundary disputes across Africa have many lessons to learn from the dispute.

The decision undoubtedly clearly raises interesting issues. For instance, is the so-called Mixed Commission an adequate mechanism to implement the ICJ decision and to serve as a template to be used in preventive diplomacy after an international court decision? In spite of the obviously interesting mechanisms to promote peaceful implementation of the ICJ judgment, such as the Greentree Agreement and the Mixed Commission, there have been some critical issues arising from the decision, especially with regard to the Bakassi Peninsula, which have caused passions to run high in Nigeria, especially concerning the perceived national shame of ceding this mineral-rich area to Cameroon. Some have gone as far as calling on the government to apply for a revision of the ICJ judgment. Others have argued that the outcome of the judgment in respect of Bakassi contravenes the 1999 Constitution of Nigeria, bringing up the important issue of the relationship between international law and municipal law. The decision also raises issues concerning the complexity involved in the case management of international litigation. Furthermore, it raises crucial issues concerning title to territory under international law and the impact of the decision on the law of the sea. It is interesting to note that the Bakassi Decision was the first decision to apply the United Nations Convention on the Law of the Sea (UNCLOS) 82 on delimitation of the Continental Shelf and Exclusive Economic Zone (EEZ), after the UNCLOS came into force. In addition, as result of the popularly held view that the Bakassi Peninsula is resource rich, it also brings to the fore the vital role natural resources located in disputed areas play in international disputes between neighbouring States. Certain Nigerians claim historical rights to live in the Bakassi area: could such Nigerians be regarded as indigenous peoples whose rights should be protected as required by international law? Additionally, there is the question of whether a joint development agreement (JDA) between the two States would have been a better option.

The book brings together a team of academics and practitioners with relevant expertise to critically explore the various issues raised above and pinpoint certain challenges and problems that have arisen because of the decision of the ICJ. The team of writers are experienced law academics, a number of whom have published widely, both academic books and articles in high-profile academic journals, as well as international affairs practitioners, some of whom have had practical involvement in the case, who have brought their wealth of professional experience and practical knowledge to bear on the project. In bringing together both academics and practitioners, this edited book also seeks to bridge the gap between academia and practice. The book, consisting of nine chapters, aims to examine certain continuing challenges in international law that have arisen from the International Court of Justice (ICJ) decision in the Bakassi case between Cameroon and Nigeria over a decade after it was published.[4] Chapter 1, written by Tim Daniel, an experienced solicitor based in London who was part of the litigation team on the Nigerian side, uses his experience with the Bakassi case to explore the challenges of case management of international litigation. Emeka Duruigbo in Chapter 2 explores whether Nigeria should have asked for revision of the ICJ decision before the expiration of the available ten-year window and engages with the issue of revision of judgments of international courts/tribunals. In Chapter 3, Bayo Ojo, who interestingly was the Nigerian Attorney-General of the Federation during the formal handover of the Bakassi Peninsula to Cameroon, using the Bakassi Decision and its implementation mechanisms as a case study, highlights the important role of preventative diplomacy in avoiding the escalation of international disputes. Nkwelle Ekaney, in Chapter 4, explores certain critical issues arising from the Bakassi Decision that are crucial to Cameroon. In Chapter 5, Hephzibah Egede engages with the issue of the indigenes of Bakassi who have a historical tie with the Bakassi Peninsula and explores whether they could be regarded as indigenous peoples under international law. Yoshifumi Tanaka, using the Bakassi Decision as a case study, in Chapter 6 explores three paradigms concerning the acquisition of title under international law. In Chapter 7, Edwin E. Egede, also using the decision as a basis for discourse, considers certain continuing law of the sea challenges, namely maritime boundary delimitation, certain domestic law of the sea impacts of the decision from the Nigerian perspective and the contentious issue of innocent passage of warships. Mark Osa Igiehon, in Chapter 8, recognising that the Bakassi dispute was not just a boundary dispute but also equally a dispute about access to the rich petroleum mineral resources of the maritime waters of the Bakassi Peninsula, explores the 'toxic' mix of various international disputes which involve both a contest for territory and mineral resources. This chapter is nicely followed by Chapter 9, jointly written by Eddy Lenusira Wifa, Mark Amakoromo and Ibiateli Johnson-Ogbo, which explores the importance of the joint development agreements (JDAs) for shared access to contested or straddling petroleum resources. The authors argue that countries in such disputes, such as that of Cameroon and Nigeria, will do well to carefully investigate the possibility of Joint Development Agreements and give this priority over international litigation.

Notes

1 See Hilary V. Lukong, *The Cameroon–Nigeria Border Dispute: Management and Resolution, 1981–2011* (Bamenda, Cameroon: Langaa Research and Publishing, 2011), pp. 1–60; Piet Koning, 'Settling border conflicts in Africa peacefully: lessons learned from the Bakassi dispute between Cameroon and Nigeria' in Jan Abbink and Mirjam de Bruijn (eds), *Land, Law and Politics in Africa: Mediating Conflict and Reshaping the State* (Leiden: Brill, 2011), pp. 191–210; and Olayiwola Abegunrin, *Nigerian Foreign Policy under Military Rule, 1966–1999* (Westport, CT: Praeger, 2003).

2 See, for example, Nsongurua J. Udombana, 'The ghost of Berlin still haunts Africa! The ICJ judgment on the land and maritime boundary dispute between Cameroon and Nigeria' (2002) 10 *African Yearbook of International Law* 13–61.

3 African Union Assembly Declaration of the Assembly of the African Union on the Peaceful Settlement of the Border Dispute between Cameroon and Nigeria: the Bakassi Case, Assembly/AU/Decl.1(XXII) of 30–31 January 2014, http://archive.au.int/collect/auassemb/import/English/Assembly%20AU%20Decl%201%20(XXII)%20_E.pdf.

4 It important to stress that this book is not intended to exhaustively engage with all the challenges arising from the case, but rather to engage with certain crucial issues, which in the editors' view highlight the fact that there are still some continuing challenges under international law several years after the decision and its implementation.

1 Bakassi case

Challenges of case management of international litigation

Tim Daniel

Introduction

I have been asked to write this chapter as the solicitor who was responsible for assembling and managing the legal team which argued Nigeria's case on Bakassi before the International Court of Justice between the years 1994 and 2002. Although the case is commonly referred to, particularly in Nigeria, as 'the Bakassi case', it was, as this account will show, a very much wider case, which was not confined simply to the issue of sovereignty over the so-called Bakassi Peninsula. The title of this chapter refers generally to 'international litigation', but its focus will be the Bakassi case and the challenges presented by that case. Those challenges will be apparent from the narrative account I give of the genesis and progress of the case during the years we were before the Court.

The Court is sometimes accused of being political. As the judicial organ of the United Nations such accusations are bound to be made. The 'permanent Bench' of the Court consists of 15 judges of different nationalities elected on a rotating basis each October during the annual meeting of the United Nations General Assembly. Although this process is designed to try to eliminate any suggestion of political bias, charges of such bias inevitably arise. This is particularly so when there is a case before the Court involving the historical colonial powers and their former colonies. Nigeria's former President, Olusegun Obasanjo, on whose watch the Bakassi case reached its conclusion and who had to deal with its aftermath, has much to say on the question of perceived bias in his recently published autobiography *My Watch*.[1] The account in this chapter will not attempt to deal with these criticisms, but it will hopefully show that every effort was made to present Nigeria's case in as comprehensive a way as was possible.

Litigating in The Hague before the ICJ does bring its own special practical challenges, as will be apparent from this account. These stem in large measure from the nature of the Court and its procedural requirements. This is a collegiate court, many of whose members have a distinguished background in academia and public life, but who may not have much, or any, litigation experience. This being the case, the pleadings are central. They are in many ways, both in appearance and content, like books containing academic texts. As such they require immense research into the historical aspects of the case and a scholarly approach to the relevant law.

Presentation of the case to the Court at the hearings requires different skill sets. Fifteen judges, supplemented by two judges ad hoc[2] chosen by the parties themselves create a mini 'audience' whose attention needs to be held over days and weeks of oral presentations, the purpose of which is to highlight and illuminate the content of the pleadings. In 2002 this was typically done by means of elaborate audio-visual presentations; the audio element being supplied by the advocates, the visual element by graphics, and sometimes, film, projected onto a large, cinema-type screen situated behind the advocate in order to give the judges a clear view. Nowadays the Court is computer-enabled, but it remains the case that this is a multi-media court, in which all the proceedings are permitted to be filmed by the parties, and in which a full transcript of the day's proceedings is produced in French and English by 7.00 pm each evening.

The background to the case

'On 16th May 1981 a Nigerian patrol opened fire on a Cameroonian vessel in waters off the Bakassi Peninsula and then tried to exploit the situation to shift the blame onto Cameroon.' This is the allegation that was made by Cameroon:[3] in fact the incident was completely the other way around. Following an unprovoked attack by Cameroon forces on a Nigerian army patrol boat which Cameroon alleged had violated Cameroonian territory, five Nigerian soldiers were killed. On 24 May 1981 Cameroon sent to Nigeria a Delegation to offer the regrets of Cameroon's President Ahidjo. President Shagari of Nigeria was not satisfied with this and President Ahidjo subsequently made a full apology to Nigeria and offered to pay compensation to the victims' families. This was duly paid.[4] Further research by the Nigerian team during the course of the case revealed that this 'incident' was almost certainly carefully planned, and designed to try to provoke Nigeria into a conflict with Cameroon.[5] One can only speculate on the reasons for Cameroon wanting to do that, but it may have been that there was a belief on the Cameroonian side that Bakassi was 'oil rich'.

This incident marks the beginning of a series of events which ultimately led to the doors of the International Court of Justice in The Hague (the World Court) in 1994.

The case widened to include not only the disputed boundary in Bakassi but the entire land boundary between Nigeria and Cameroon which stretches from Lake Chad on the fringes of the Sahara desert to Bakassi in the south – a distance of some 1,800 kilometres. Peninsulas are normally joined to the mainland from which they jut out into the water: Bakassi is not so much a peninsula as a group of low-lying islands divided by mangrove-lined creeks where the boundary enters the sea. The maritime boundary was also put in dispute by Cameroon for resolution by the Court. In the north, in Lake Chad, there was a dispute over where the boundary commenced and ran. This dispute came about as the result of the climatic changes which had caused a dramatic shrinkage of the lake in the 25 years before the case came to the ICJ.

In those 25 years the process of sahelisation had shrunk the lake from being over 25,000 square kilometres to less than 2,000 square kilometres, with drastic effects on the local population, who had moved across the lake bed setting up farms and villages as the lake receded. The majority of these people were Nigerians and many of them created settlements on the lake bed and became farmers, where they had previously been fishermen.

The result of the physical changes was to produce a question as to where the boundary now ran; originally the boundary had been drawn by the colonial powers when Lake Chad was still a lake.

In addition to these geographical disputes there was a long history of unrest in border areas and of incidents of varying degrees of seriousness, from cattle rustling to murder. These incidents became the subject of claims of State Responsibility made by each country against the other in an effort to win compensation for losses suffered. The claims themselves may be found in Part V of Volume III of the Counter-Memorial and Rejoinder.

On the land boundary itself there were some 17 disputed areas. The disputes had come about for a variety of reasons, including inadequate mapping by the colonial powers leading to defective delimitation and, according to Nigeria, the failure by Cameroon correctly to apply the delimitation agreed under the relevant treaties. These defects are set out in detail in Part III of Volume II of the Counter-Memorial and Rejoinder.

Referral to the International Court of Justice

The immediate run-up of the case to the ICJ commenced in 1993, when Nigeria, whose Head of State at the time was General Sani Abacha, sent in some 3,000 troops to secure the Bakassi area for local Nigerians. There had been an increasing number of incidents taking place, and Nigeria maintained that it was necessary to restore law and order. The arrival of these troops was inevitably characterised by Cameroon as an 'invasion' and on 29 March 1994 Cameroon lodged with the Registry of the Court an Application which stated that the dispute was 'essentially on the question of sovereignty over the Bakassi Peninsula'[6] and the 'maritime boundary ... up to the limit of the international zones which international law places under their respective jurisdictions'.[7]

This Application took Nigeria completely by surprise.[8] Nigeria had no inkling that Cameroon had signed up to the so-called 'optional protocol' which, under the Statute of the Court, allows States to accept the jurisdiction of the Court. The jurisdiction of the ICJ is voluntary, not compulsory. Thus either the States have to be parties to the Optional Protocol or they have to agree to take a dispute to the Court.[9] Nigeria had signed up to the Optional Protocol shortly after achieving independence, in 1964.[10]

Barely ten weeks later, on 6 June 1994, Cameroon filed a further Application. At a meeting between the President of the Court[11] and the representatives of Nigeria and Cameroon held at the Court on 14 June, Cameroon informed the President that this Additional Application was intended as an amendment to the original Application. Nigeria made no objection, and the Court, by an Order dated 16 June, directed that the Additional Application be treated as an amendment to the initial Application, and that it would deal with the whole as one case. Cameroon was ordered to file its Memorial by 31 March 1995.

In the Additional Application the Court was asked not only to adjudge and declare 'that Cameroon has sovereignty over the disputed parcel in the area of Lake Chad', but also 'specify definitively the frontier between her [Cameroon] and the Federal Republic of Nigeria from Lake Chad to the sea'.[12]

Nigeria was notified by the Registrar of the Court of Cameroon's Application in April 1994. In June, the former Attorney General, Chief Richard Akinjide SAN, contacted me in order to enquire whether we still had copies of a Report which had been requested by him ten years previously when he was Attorney General under President Shagari. That Report had been commissioned by Chief Akinjide as the result of the Bakassi incident described above. He had realised that there was uncertainty about the border and he wanted to try to ascertain just what the status of the boundary was.

At that time my firm had been acting for a number of years for the Nigerian Government, assisting them in resolving the issues which arose out of the so-called 'Cement Armada' which had paralysed Nigeria's ports in the mid-1970s. Extensive litigation had arisen following Nigeria's cancellation of some 85 substantial cement contracts.[13] Following the ultimate failure in the English courts of Nigeria's sovereign immunity plea[14] and the passing of the UK State Immunity Act in 1978, Nigeria was plunged into a series of arbitrations and court cases which went on for about 15 years. The result of all this had been that my firm was well known to the Ministry of Justice in Nigeria and so, when Chief Akinjide sought legal advice following the border incident, he came to us.

When he called I was able to tell him that, fortunately, I had taken copies of the Report and of all the research materials with me from my old firm to my new, 50-partner firm, DJ Freeman. I had moved to DJ Freeman in 1988, together with three of my partners from my former firm, Hedleys, which was a very much smaller (five-partner) firm. The increase in size and scope of the firm was to become an important factor in the preparation of the case for Nigeria, simply by virtue of the increased resources available for management of a case the size of which the Nigeria/Cameroon case became. Cases before the ICJ can be, and frequently are, conducted by counsel with a small team of technical experts. The size and composition of teams depends very much on the complexity of the case, how much research needs to be done, timing and the preferences of the governments concerned. Budgetary considerations may also play a part, but States will generally be reluctant not to commit the required resources bearing in mind the importance of the issues at stake.

Choice of counsel

In addition to locating copies of the Report, thought was being given to the composition of Nigeria's team of counsel. This is a key point in the preparation of any case going before the ICJ, or any other international tribunal, and it can be quite a challenge to find the right people. There had been consultation by the government with Prince Bola Ajibola SAN, who was at the time a judge at the ICJ.[15] A distinguished public international lawyer, he had been Attorney General under General Buhari's first government, as successor to Chief Akinjide in the Shagari Government. Prince Ajibola already knew the major players at the International Court, and had immediately been in touch with Ian Brownlie QC who was Professor of International Law at Oxford. Author of 'African Boundaries',[16] Brownlie had unrivalled knowledge of Africa and had appeared in more cases before the ICJ than any other practitioner.

The services of James Crawford SC, Professor of Public International Law at Cambridge, were also secured. Younger than Brownlie, who had been his PhD supervisor, he already enjoyed a considerable reputation.[17] In 2014 he was elected to the bench of the ICJ as Australia's judge.

To these two formidable practitioners the extremely distinguished Sir Arthur Watts KCMG QC was added, on his retirement as Legal Adviser to the Foreign and Commonwealth Office.

When taking a case to the ICJ it is important to remember that the Court operates in two languages, both English and French: it is therefore desirable to have an experienced French lawyer on the team. Such lawyers are not as abundant in France as they are in England; our first choice regarded himself as conflicted by virtue of academic articles he had written which he thought would be less than helpful to Nigeria. Our second choice became ill and was unable to continue: we were fortunate ultimately to secure the services of Professor Georges Abi-Saab, a distinguished practitioner of Egyptian parentage who was a leading academic at the Graduate Institute of International Studies in Geneva and a judge at the WTO Tribunal.[18]

On the Cameroon side, the team was led by France's leading public international law practitioner, Professor Alain Pellet; he was assisted by Professor Jean-Pierre Cot, now a judge at the International Law of the Sea Tribunal. They were joined by Sir Ian Sinclair, also a former Foreign Office Legal Adviser, Professor Malcolm Shaw of Leicester University,[19] Professor Maurice Mendelsohn of Oxford, and Professors Maurice Kamto and Peter Ntamark, from the University of Yaoundé, the only indigenous lead lawyers in either team.

Interlocutory proceedings and the progress of the case before the Court

In accordance with the timetable set by the Court, Cameroon duly served its Memorial on 16 March 1995. Written in French, it ran to 688 pages and had six volumes of Annexes. It had all the hallmarks of a document produced in a great hurry, with the result that, for example, almost none of the cross-referencing or references to Annexes were correct, and many appeared to be missing. It was a considerable challenge to make any kind of sense of it at all. I wrote to the Cameroon side with a long list of queries, which were ultimately answered.

The difficulty of deciphering Cameroon's Memorial, coupled with huge gaps in Nigeria's knowledge of issues which she had never hitherto had to address in any coherent fashion, meant that Nigeria's team desperately needed time to collect evidence and conduct interviews in Nigeria. At the same time, there were some very real issues which needed, in Nigeria's view, to be addressed by the Court before the case could proceed. Thus, Nigeria did not set about preparing and serving a Counter-Memorial immediately. Instead, on 18 December 1995, Nigeria filed with the Registry Preliminary Objections to the jurisdiction of the Court and the admissibility of Cameroon's claims.[20]

The effect of lodging Preliminary Objections was to stop the clock as far as the main pleading process was concerned. As we have seen, the scope of the case had been very considerably extended by Cameroon putting the entire land boundary in issue. It was also apparent that dealing with the sovereignty issues on Bakassi and in Lake Chad would require an extensive evidence-gathering exercise for Nigeria. Working out how this evidence was going to be obtained was the next big challenge for us as the solicitors, and will be dealt with further below.

Within two months of Nigeria's Preliminary Objections being lodged, on 10 February 1996, Cameroon launched a Request for the Indication of Provisional Measures under Article 41 of the Statute of the Court. This is the equivalent of injunctive proceedings before the ICJ. The reason for Cameroon issuing this request was that there had been a flare-up in Bakassi, with a confrontation between the Nigerian forces stationed there and the Cameroonian army. Exchanges of mortar fire had taken place and there had been casualties. The Cameroonians were keen to secure a cease-fire, as indeed were the Nigerians. Although there might have been talk among the Nigerian military of an all-out assault on Bakassi, this fortunately never materialised and both sides had been maintaining an unofficial truce which had been generally well respected.

Nigeria had very little time to prepare for the Provisional Measures hearing. Notice was only given two weeks before the hearing was due to take place. Getting a team over from Nigeria at such short notice was extremely challenging. It was as well that the hearings were taking place in The Hague because while Abacha was in power there were travel restrictions on government officials travelling to the UK.[21]

The hearings on Provisional Measures lasted for three days and involved both counsel (Ian Brownlie and James Crawford) and ourselves as solicitors. The preparations of the London team for the hearing had to be carried out at great speed, with many practical considerations, such as which hotel would house both the legal team and Nigerian officials, to be taken into account: these fell to be resolved by us as the solicitors.

The legal team was heavily dependent on receiving material quickly from Nigeria in order to put its case to the Court. The military personnel in particular brought with them copies of telex exchanges which had taken place between the two sides. It was also necessary for this hearing to obtain detailed information on troop dispositions, particularly from the senior army officers involved in the occupation of Bakassi. Although the initial application was made by Cameroon, Nigeria was not so much opposing it as keen to ensure that any Order made by the Court did not disadvantage Nigeria. In effect, this meant maintenance of the status quo on Bakassi. That status quo had developed into a de facto cease-fire line which was at the time of the Application respected by both sides. The Court's Order duly adopted that line, which held for the rest of the case.

There were obviously security concerns on both sides, each being reluctant to give away too much about their troop dispositions. It was necessary to understand the geography of Bakassi and quickly to familiarise ourselves with the main place names. At that time we only had one A4-sized map of Bakassi, which was photocopied from part of an Admiralty chart. It being an Admiralty chart, as opposed to a land map, there were almost no place names locating settlements on the peninsula itself. These had to be written in by me in manuscript based on the information given to me by the army officers. This rather home-made effort was the map which was used by the Court to make its Order regarding the cease-fire.[22] The Court's Order on Provisional Measures was made on 15 March 1996.[23]

On 30 April 1996 Cameroon served a written statement of its Observations on Nigeria's Preliminary Objections, but due to the exigencies of the Court's own timetable the oral hearings on the Preliminary Objections did not take place until March 1998, almost two years later.[24] The Court handed down its Judgment on Nigeria's Preliminary Objections on 11 June 1998.[25] Seven of Nigeria's Objections were rejected by the Court, and the Court declared that the eighth Objection did not have an exclusively preliminary character. The Court found that it did have jurisdiction to adjudicate upon the dispute and that Cameroon's Application and Additional Application were admissible. The eighth Objection concerned Cameroon's neighbour, Equatorial Guinea. Equatorial Guinea is a country divided into two geographical parts. The major part is the large island of Bioko (formerly Fernando Po, a Portuguese colony), which is opposite Cameroon's coast, and south of Bakassi. The lesser part is Rio Muni, a tiny coastal enclave on the mainland below Gabon. Nigeria correctly adjudged that any determination of the maritime boundary as between Nigeria and Cameroon would almost certainly have a potential impact on Equatorial Guinea's maritime space. The Court (correctly) declined to deal with this on the basis of Nigeria's Preliminary Objection, but stated that this was a matter in respect of which Equatorial Guinea itself might wish to make an application to the Court.[26] In due course Equatorial Guinea did precisely that, becoming the Intervener in the case.

On 1 July 1998 the Court fixed 31 March 1999 as the time limit for the filing of Nigeria's Counter-Memorial. But Nigeria was not done with interlocutory applications, and on 28 October 1998 filed an Application requesting an interpretation of the Court's Judgment of 11 June on Nigeria's Sixth Preliminary Objection, namely that: 'There is no basis for a judicial determination that Nigeria bears international responsibility for alleged frontier incursions'. Although the Application was genuinely made, it did make it possible for Nigeria to apply for a much-needed extension of time for service of her Counter-Memorial. This was duly granted and the time was extended from 31 March 1999 to 31 May 1999 – a vital extra two months. On 25 March 1999 the Court had declared Nigeria's Request for Interpretation inadmissible.[27]

In due course, on 30 June 1999, Equatorial Guinea filed an Application for Permission to Intervene in the case. The Court duly allowed Equatorial Guinea's request on 21 October 1999 after written statements by both Nigeria and Cameroon. The Court also fixed 4 April 2001 as the time limit for the filing of a written statement by Equatorial Guinea and 4 July 2001 as the time-limit for the filing of written observations by Cameroon and by Nigeria on that statement.

Also on 30 June 1999 the Court fixed 4 April 2000 for Cameroon to file a Reply and 4 January 2001 for Nigeria to file a Rejoinder. Cameroon duly filed its Reply on 4 April 2000, and Nigeria filed her Rejoinder on 4 January 2001, thus concluding the pleadings stage of the case.

It was just over five years following the lodgement of Cameroon's Application at the Court before Nigeria had to file her Counter-Memorial. Nigeria made good use of that time, as will become apparent below. The nine month time limit imposed by the Court for service of Nigeria's Rejoinder was very tight, but by that time we had collected most of the evidence we required and were in a good position to meet the Court's timetable.

The pleadings

Nigeria had been happy not to oppose extending the case to cover the entire land boundary because there did exist considerable uncertainty about portions of the boundary and it was felt that it would be sensible for both sides to cooperate in endeavouring to establish definitively the line of the boundary in order to avoid possible future conflict.

At a relatively early stage the case was divided up into five main sections. In both the Counter-Memorial and the Rejoinder Volume I dealt with Bakassi and Lake Chad, Volume II dealt with the Land and Maritime Boundaries, and Volume III dealt with State Responsibility and Counterclaims, as well as containing Nigeria's Conclusions and Submissions. Each of these topics was allocated a lead counsel; thus Ian Brownlie was mainly responsible for Bakassi and Lake Chad, Sir Arthur Watts was mainly responsible for the land boundary, and James Crawford was responsible for the maritime claims and state responsibility. However, each counsel critically appraised the drafting of his fellow counsel so that all three counsel both had input and knew what was being pleaded on each topic. Each counsel had members of the team working for them at different times; the drafts were based on materials fed to them by the solicitors, who in turn gathered the material from Nigeria and from sources available in the UK and elsewhere.

Each of the five main issues in the case could have been the subject of a separate set of proceedings. In many ways the team was dealing with five cases at once – all interlinked, but with quite separate sets of facts. All of these features made this possibly the largest and most complex case ever to come before the Court. Each pleading ran to several hundred pages: the Counter-Memorial was 835 pages long, and the Rejoinder 766 pages. The Counter-Memorial had eight volumes of Annexes containing 410 individual documents, running to 2,957 pages; the Rejoinder had six volumes, containing 225 documents, which ran to 1,857 pages. The production of such volumes required extremely careful planning. The Cameroonians pleaded in French, and Nigeria in English. It was thus necessary for translations to be prepared of each pleading. Cameroon's pleadings were also in excess of 1,000 pages in all: a considerable translation job, which had to be carried out quickly and accurately within the allowed time. Nigeria was fortunate in having in her team a partner at DJ Freeman who was effectively bilingual.[28] He was able to produce translations from French into English swiftly and to a very high standard.[29] In fact, such was the standard of his translations that the Registrar of the Court asked if they could be adopted by the Court as the official English translations of Cameroon's French pleadings. This was the first time that such a request had been made; it proved highly successful and has been used in subsequent cases where a party produces translations of a sufficiently high standard.[30]

Running a multi-disciplinary team of this nature required much organisation, and this was essentially carried out at my offices using a legal team consisting of two partners, two assistants, numerous trainees over the years and large numbers of paralegals. The paralegals were particularly useful in indexing the mass of documentation which was assembled. In all over 10,000 documents and maps were gathered. All of these documents had to be identified and indexed. This required painstaking work by the paralegals, carried out over the years in which the case was active. That archive became of course invaluable to Nigeria's team and was only possible with the advent of sophisticated computer technology, which enabled the documents to be scanned into the database and electronic lists to be compiled and the documents accessed with relative ease.

The production schedule was the equivalent of a major publishing exercise. In effect there was a nine-month period allotted to the preparation of each round of pleading. There had first of all to be the translation of the French pleadings of Cameroon, then a consideration of the content of those pleadings, then preparation of Nigeria's pleadings and accompanying evidence in response. Numerous meetings and interviews had to be held, both in London and in Nigeria, to discuss the content of both Cameroon's and Nigeria's pleadings. Then there was the actual drafting of the pleadings by counsel, and assembly and collation of all the evidence preparatory to the creation of the volumes of Annexes. Six weeks were needed for the actual printing, copying and delivery of the pleadings to the Court. When the case began, the Court required 125 hard copies of each side's pleadings. For Nigeria's Counter-Memorial this meant delivery of 6,413 volumes plus 250 copies of her atlas.[31] This was to ensure that there were not only copies for use in the Court during the hearings, but also archive copies, including copies to be sent to other States which might in the future be embarking on proceedings before the ICJ and need examples of previous pleadings. Nigeria herself was provided with such pleadings at the outset, which was extremely helpful. The documents which go before the Court have to be in a particular format, using bound volumes. All of this took considerable planning and preparation, with the use of outside contractors to do the binding. DJ Freeman's print room worked around the clock for the whole six weeks prior to the delivery of each round of pleading. Coupled with the physical production of the pleadings and annexes, there had to be constant proofreading and cross-referencing of texts. For the most part, there were three or four different authors, each working on their own part of the pleading. Inevitably there was cross-referencing between each part and this could not be completed until the texts themselves were complete. Nigeria was extremely fortunate in having as its three main counsel draftsmen of the highest quality who were able to produce drafts to tight schedules in a form which required very little, if any, subsequent textual alteration: this greatly facilitated the cross-referencing task. The secretarial team at DJ Freeman were responsible for the formatting and production of documents with a homogenous look and consistent in layout and headings. Again, this was a huge task, involving very long hours.

The atlas

In any boundary matter the use of maps forms an essential part of the presentation of the case. The maps used fell into various categories:

- Historical maps: these were to show how the portrayal of what are now Nigeria and Cameroon progressed from the art of cartographers active in the sixteenth and seventeenth centuries through to the maps produced by the colonial powers in the nineteenth and the beginning of the twentieth centuries.
- Modern maps: these tend to be those produced by national survey bodies, both civilian and military.
- Illustrative maps or graphics: these are maps produced specifically to accompany the pleadings.
- Satellite imagery: very useful for giving photographic images of remote terrain.

In London the team had been augmented by the appointment of Alastair Macdonald, the former Deputy Director of the UK Directorate of Overseas Surveys (DOS), which existed for 38 years from 1946 until 1984. The DOS mapped many parts of the world, focussing mainly on Britain's erstwhile colonial territories, which of course included Nigeria. The majority of the maps used in the case had been produced by the DOS for the Nigerian Government between 1965 and 1969 at a scale of 1:50,000. This scale was ideal for use in making up an atlas to show the eastern boundary of Nigeria with Cameroon in sufficient detail to enable identification of the physical features described in the treaty wordings. These included mountains, rivers and watersheds, as well as some place names.

In many instances, however, the names of settlements had changed or the settlements themselves had moved. This was particularly so on the bed of Lake Chad. Nigeria's team gradually came to include government surveyors from the border States. These knowledgeable people (both male and female) were able to update names for us and, in the case of the Lake Chad bed, to identify and give co-ordinates for settlement sites. All of this involved a considerable amount of fieldwork, travelling to what were often very remote locations with GPS equipment. Detailed information had then to be transposed onto the 1:50,000 topographical sheets. This was done mainly by Alastair Macdonald. It had to be done with pinpoint accuracy, because only in this way could anomalies be discovered and made the subject of particular land boundary claims. Again, such exercises only really became possible with the advent of Geographical Information Systems based on digital technology and the use of laptop computers. It was all pretty cutting-edge stuff at the time.

A graphic showing the different numbered sheets making up the map of the border appears at the beginning of the atlas: in all, there were over 60 sheets. Assembling these DOS topographic sheets was itself a considerable feat of research. It rapidly became clear that the Department of Federal Surveys in Nigeria was not able to supply a complete set – or, indeed, any – of the maps which had been made for them by the DOS.[32] The team in London had at an early stage identified the International Boundaries Research Unit (IBRU) at Durham University as a helpful body to become involved in the case.[33] This was particularly so as Durham had in its archive a fairly complete set of DOS map sheets covering much of the border.[34] Those sheets that were missing had to be tracked down to other locations, including the DOS archive situated at the headquarters of the Ordnance Survey in Southampton. The DOS had not in fact mapped the entire boundary, owing to the technical difficulties of overflying some of it.[35] The missing sectors were supplemented by the use of Russian military maps[36] compiled from Nigerian and Cameroonian map material gathered by the Russian authorities.[37] This is why the atlas has some maps in the southern sector with place names in Russian.

The northern and western boundaries of the Bakassi Peninsula are formed by a river, the Akwayafe, which flows into the Cross River estuary. The course of the river at this stage is studded with islands, and the description of the boundary in the 1913 Anglo-German Treaty contains detailed references to the islands between which the boundary weaves. No modern mapping was available to show this part of the boundary and it was therefore necessary to refer to the copy of the original treaty held at the former Public Record Office[38] at Kew, outside London. As with many of the colonial treaties drawn up at the end of the nineteenth century and in the early twentieth, a detailed map,[39] signed in this case by the German and English military surveyors who had carried out the field survey work, was appended to the treaty. That map was at a scale of 1:100,000, and had to be digitised and reproduced at the 1:50,000 scale required for the atlas. The maps were considered by the Nigerian team to be models of their time, and of sufficient accuracy to represent the boundary without ambiguity. Their use was not challenged by Cameroon.

Cameroon relied in her maps on French cartography produced by the IGN (Institut Geographique Nationale). Much of this mapping was at a scale of 1:100,000 and accordingly had also to be scaled up to match Nigeria's 1:50,000 mapping. In the end, a comprehensive atlas covering the entire boundary was assembled. Alastair Macdonald was the mastermind behind the production of this atlas. One or two of the sheets comprised integrated English and French mapping. The final versions of the atlas served as part of Nigeria's pleadings in the Rejoinder. They were printed on A3 sheets with wire spiral binding, enabling them to be laid out flat on the judges' desks at the Court during the hearings.[40]

The decision was taken to mark the boundary on the maps in the Rejoinder Atlas in an effort to 'to specify the frontier definitively' as stipulated in Cameroon's Additional Application. This is worthy of note because it was not usual for the DOS to mark boundaries on maps precisely because of the political difficulties that might ensue. The team thus had to create the entire boundary line from scratch. Cameroon also produced an atlas,[41] which helped to pinpoint where differences arose.

As time went on, other imagery, in particular satellite imagery, became available to the team. The team was joined in England by personnel from a satellite imaging company called Nigel Press Associates. One of their personnel, Dr Robin Cleverley, became an essential member of the team. He not only had satellite imagery knowledge but had previously worked as a petroleum geologist for BP. His knowledge and experience was invaluable in dealing with the maritime aspects of the case, involving, as they did, offshore oil fields. As the case went on Dr Cleverly worked more and more closely with members of the UK Hydrographic Office (UKHO), using specialist maritime boundary software which is now an essential tool for maritime boundary delimitation.[42] He subsequently joined UKHO and became head of their Law of the Sea division.

The physical printing of the maps comprising the atlas was carried out by a specialist cartographic company based in the United States, Maryland Cartographics. The reason for using that company was their expertise in handling the map presentations in the Court. Mention has already been made of the fact that the Court is a multi-media centre. Maryland possessed the specialist equipment required at that time to project the map sheets and other graphics onto the cinema-sized screen in the courtroom. Handling these projections was in itself a highly skilled task, involving a control board not dissimilar to those found in modern theatres. As in the theatre, all the projected images have to be cued in right on time, in accordance with the advocate's 'script', so that the images coincide exactly with the passage in the speech which is illustrated by the particular image.

Political background

The case before the Court began, as we have seen, early in 1994, shortly after General Sani Abacha, Nigeria's Head of State, sent the army into Bakassi. Abacha was the latest in the line of military rulers who dominated Nigeria's political scene almost from the time she achieved independence from Britain in 1960.

He has become known as the most notorious of Nigeria's military rulers. Brutal and corrupt, it was he who ordered the hanging of the Igbo poet Ken Saro-Wiwa and eight other Ogoni activists on the eve of the Commonwealth Heads of Government Meeting due to be held in New Zealand in October 1995. The resulting outrage caused Nigeria to be suspended from the Commonwealth. It is estimated that he looted $5 billion from Nigeria during the four and a half years he was in power.

Abacha died on 8 June 1998. This was helpful to Nigeria in the sense that it lifted from her the aura of a 'pariah State' with the concomitant hostility that that label evoked. General Abdulsalami Abubakar took over as interim Head of State, and Nigeria returned to the Commonwealth and was returned to civilian rule, which was achieved in 1999 with the election of another former General, Olusegun Obasanjo. Abacha never attempted to meet Nigeria's team; Abubakar did, and Obasanjo took a close interest in the case. He in fact used it as a springboard to negotiate maritime boundaries in the Gulf of Guinea with Nigeria's other neighbours, Equatorial Guinea, Sao Tome and Principe and Benin.

Those negotiations started while the case was still before the Court, and agreement was reached with Equatorial Guinea shortly before the hearings were due to take place. Agreement with the other two States followed within the next two years. The negotiations added considerably to the workload of the team while the case was on, but it made a lot of sense to conduct them while Nigeria had at her disposal all the expertise needed to bring them to a successful conclusion.

Mention should also be made in this section of General Yakubu 'Jack' Gowon, the victor of the Biafra conflict.[43] During his period in office, in 1975, Gowon signed the Maroua Declaration, which was a major stumbling block for Nigeria's case in that it consisted of an agreement made between the two then Heads of State, General Gowon for Nigeria and President Ahidjo of Cameroon, that the boundary should continue down the middle of the estuary of the Akwayafe River and Cross River, which lies to the west of Bakassi, right out to a point which was to the south of the southernmost limit of the Bakassi Peninsula. This agreement effectively continued the line which had stopped with the colonial treaties at the point from which Nigeria had to try in the case to fashion a revised boundary. It was of course extremely difficult for Nigeria to argue against an agreement which had been reached by Heads of State with full ostensible authority and in recent times. In the end she was not successful, and sovereignty over Bakassi was awarded to Cameroon. As far as the legal team was concerned, every effort was made to try to find a convincing way of nullifying the effect of the Maroua Declaration, including seeking an interview with General Gowon himself. That interview was conducted through senior Nigerian officials and lawyers, not with the London legal team. The upshot was that General Gowon appeared not to have appreciated the full significance of the line in the Maroua Declaration to which he was asked to put his signature by the surveyors on each side. It was, from Nigeria's point of view, a catastrophic error of judgement, the full significance of which only became apparent during the course of the case. Although some have claimed that the Maroua Declaration led to the downfall of General Gowon, it is doubtful that that was the sole cause of his being ousted in a bloodless coup while on a state visit to Tanzania.[44]

The Nigerian team

Nigeria's team went through a number of changes over the years. Every State which comes before the ICJ has to appoint an Agent.[45] This is the person with whom the Court communicates during the proceedings. Such communications include the setting up of appointments with the President of the Court to give agreed directions as to the future delivery times for service of pleadings, for example. The pleadings themselves are always delivered in the first instance to the Registrar of the Court, who then arranges for service on the other party's Agent at an agreed address, frequently the party's Embassy in The Hague. In Nigeria's case, the Agent was always the Attorney General and Minister of Justice, but the address was the Embassy in The Hague. Having the Attorney General as Agent provided continuity of office, but not necessarily of knowledge of the case. For this reason, Nigeria appointed as Deputy Agent Chief Richard Akinjide, who, although in private practice, had, as has been seen, a considerable knowledge of the case. During the course of the case, Nigeria had three Agents, one of whom, Bola Ige, was assassinated on the day before Christmas Eve 2001.[46] The Agent for the hearings, whose term in office straddled both military and civilian rule, was the extremely sensible and pragmatic Abdullahi Ibrahim SAN.

Chief Michael Agbamuche SAN was the first Agent appointed by Nigeria. By the time he was appointed he was already an elderly man and was largely a figurehead. The Ministry of Justice itself did not have the capability to handle a case of this magnitude and initially assistance was provided by the military. Fortunately, it was not long before the National Boundary Commission (NBC) was appointed effectively to administer the case in Nigeria. The NBC had far greater resources than the Ministry of Justice and is run out of the President's Office. The Director-General of the NBC was Alhaji Dahiru Bobbo, and he essentially became the contact person in Nigeria for the team in London. He was a very experienced administrator, extremely hard working, with an engaging personality, and very dynamic: he commanded respect and was a person who got things done. Such a person is a huge asset to any team preparing a case for the ICJ. Thus, not only did he locate and appoint personnel but he also saw to it that the field trips in Nigeria, which took place at this time, were properly organised and carried out.

The composition of Nigeria's team from time to time is recorded at the commencement of the various Judgments and Orders made during the course of the case. Two of the core members of the team were a law professor with an interest in the law of international boundaries, Anthony Oye Chukwurah of Imo State University, who also acted as a Boundary Commissioner with the NBC and who had collected many documents relating to Nigeria's boundaries, both national and international. There was also the Head of the Nigerian Institute for Advanced Legal Studies, Professor Ignatius Ayua. Professor Ayua's background was, however, in commercial law – Public International Law was a new discipline for him. Both were intelligent and helpful colleagues, but, like the other lawyers assigned to the team from time to time, none had specialist knowledge.[47]

In the early days the field trips were accompanied by large numbers of soldiers and there were convoys of vehicles numbering anything up to 30 or 40. Such was the size of these convoys that Cameroon at one point during the Preliminary Objections hearing said that she had feared that she was being invaded by the Nigerian army, when in fact it was the legal team on a field trip to a particularly remote and hilly part of the boundary.[48]

Sources of evidence

The principal source of material in any case involving colonial boundaries is what is now known as The National Archives at Kew near London, of which mention has already been made. In earlier days this was known as the Public Record Office (PRO). A huge amount of research was carried out at the PRO, looking at the colonial archive, which is very extensive. The research for the case was greatly assisted by having the earlier Report which had been prepared back in the 1980s and was very much based on the material at the PRO. The records at Kew typically include not only correspondence between the Colonial Office in London and the government in Nigeria, but also contain copies of treaties and maps. These historical maps can be of great significance. The staff at Kew are always outstandingly helpful when research of this kind is being carried out, but it does take time, as only three files at a time can be made available to the researcher. Again, the advent of computer technology has made the searching of the archives very much more straightforward. At the beginning of the case, many of the records were accessed through the use of card indexes. It is essential in a case of this kind to have members of the team who are thoroughly familiar with conducting this type of research.

Research was also carried out at other institutions, such as the Royal Geographical Society, the British Library, the Library of Congress in Washington, DC, the French Colonial Archive at Aix en Provence, the Berlin State Library and various university libraries. In addition to Durham, the library at the LSE was important, as it is there that the archive of the League of Nations is to be found. The United Nations archive in London also had to be checked.[49]

Extensive research in Nigeria was also carried out and was on occasion quite challenging, particularly where the detailed evidence required for effectivités (see 'Effectivités', below) was concerned. Regional archives are not a high economic priority and seldom have electricity, let alone computerised records. All searches had to be done using record books compiled in manuscript, the only key to which were the (usually aging, but very knowledgeable) archivists themselves. In Enugu I found that much of the archive I wanted to see had been eaten by termites.

The sovereignty disputes

At either end of the boundary, Lake Chad in the north and Bakassi in the south, the dispute was over sovereignty, i.e. was the territory part of Nigeria or part of Cameroon, and to which of those two countries did the local population owe their allegiance? Sovereignty can be shown in a number of ways. Maps are clearly an important aspect but they do not tell the whole story. It is necessary also to go into the history in detail and, in this case, the relevant history begins largely with the colonial era and the division of Africa between the European powers.

Nigeria also endeavoured to introduce as much local history as she could in order to demonstrate the strong tribal affiliations that existed before the colonial era. Such information was not easy to come by and the team were reliant on accounts given by early explorers, as by and large there was no written history pertaining to the areas in question.[50] Three colonial powers had been involved in the division of Nigeria and Cameroon. Initially, in broad terms, Britain had colonised Nigeria and Germany colonised what was then known as Kamerun. It was necessary to look at the colonial era up to the outbreak of the First World War, and then, after Germany lost the war, the boundary area became a

League of Nations mandated territory with administration of the former German colony passing to the French. Thus, French is still the national language for much of Cameroon. After the Second World War the boundary area became a United Nations Trust territory. Both the League of Nations and the United Nations have archives relating to the periods of the Mandate and the Trust. These also had to be researched.

In July 1961 a plebiscite organised by the UN was held in both the northern and southern parts of the jointly administered territory in order for the local inhabitants to say whether they wanted to become a part of Nigeria or of Cameroon. Much to everyone's surprise, the North went with Nigeria, and the South with Cameroon. The team scrutinised those results closely.

Effectivités

Perhaps the most telling evidence of sovereignty is the hard evidence produced by administration of territory. This was looked at in great detail by the Nigerian team. Cameroon was asserting sovereignty over Bakassi and Lake Chad by virtue of the treaty evidence, Nigeria asserted such sovereignty by virtue of having been the de facto administration in both areas. The challenge therefore was to produce evidence of which side was actually conducting the administration. In order to do this it was necessary to examine many aspects of local administration. This was the main thrust of the field trips which were conducted both in the Bakassi area and in and around Lake Chad. Sovereignty was also an issue at some of the disputed areas on the land boundary, but tended to be much more limited, being confined perhaps to the administration of a particular village or, in one or two cases, a town.

Key to Nigeria's claim to sovereignty over Bakassi and Lake Chad was the concept of historical consolidation of title. This has been described as the continuous display of title as evidenced by recognition, acquiescence, possession, administration, affiliations of inhabitants in the disputed territory, geographical considerations, economic considerations and historical considerations. In order to demonstrate these historical and administrative links it was necessary to examine closely the history of the areas in question and the pattern of administration.

Thus, in the case of Bakassi the elements of historical consolidation of Nigerian title included the following:

i The original title of the city states of old Kalabar
ii The attitude and affiliations of the population of Bakassi
iii The toponomy of Bakassi
iv The administration of Bakassi as part of Nigeria in the period 1913 to 1960
v The exercisable authority by tradition or rulers
vi The jurisdiction of customary law courts
vii The settlement of nationals of the claimant state (Nigeria)
viii Acts of administration by Nigeria after independence in 1960.

This last heading included the following aspects of administration:

a The evidential sources
b The maintenance of public order and the investigation of crime
c Taxation

d The exercise of ecclesiastical jurisdiction
e Delimitation of electoral wards
f Participation in Parliamentary elections
g Census taking
h Public works and development administration
i The exercise of military jurisdiction
j Public education
k Provision for public health
l The granting of oil exploration permits and production agreements
m The Rio del Rey port
n The collection of customs duties
o The use of Nigerian passports by residents of the Bakassi Peninsula
p Immigration
q Local administration
r Internal Nigerian state rivalry over Bakassi.

Evidence under each of these headings required visits to be made to local government offices, courts, police stations, military outposts, tax and customs offices, schools, medical centres, the local postal offices, and archives containing census records. These tended to be quite spread out and frequently divided between different centres. Documentary evidence needed to be gathered up, copied and returned to the offices from which they came. Statements had to be taken from officials, local Chiefs and Headmen. Photographs were taken of many of these witnesses. Digital photography using, for example, mobile telephones would have greatly facilitated these tasks, but had not at that time come onto the scene.

The copy documents contained in Nigeria's Annexes are witness to the detail and depth of information obtained. Cameroon were quite unable to match it. Unfortunately the Court remained unpersuaded, ruling that the treaty lines were definitive, no matter what the reality was on the ground.

The land boundary

The land boundary also presented particular challenges. The main treaty document was the Thomson/Marchand Declaration. Drawn up by the British and French in 1929–1931, it provided a detailed clause-by-clause description of the course of the boundary. It consisted of more than 100 clauses, each one containing a detailed description of the course of the boundary over the terrain in question. This included watersheds, rivers, rocks and even trees. It was necessary for the team to identify all these features on the topographical sheets, in so far as that was possible, and, in the cases of the greatest doubt, to visit the locations in question in order to check out how the land actually lay.

There were frequent meetings between Alastair Macdonald and Sir Arthur Watts, counsel responsible for drafting the land boundary part of the pleading. In addition to those meetings in London, Alastair Macdonald and an assistant solicitor and sometimes one of the partners would meet with members of the NBC in Nigeria in order to go through the topographical maps sheet by sheet, projecting the images of the maps onto large screens and painstakingly going through the features and the description contained in the treaty. These meetings were always attended on the Nigerian side by local government surveyors, who had a detailed – and often encyclopaedic – knowledge of the areas in question and were able to provide much useful additional information, particularly regarding the movement of people in the areas in question and whether or not settlements were in fact on the 'correct' side of the line, or whether roads actually followed the boundary or deviated, purporting to form a boundary different from the one described in the treaty.

Assiduous research at Kew in particular yielded additional material in the form of sketch maps and notes made by the surveyors who originally drew up the clauses in the treaty. These were invaluable for reviewing decisions – and, in some cases, mistakes – made.

Ultimately, as mentioned, the team, led by Alastair Macdonald assisted by the cartographers from Durham University in the early stages, and subsequently using digital GIS technology on laptops, was able to produce a putative boundary line on the 1:50,000-scale maps. This was the line which Nigeria maintained should be the boundary in accordance with the relevant articles in the treaty. The description in each treaty article appeared on the map sheets so that it was possible, with assistance from Alastair Macdonald in particular, for the Court to follow on the maps what was being described in the treaty. This was a process which was rehearsed over a period of months and years, as Alastair gave presentations to NBC officials and local surveyors. Those sessions were often lively discussion meetings.

In addition to showing where Nigeria thought the line should be drawn (in red), there was a blue line which was Nigeria's best effort at drawing the line put forward by Cameroon. This was necessary because, initially, Cameroon was extremely reluctant to be specific about where the line ran. Ultimately Cameroon did produce its own atlas which made it possible to compare both lines, and a composite atlas was produced by Nigeria which highlighted the differences between the two parties. Where those differences appeared on the maps, the Court was ultimately taken through them and these provided the focal point for the arguments before the Court.

The differences arose not only as the result of local custom and practice – i.e. where people from one side or the other actually established their settlements – but also from mistakes made by the early surveyors. Where settlements had come into being in apparent contradiction to the terms of the treaty, it was often the case that practical considerations had prevailed, such as the necessity to travel to market, draw water, etc. It should always be borne in mind that the peoples on either side of the border frequently knew each other extremely well and, for the most part, lived a peaceful co-existence, with their families frequently inter-marrying. The vast majority of the border was like that and it was only in a very small number of places that differences over the course of the boundary had led to actual disputes, and in some cases fighting and even murder. Such instances were fortunately few.

The meticulous work carried out by Nigeria's team paid dividends: Nigeria prevailed on all but three of the disputed land boundary segments.

Maritime boundary

Offshore

One of the great myths that arose around the case was that the Bakassi Peninsula itself was 'oil rich'. It was always referred to as such in the Nigerian press. In fact, the team established fairly early on, through research into oil company records, that this was not the case and that all that existed below the surface of Bakassi was a certain amount of gas, which was not present in commercial quantities. That picture changed the further out to sea one went and there were indeed some large offshore fields which were close to the boundary. This was without a doubt the most valuable part of the boundary in economic terms.

The offshore area below Bakassi was the subject of a de facto, informal, line drawn by the oil companies with concessions in the area. The official data for the Nigerian fields is held by the Department for Petroleum Resources, and the officials there were always extremely helpful in explaining exactly where fields lay, giving precise co-ordinates for the limits of the fields. This is commercially sensitive information which is not normally released. Negotiations had to take place with senior management in the oil companies at their offices in Lagos or Port Harcourt. The visits to the oil companies were always amicable – it is a fairly tightknit community, with the operators in the region knowing each other well.

The oil fields along this line represent more or less the easternmost limit of prospective offshore fields. This is because of the volcanic chain comprising basalt rock formations running from Mount Cameroon through the Equatorial Guinean island of Bioko to Sao Tome and Principe and on to Annobon. Cameroon was desperate to try to achieve through the proceedings what it termed an 'equitable solution'. By this Cameroon meant, effectively, that the offshore area should be divided up into blocks in such a way that Cameroon would receive at least a share of the offshore fields. Cameroon was undoubtedly geographically disadvantaged and was desperate to try to increase offshore oil production. When judgment in the case had been given in October 2002, a senior member of Cameroon's team said to Nigeria's Agent that while Cameroon might have won the argument on sovereignty over Bakassi, she had lost the economic argument. He was right: the rejection of Cameroon's arguments meant that even at that time Nigeria's reserves in the disputed area were worth in excess of US$30 billion to her.

The other player in this scenario was Equatorial Guinea who, as mentioned above, intervened in the case. Their most valuable oil field, the Zafiro (Sapphire) Field, actually straddles the boundary with Nigeria. Separate negotiations took place between Nigeria and Equatorial Guinea while the case was in progress, in order to establish a maritime boundary line between the two countries. This, as mentioned, was successfully achieved in 2001, shortly before the hearings took place. Thus, by the time the Court came to deal with Equatorial Guinea's Intervention, Nigeria and Equatorial Guinea had resolved their boundary issues, which simplified the situation. Where a party intervenes, it does so in order to make its position known to the Court, so that the Court should not infringe on its space by whatever Order the Court makes. This gives the Intervener a right of audience, but the Intervener does not generally agree to be bound by whatever decision the Court reaches, because it is not a party to the main proceedings. The boundary between Nigeria and Equatorial Guinea is thus now established by treaty, although there is some uncertainty over the end point of the boundary. The maritime boundary is a prolongation of the land boundary; it was thus critical to determine where the boundary ran through Bakassi.

Nigeria's technical depiction of the offshore area was largely in the hands of the UKHO, whose Law of the Sea specialist, Commander Chris Carlton, became a valued member of the team. Other specialists were provided on the Nigerian side by the Nigerian National Petroleum Corporation (NNPC) and, in particular, the Department of Petroleum Resources (DPR). James Crawford of counsel was, as mentioned, in overall charge of the maritime boundary part of the case.

Bakassi

As far as Bakassi itself was concerned, Nigeria found herself in the position of having to 'create' a boundary. The wording of the colonial treaties of 1911 and 1913 were clear, and unhelpful to Nigeria's contention that Bakassi belonged to Nigeria. However, the treaty line actually stopped at a point in the estuary of the Akwayafe/Cross River which forms the northern boundary of Bakassi. From that point Nigeria constructed a line running through a convoluted but continuous line of creeks to the head of a creek known since the nineteenth century as the course of the Rio del Rey. This was the first boundary identified by Victorian explorers: it only became apparent at a later date that the so-called Rio del Rey was in reality only a creek, which led nowhere.

The Judgment followed the treaty lines, as extended by the Maroua Declaration, thus awarding sovereignty over Bakassi to Cameroon.

State responsibility claims

Cameroon, in its Memorial and Reply, raised a whole series of incidents which were alleged to have taken place on or near the boundary, and in respect of which it claimed Nigeria bore state responsibility. Each one of those incidents had to be investigated by Nigeria. Many of them took place in very remote locations and gathering evidence about them was not straightforward. This was particularly so when many of them were supposed to have occurred in the distant past. On closer examination, Nigeria found that the great majority of the allegations made were without merit, because they related to unspecified locations, were in localities unconnected with the dispute and were unsupported by first-hand evidence. In the instances where incidents were found to have taken place, Nigeria characterised them as 'trivial, occasional and ephemeral'. Nigeria also found that neither persons nor property had been harmed, and that for the most part the incidents had been resolved locally at the time, or subsequently by agreement between the two States.[51]

The Court took a similar view, and in its Judgment basically dismissed the state responsibility claims and counterclaims as cancelling each other out and not being sufficiently proven to merit a ruling by the Court.[52]

The Court's Judgment of 10 October 2002 and subsequent developments

As has been indicated above, Nigeria lost the arguments on sovereignty over Bakassi and Lake Chad. She won all but three of the land boundary claims, thus acquiring sovereignty over some 17,000 hectares of territory; Cameroon won 4,000 hectares. Cameroon's attempts to acquire sovereignty over large maritime areas south of Bakassi were rejected in their entirety. The Court rejected all state responsibility claims on both sides.

A maritime boundary between Nigeria and Cameroon was established, the end-point of which has yet to be determined, involving, as it does, a tri-point with Equatorial Guinea. Nigeria maintains that the calculation of the median line adopted by the Court is flawed, but only by a few hundred metres – not enough to merit a return to the Court.

A definitive land boundary was also for the most part established. The UN set up a Mixed Commission to produce a definitive map of the boundary and to iron out any remaining uncertainties. Some of these uncertainties have arisen as the result of what Nigeria maintains were the result of a flawed understanding by the Court of the technical evidence presented by Nigeria. The Mixed Commission consisted of representatives of both States and a UN Commissioner, Ambassador Ould Abdallah of Mauretania. The Mixed Commission worked with a UN-led cartographic team to produce a definitive boundary map, using satellite imagery. The work of the Mixed Commission is the subject of a separate chapter in this book.[53]

As far as Lake Chad was concerned, notice of the Judgment and its effect was given to the local population. All Nigerian citizens were given the opportunity to resettle, or remain living under Cameroonian sovereignty, like many of their fellow countrymen.[54]

Bakassi has been the subject of a far more protracted post-judgment process, involving the UN and the drawing up of a formal agreement.[55] This agreement led to a peaceful withdrawal of Nigerian troops and of the Nigerian Administration from Bakassi. The troop withdrawal was finally accomplished on 14 August 2006. An excellent account of the whole political process involved is given in former President Obasanjo's autobiography.[56]

Impact of the case and subsequent jurisprudence

Citations of the case have mainly taken place in the area of maritime delimitation and are the subject of a separate chapter in this book.[57] The impact on international law and sovereignty is also dealt with in a separate chapter.[58] Brief mention has also been made of the impact of the case on the procedure of the ICJ. Practice Directions IV (Use of translations), V (Time-limits for Preliminary Objections) and VI (Subject matter of oral statements before the Court), came into effect in October 2001,[59] and could all be said to have been given, at least in part, as the result of the Court's experience in the case.

There can be little doubt that the Nigeria/Cameroon case was one of the most complex and challenging boundary cases to come before the ICJ. This was so not only in terms of the variety of the terrain involved, some of which is extremely remote, but also, and particularly, in terms of the detail and lack of accessibility of the evidence which Nigeria had to adduce in support of its arguments on effectivités, and state responsibility. The long-term ramifications of the case as far as Nigeria has been concerned include the concerted efforts by the National Boundary Commission and its surveyors to undergo training, particularly under the auspices of the International Boundaries Research Unit at the University of Durham (it is still probably the only such dedicated institution of its kind in the world). Many practical lessons were learned from the case, and it will be good if Nigeria's newfound expertise in this area can be put to use, not only in and around Nigeria, but also in other parts of Africa where there is a need for boundary expertise.

Notes

1 *My Watch* (Lagos: Prestige, 2014). See, in particular, Volume 2, *Political and Public Affairs*, pp. 279–287.

2 Under Article 31 of the Court Statute each party is entitled to appoint a judge ad hoc where it does not have a judge of its own nationality on the Court. Such a judge may be a national of the party (or of a nationality closely associated with the party). Ideally, they will have had judicial experience in the field of public international law. Their function is to provide the bench sitting on a particular case with 'local' knowledge regarding the background to the case. They will frequently, but not invariably, give a judgment supporting the party that has appointed them, but their bias is expected. It is my belief that they fulfil a very useful function, providing context for the bench, whose members may be from cultures totally alien to the parties.

3 Cameroon Memorial paras 6.13–6.27. All the pleadings appear in pdf format on the ICJ website, www.icj-cij.org/en/case/94.

4 Nigerian Counter-Memorial paras 24.65–24.67. Nigeria was able to exhibit not only the correspondence exchanged between the two Presidents, but also the cheque, which was for $48,000.
5 See Nigeria's Rejoinder Volume 3 (State Responsibility) pp. 611–615 and 631–640, esp. para. 41.
6 Application para. 1.
7 Application para. 20.
8 It became to be widely believed that the reference to the Court was the result of a discussion Cameroon had with the then President of the Court, Mohammed Bedjaoui of Algeria.
9 Statute of the International Court of Justice, Article 36; www.icj-cij.org/en/statute.
10 This 'ambush' was subsequently the subject of Nigeria's First Preliminary Objection (see below). The Optional Protocol is dated 3 March 1994 and Cameroon's Application was dated 29 March 1994. States now commonly insert wording which requires at least one year from lodgement of a Protocol before an Application is filed. See, e.g., Australia's Protocol, www.icj-cij.org/en/declarations.
11 President Bedjaoui.
12 Additional Application para. 17 (f).
13 Each contract was for 250,000 tonnes of Portland cement ordered to build military barracks all around the country. Nigeria was enjoying newfound wealth in the wake of the hike in oil prices initiated by OPEC in the early 1970s. Many other oil-producing States finding themselves in the same position had embarked on massive infrastructure projects, necessitating the purchase of large quantities of cement, leading to a worldwide shortage of cement. Nigeria was advised to order approximately ten times as much cement as she actually needed in order to ensure delivery of the amount she required. The result was that by the beginning of 1976 there were over 400 ships waiting to discharge cement at Lagos/Apapa, which could at that time discharge only one cement vessel a week.
14 See *Trendtex Trading Corporation v. Central Bank of Nigeria* [1977] 2 *WLR*.
15 Bola Ajibola was Nigeria's judge at the ICJ from 1991 to 1994.
16 Ian Brownlie, with the assistance of Ian R. Burns, *African Boundaries: A Legal and Diplomatic Encyclopedia* (London: C. Hurst, 1979).
17 His doctoral thesis was *The Creation of States in International Law* (Oxford: Oxford University Press, second edition, 2007).
18 For more on Georges Abi-Saab see http://legal.un.org/avl/faculty/Abi-Saab.html.
19 Author of *Title to Territory in Africa: International Legal Issues* (Oxford: Clarendon Press, 1986).
20 The Preliminary Objections are available on the ICJ website at www.icj-cij.org/docket/files/94/8598.pdf.
21 Meetings with the London team had to be held either in The Hague or in Geneva during this period.
22 All of this was to change during the course of the proceedings, as digital mapping became available, making it possible for our technical experts to create maps on their laptops.
23 Request for the Indication of Provisional Measures, Order of 15 March 1996, www.icj-cij.org/docket/files/94/7425.pdf.
24 This would be very unlikely to happen nowadays. In those days the Court only sat in the mornings from 10.00 am until 1.00 pm, with a 20-minute coffee break in the middle. Now, the Court frequently sits in the afternoons as well, doubling the amount of time available for hearings.
25 Preliminary Objections, Judgment of 11 June 1998, www.icj-cij.org/docket/files/94/7473.pdf.
26 See Preliminary Objections Judgment, para. 116.
27 Request for Interpretation of the Judgment of 11 June 1998 in the Case concerning the Land and Maritime Boundary Between Cameroon and Nigeria, www.icj-cij.org/docket/files/101/7631.pdf.
28 Alan Perry, who could also read German and spoke passable Spanish, with an understanding of Portuguese. All these languages were to be deployed in resolving Nigeria's maritime boundaries in the Gulf of Guinea.
29 Almost none of the Nigerians in the team spoke any French; most of the Cameroonians spoke some English.
30 Practice Direction IV of the Court issued in October 2001 now requires the parties to provide to the other side translations where they exist. It has of course always been a requirement that translations be provided of documents in languages other than English and French.

31 Each round of pleadings filled a large Transit van, which I drove to The Hague each time in order personally to deliver them to the Court.
32 This was perhaps hardly surprising. Alastair Macdonald did visit them in Lagos, but the archive was plainly deficient, maps having no doubt been 'lent out' to district surveyors over the years.
33 Not only were IBRU extremely helpful in locating maps, they were able to carry out some of the early cartographic work required in producing graphics for pleadings. One of their senior staff, Clive Schofield, at that time a lecturer in the Geography Department, later participated in the field trips to remote border areas, where his expertise in a number of areas, including the use of Geographical Information Systems (GIS), was invaluable.
34 These were loaned to the legal team, enabling us to have them scanned and digitised, a vital step in the process of producing the annotated maps used in the atlas, with the various boundary lines drawn on them.
35 Mainly the weather which, with mountain ranges so close to the equator, was invariably too cloudy to obtain the required high-definition photographs for the production of maps using photogrammetry.
36 Obtained for us by IBRU through their worldwide network of geographical contacts.
37 The production of detailed maps by Russia during the Cold War era was clearly high on their security agenda.
38 Now The National Archives (TNA).
39 Described in the atlas as a 'form-lined strip map'.
40 The atlases produced by Nigeria for her Counter-Memorial were printed on A2 sheets contained in large and unwieldy ring binders, which made it almost impossible for the judges to open them in court: fortunately this did not matter too much because it was the Rejoinder maps that were relied on at the oral hearings.
41 But the IGN maps had marked boundaries.
42 This software was being pioneered at the time by a firm called Caris Lots, based in Canada.
43 The Biafran civil war in the late 1960s, the result of an attempt to create a breakaway oil-rich State, resulted in terrible suffering among the Igbo people, who lost well over one million dead and wounded.
44 The 'Cement Armada' also played a part.
45 A useful description of ICJ Agents is on the Court's website, under 'How the Court Works' in the contentious cases section.
46 The assassins were never found but it was widely believed that the motive had to do with in-fighting between Nigerian political factions.
47 The picture would be different now: the case provoked great interest in Nigeria, and members of the NBC have been regular attendees of international seminars, particularly those given by IBRU in Durham.
48 Near the village of Lip (see Rejoinder, p. 362).
49 See further below.
50 The best descriptions of the ancient civilisations which dwelt on the shores of Lake Chad are found in the writings of the nineteenth-century German explorer Heinrich Barth.
51 Rejoinder, pp. 715–717.
52 Judgment, para. 324.
53 Chapter 3 of this book.
54 It is estimated that one-third of Cameroon's 12 million population consists of Nigerians.
55 The Greentree Agreement.
56 Volume 2, pp. 286–301 (see note 1 above).
57 Chapter 7 of this book.
58 Chapter 6 of this book.
59 See the ICJ website.

2 Should Nigeria have sought revision of the Bakassi Decision by the International Court of Justice?

Emeka Duruigbo[1]

Introduction

Questions over the ownership and control of the oil- and gas-rich Bakassi Peninsula have lingered for some time.[2] In 1994, following Nigerian military presence on the peninsula in response to Cameroon's placing of police and administrators in the area, Cameroon invited the intervention of the International Court of Justice (ICJ).[3] In its application to the Court, Cameroon sought the determination of the sovereignty of the entire land and maritime boundary between Cameroon and Nigeria.[4] In October 2002, principally relying on agreements in the colonial era between Great Britain and Germany, the ICJ decided that the Bakassi Peninsula was an integral part of Cameroon's territory.[5]

Nigerians greeted the loss at the Court with a range of emotions, from anger to anxiety and from despair to sadness. Beyond the rage and outrage, questions surfaced as to what could be done to remedy the unpalatable, if not unacceptable, state of affairs.[6] One option that featured prominently in the discourse was the remedy of revision under international law.[7] Revision of judgments (which also exists under national judicial systems) is one of the remedies that a party to an international dispute may utilize to address some discomfort emanating from the judgment. Simply put, revision refers to "the power of a tribunal to revise its judgment or award."[8] Revision has a long history as an international adjudication remedy,[9] although its modern history at the International Court of Justice dates to the mid-1980s when the ICJ gave its first judgment on the issue of revision in the application by Tunisia seeking, *inter alia*, the revision of the Court's judgment in the Tunisia–Libya Continental Shelf case.[10] While not limited to boundary and territorial decisions, resort to this remedy features prominently in decisions in that area. This development is understandable because boundary and territorial disputes raise questions of title and territorial sovereignty that strike at the heart of statehood, creating a fertile ground for prolonged conflicts inside and outside the Court.[11]

Some Nigerian and foreign scholars, including the present author, recommended pursuit of the remedy of revision before the expiration of the ten-year period, within which the country could invoke its right to seek the remedy at the ICJ.[12] In its wisdom, the Government of Nigeria, under President Goodluck Jonathan, decided not to pursue the option. During a visit to Cameroon in August 2015, the current President of Nigeria, Mr Muhammadu Buhari, reassured Cameroon that Nigeria would continue to respect the Bakassi judgment.[13]

Nigeria's willingness to comply with the decision is consistent with the modern practice of States which generally accord a reasonable degree of deference to the judgments of the ICJ, although some cases of noncompliance or partial compliance also exist.[14] Yet, the step taken by Nigeria in this regard is remarkable because disputes adjudicated by the ICJ that involve land boundaries and a history of armed conflict have been greeted by the lowest levels of compliance.[15] Moreover, some analysts expected Nigeria not to comply with the decision, citing its relative advantages over Cameroon, including a larger population, resource endowment, and military prowess.[16] In all of these analyses, one cannot overlook the roles played by diplomatic pressure and Nigeria's reputation as an African leader in leading Nigeria to comply.[17] While the issue of lodging an application for revision of the Bakassi Decision is now moot from the political and legal angles, its academic relevance retains considerable force.

This chapter examines the remedy of revision and assesses Nigeria's chances of success had it elected to invoke this review procedure in the Bakassi case. It is hoped that the discussion presented here will serve as a valuable guide to policymakers faced with similar circumstances or wrestling with thorny questions surrounding seemingly intractable boundary problems, even in slightly different contexts.[18]

The rest of the chapter is organized into four parts. The first highlights some preliminary points about the concept of revision. This synopsis provides a guide as to the rationale and scope of the remedy. The second part discusses the notion of revision in general and its specific application under the ICJ system. It outlines the standards for the revision remedy in international adjudication, referencing past judicial and arbitral experiences and scholarly submissions. The third part applies the requirements to the case of Nigeria to ascertain whether Nigeria would have fared favorably or not in the pursuit of the remedy in the Bakassi case. It discusses possible arguments by Nigeria to support a revision of the judgment. The final part is the Conclusion.

Preliminary points about revision

The rationale for the right or remedy of revision in international law is almost unassailable. Revision provides a comfortable middle ground between allowing an unjust result to stand and maintaining uncertainty in the resolution of differences between the parties to a dispute.[19] If there is a valid basis for asking a tribunal to revise a decision reached in error, it stands to reason that such a submission should be entertained, so that an obvious act of injustice is not allowed to remain in place. If a form of redress can be found, it should be provided. At the same time, it accords with common sense and sound reasoning to bring every dispute to a point of finality or a terminal date. The right of revision, therefore, appears to be grounded in fairness, justice, and prudence.[20]

One of the first things to understand about revision is that it is a remedy that is not lightly provided. Instead, it may only be exercised in exceptional circumstances.[21] Indeed, one scholar argues that great caution is called for in the Court's exercise of the power of revision, considering that in applying for revision, the clear objective of the party seeking it is to change the judgment or award completely or partially.[22] More significantly, in the case of boundary disputes, revising the judgment would almost invariably affect the location of a country's boundary.[23]

Another pertinent point about the concept of revision is that a tribunal does not have an inherent power to revise its decisions.[24] In reality, the power of revision is generally found in the constitutive instrument of the tribunal or founded upon the mutual consent and agreement of the parties to the dispute to confer such power on the tribunal.[25] There may be exceptions to the general rule, such as decisions induced by fraud.[26] For the ICJ, where the power exists, the Court may then consider whether the conditions for exercising the power under its constitutive instrument have been met.[27] In exercising the power, there are two stages to the revision process. The first stage deals with questions of admissibility, while the second stage is devoted to the merits.[28] To be admissible, the application needs to meet the basic conditions for revision. No matter the apparent strength of the case on the merits, if the preliminary conditions are not satisfied, the Court will not accept the case nor bother to delve into the merits. The recent application for the revision of the judgment delivered on February 26, 2007 in the Bosnian Genocide Convention Case (*Bosnia and Herzegovina v. Serbia*) is instructive.[29] In a statement issued by the President of the ICJ on March 9, 2017, it was announced that the application by Bosnia for revision was rejected by the ICJ on the ground that the agent who filed the application on behalf of Bosnia did not have the authority of the Bosnian Government.[30]

An important preliminary point that deserves reference is that in seeking revision of a judgment, the party making the application accepts the tribunal's decision as valid. That is, the party is not claiming that the decision is null and void.[31] Accordingly, revision differs from the related concept of nullity,[32] which is deployed to attack the prior decisions themselves, whereas revision does not attack the prior decisions.[33] Revision is also different from the connected and overlapping concept of interpretation of judgments.[34] It should also be pointed out that the scope of revision does not necessarily embrace every category of relief that common usage would assign to it, such as correction of errors in the judgment. These reliefs do not fall under revision by the standards of contemporary international law.[35]

Additionally, it should be noted that the existence of the remedy of revision is not contingent on the availability of the remedy of appeals. Revision is available even when the option of appealing a tribunal's judgment is not available.[36] This position is certainly the case with the ICJ, whose judgments are not subject to appeal.[37] In *Genie Lacayo v. Nicaragua*,[38] the Inter-American Court of Human Rights, while holding that it has the power of revision despite the non-existence of any such power in its constitutive instrument, also held that "the decisive or unappealable character of a judgment is not incompatible with the existence of the remedy of revision in some special cases."[39] Viewed from this perspective, revision assumes a position of tremendous importance as a losing party, unable to appeal an unfavorable decision, may explore the route of revision and utilize it in accomplishing substantially the same objective afforded by an appeal, which is to avoid the burdens imposed by the decision. In fact, similarly to an appeal, a revision can lead to overturning of the court's judgment.[40]

It should be emphasized at this point, however, that revision differs from an appeal on several grounds. In the Laguna del Desierto Arbitration,[41] the tribunal highlighted the distinguishing features between revision proceedings and appellate proceedings. A court handling an appeal "is entitled to make good any error of fact or law contained in the judgment under appeal."[42] In appellate proceedings, the court is also entitled to "re-examine the evidence, correct the original reasoning and amend the decision, replacing it by a fresh decision."[43] On the other hand, the role of a court or tribunal in a revision proceeding is much more limited. In revision, the tribunal lacks the "power to correct errors of law, or to re-examine the evidence, or to alter the reasoning on which the judgment is based, or to adopt definitions of terms differing from those used in the judgment."[44] Accordingly, the revision procedure simply enables the tribunal only "to amend the judgment in so far as it was given in consequence of an error resulting from an act or document of the proceedings."[45]

One other important point that should not be glossed over is the uncomfortable co-existence of the remedy of revision with the doctrine of *res judicata*.[46] The concept of *res judicata* encapsulates the notion that final judgments of a court or tribunal should be respected as such, thereby eschewing the scepter of endless litigation. The doctrine posits that "an earlier and final adjudication by a court is conclusive in subsequent proceedings involving the same subject matter or relief, the same legal grounds and same parties."[47] *Res judicata* is a firmly established principle of international law.[48] As one tribunal has remarked: "There is no doubt that res judicata is a principle of international law, and even a general principle of law within the meaning of Article 38(1)(c) of the Statute of the International Court of Justice."[49] *Res judicata* is justified on the grounds that the society has an interest in bringing a court action to an eventual conclusion and that litigants enjoy a right not to be dragged into a judicial forum repeatedly for identical reasons.[50] In the international arena, finality of decisions promotes stability in international relations.[51]

Some scholars contend, however, that the co-existence of the two notions can be justified. They accept as sound the idea of holding that a decision is final and disposes of the issues presented by the parties.[52] Nonetheless, they do not think that the doctrine should be elevated to a sacred status.[53] If there are good reasons to obtain real justice, such as the presence of bribery or prejudice in the bench, the rule of *res judicata* should not provide a ground for injustice to stand.[54] In that connection, Professor Michael Reisman has observed that

> tribunals faced with what they deem to be faulty past decisions will devise methods of avoiding them. Certainly such independence is preferable to slavish maintenance of an error or an injustice out of an obsessive loyalty to a secondary policy as an instrumentality of justice.[55]

Another scholar, in underscoring the point, notes that "in international law, as in all legal systems, the adage is valid that 'nothing is settled until it is settled right.'"[56] Furthermore, where neither possibility of appeal nor a form of review exists, parties may be reluctant to authorize a tribunal lacking such processes to hear its disputes.[57] Moreover, while there is validity to the claim that finality may have a stabilizing effect in international relations, the problem is that the conclusion of adjudication does not necessarily equate to an end of the conflict.[58]

The major point is to strike a balance in which parties have a right to revision but not in a way that makes it easy for parties to abuse the process, use it as dilatory tactics or extend the dispute for an unreasonably long period of time. A losing party in a judgment or award should therefore not continue to avoid compliance with the verdict, using the assertion of revision as a delay stratagem. One final point on this issue touches on the relationship between *res judicata* and revision under the ICJ process, concerning Article 59 of the ICJ Statute, which provides that the decisions of the Court have binding effect only on the parties and with respect to the particular case.[59] On that score, the following observation has been made:

> In the ICJ context, a judgment is subject to res judicata when it is rendered and will remain so even if a successful application for revision under Article 61 is made. This is because revision proceedings are considered a separate "particular case" and thus outside the bounds of Article 59.[60]

It is important to stress that this result is only applicable to the ICJ, because of the nature of its judgments whose binding effect is limited to the parties and to the particular case.

For other international tribunals, the result may be different. For instance, under the ICSID Convention, the original decision would not remain *res judicata* if it is successfully revised or annulled.[61]

The following section provides a more detailed discussion of revision, including elements that must be satisfied for its application under the rules of the International Court of Justice. Without establishing these grounds, a party seeking revision is not likely to receive the attention of the Court, or if it gets its initial attention is unlikely to prevail at the conclusion of the process.

Requirements for revision

As stated earlier, revision denotes the power that a court or tribunal can exercise to revise a judgment or award earlier given by it. It could be further described as "the act of examining the judgment or award on the basis of the discovery of a hitherto unknown but decisive fact relevant to the decision, provided certain criteria are fulfilled."[62] Within the context of our discussion, the legal basis for seeking revision of a judgment of the ICJ is contained in Article 61 of the Statute of the International Court of Justice.[63] The Article provides as follows:

1 An application for revision of a judgment may be made only when it is based upon the discovery of some fact of such a nature as to be a decisive factor, which fact was, when the judgment was given, unknown to the Court and also to the party claiming revision, always provided that such ignorance was not due to negligence.
2 The proceedings for revision shall be opened by a judgment of the Court expressly recording the existence of the new fact, recognizing that it has such a character as to lay the case open to revision, and declaring the application admissible on this ground.
3 The Court may require previous compliance with the terms of the judgment before it admits proceedings in revision.
4 The application for revision must be made at latest within six months of the discovery of the new fact.
5 No application for revision may be made after the lapse of ten years from the date of the judgment.

Accordingly, for an applicant to attract the Court's interest, and ultimately prevail, the application must demonstrate the discovery of a new fact, i.e. a fact that was in existence at the time of judgment but unknown to both the tribunal and the applicant State at the time the judgment in the case was delivered, the absence of negligence in discovering the fact and the decisive influence of the discovery on the judgment sought to be revised. It bears mentioning that several other tribunals have also adopted the ICJ's approach to revision.[64] The requirements are discussed in greater detail below.

Emergence of new facts

The discovery of new facts is a crucial factor in revision and this requirement is applied with strictness.[65] Professor Reisman remarks that "revision is usually limited to a new fact contingency."[66] Pelletier and Lazare (*United States v. Hayti*) involved the arbitration of claims for compensation based on acts of the Government of Haiti.[67] Subsequent to the delivery of the award, Haiti brought a petition for a rehearing on the ground of evidence discovered after the award. The arbitrator rejected the petition on the basis that his task had been completed and the tribunal had dissolved; thus, he lacked the power to continue to handle the matter.[68] Nevertheless, the United States decided against enforcing the award, accepting that the claim for revision was well founded.[69] The action of the American Government placed an important imprimatur on the use of subsequently discovered evidence as a basis for revision of a validly rendered judgment or award.[70]

The meaning of "new facts" is not always clear. A narrow definition limits a new fact to "one which had occurred but which was unknown at the time of the award."[71] New facts have also been given a broader definition to encompass "*ante*judicial facts, facts arising from the process itself as well as unforeseen effects of a decision."[72] This more expansive approach to defining the term is anchored on the understanding that

> [t]he concept was introduced in order to avoid miscarriage of justice; new facts whose import is dogmatically excluded, in any of these sequential phases, can cause just that and must be included in order to conform to the principle underlying revision.[73]

In reality, the ICJ position is that these facts must have been in existence at the time of judgment. In *Bosnia and Herzegovina v. Yugoslavia*,[74] the ICJ emphasized that the discovered fact must predate the judgment.[75] In that case, Yugoslavia based its revision application on facts that occurred in 2000, namely the admission of the Federal Republic of Yugoslavia into the membership of the United Nations, even though the Court rendered its judgment in 1996.[76] The ICJ held that Article 61 of the ICJ Statute refers to

> a fact existing at the time when the judgment was given and discovered subsequently. A fact which occurs several years after a judgment has been given is not a "new" fact within the meaning of Article 61. This remains the case irrespective of the legal consequences that such a fact may have.[77]

Accordingly, the Court decided that the presented fact could not be regarded as "a new fact within the meaning of Article 61 capable of founding a request for revision of that Judgment."[78] In a decision issued on June 12, 2015, an arbitral tribunal of the International Centre for the Settlement of Investment Disputes (ICSID) cited this particular ICJ holding with approval.[79]

The definition or requirement of a new fact excludes "facts" that are generated "in terms of commissioning of reports, surveys, and a variety of instruments and documentation."[80] On the other hand, knowledge of the existence of a document, such as a map, governmental record, or very old historical texts or instruments, does not preclude the discovery of facts within them unknown at the time of judgment. In essence, the focus is on the document's contents, not the document itself.[81] This scenario may play out where a party had refused to produce a document in contravention of the Court's request to produce it.[82]

Facts may be defined to include all means of proof, including documents that pertain to questions of law.[83] The fact or evidence claimed to have been discovered must be new. Presenting new documents is not synonymous with presenting new facts. Parties and tribunals may be apprised of some facts without access to, or knowledge of, all the documents harboring those facts.[84] Therefore, a key point here, after establishing the prior existence of the document, is what the court or tribunal knew at the time of judgment. In *Battus Case*, the Franco-Bulgarian Mixed Arbitral Tribunal held in 1929 that "the use of the word 'discovery' implies unquestionably the existence of the fact, which was unknown to the Tribunal, at the time when it gave the decision."[85]

Deploying the emergence of new facts to defeat an earlier decision seems to offend the notion of *res judicata*. The argument can be made that parties should be entitled to know that the victory they obtained is certain and final, after a thorough examination of the parties' submissions in court. Nevertheless, as stated earlier, the doctrine of *res judicata* should not be canonized to the extent it becomes a weapon for promoting unjust outcomes.[86] If new facts justify revisiting a case, at least within a specified period and applying strict scrutiny in entertaining it, an opportunity to revise should not be extinguished lightly. Indeed, it should be emphasized that the facts sought to be used to revise the judgment of the ICJ must have been discovered not later than ten years from the date of the ICJ decision.[87]

Newly discovered facts must be of decisive character

The ICJ is only likely to revise a judgment where the newly discovered fact or evidence was fundamental to its earlier decision. That is, the fact would have had substantial influence in arriving at its decision, had the tribunal known of its existence. Accordingly, facts that only would have had infinitesimal influence or would have had a tangential connection to, as opposed to a direct bearing on, the decision cannot successfully support a claim for revision.[88] In the *Application for Revision and Interpretation of the 1982 Judgment* between Tunisia and Libya,[89] the ICJ held that

> what is required for the admissibility of an application for revision is not that the new fact relied on might, had it been known, have made it possible for the Court to be more specific in its decision; it must also have been a "fact of such a nature as to be a decisive factor."[90]

In *Lehigh Valley R.R. v. Germany*,[91] which involved acts of wartime sabotage by German spies within the United States during World War I, the German–US Mixed Claims Commission reopened the case after evidence of perjury and fraud in the original proceeding was presented and substantiated by the US side.[92] There, a spy and confessed saboteur, who had been accused of falsely informing the tribunal in the original proceeding that he was involved in the destruction of a munitions depot in New Jersey in 1916, supplied evidence to buttress his involvement after a final decision had been reached. The evidence was in the form of a written message sent earlier by a fellow German spy, who also became a confessed saboteur, in which the latter had referenced the New Jersey explosion and requested funds to execute another attack. On the basis of the newly presented evidence, the tribunal vacated its previous findings and ruled against Germany, holding it liable for sabotage operations inside the United States during the First World War, and awarding tens of millions of dollars in damages.[93]

Absence of negligence in discovery of facts

Scientific and technological improvements, not available at the time of judgment, may make it possible to discover facts afterwards.[94] Relevant data, in possession of another State, may also have been classified in furtherance of national security, thus making it inaccessible at the time it was needed. Should the documents be declassified or otherwise become accessible, a party may stake its claim on such a document, all other things being equal.[95] In such instances, the State requesting revision could rightfully argue that the lack of earlier discovery was not occasioned by negligence or absence of diligence on its part. Indeed, the onus is on the requesting party to show that its claim is not tainted or marred by negligence in the discovery of the "new" fact.

It should also be noted that the ICJ may dispense with inquiring into the diligence or absence of negligence in the fact discovery, if it determines that the fact in question is neither new nor decisive.[96] That was the conclusion reached and approach adopted by the ICJ in *El Salvador v. Honduras.*[97] In imposing the negligence criterion, it seems that the plight of the respondent State is being given due consideration. It is certainly equitable to look at the burden that the respondent faces in protecting a judgment given in its favor, if the new proceedings result from the requesting State's shortcomings in preparing its case in the original proceedings. Giving attention to the interest of the respondent State, in such circumstances, protects the notion of justice, thereby justifying a requirement of heightened scrutiny in approaching the discovery of new facts or evidence. All States, including an applicant State, should welcome the imposition of a duty to demonstrate that the discovery of new facts or evidence was not accompanied by negligence.

Indeed, revision, by its nature of upsetting the finality of judgments, calls for exacting scrutiny at every step. As the European Court of Human Rights has observed:

> The Court notes the embodiment of the principle of the finality of judgments in the present Article 44 of the [1951 European Convention on Human Rights] and recalls that, insofar as it calls into question the final character of judgments of the Court, the possibility of revision is considered to be an exceptional procedure. Requests for revision of judgments are therefore to be subjected to strict scrutiny.[98]

A similar observation was made many years earlier by the European Court of Justice in *Riseria Modenese Srl v. Council*[99] that "[t]he strictness of [the criteria for revision] is due to the fact that an application for revision is not a means of appeal but an exceptional review procedure which may render inapplicable the principle of res judicata."[100]

Assessing Nigeria's case for revision

One scholar has noted that

> [t]he importance of territory to a state's political, economic, and military power, as well as to its cultural identity and national pride, puts international boundary disputes in a league with those disputes that are the most difficult to settle definitively in a single, unified decision process.[101]

It is perhaps a reflection of this observable fact that many stakeholders campaigned for a rejection or revision of the Bakassi Decision, unwilling to accept the conclusion of the matter at that point.[102] Nigeria could have presented a case relying on the grounds of discovery of new facts and equity.

Discovery of new facts

As should be clear from the foregoing discussion, if a State has not discovered new facts in its favor subsequent to the decision of the Court, it would be futile to pursue a revision application.[103] Nor the point that all the other requirements associated with the discovery must be met, including the fact that the application must be made within six months of the discovery of the new fact. In March 2017, the ICJ announced that Malaysia had filed, on February 2, 2017, an Application for Revision of the Judgment delivered by the International Court of Justice on May 23, 2008 in the case concerning *Sovereignty over Pedra Branca/Pulau Batu Puteh, Middle Rocks, and South Ledge (Malaysia/Singapore)*.[104] Malaysia filed the application following the discovery of three documents at the National Archives of the United Kingdom, "namely internal correspondence of the Singapore colonial authorities in 1958, an incident report filed in 1958 by a British naval officer and an annotated map of naval operations from the 1960s."[105] Malaysia contends that these documents establish the new fact about the knowledge of top British colonial and Singaporean Administration officials that the disputed area was not part of Singapore's sovereign territory.[106]

One of the facts that would have featured in an application for revision is the existence of treaties that were not brought to the attention of the court. A group of Nigerian and foreign scholars canvassing support for revision framed it in that light. According to the scholars, a number of treaties relevant to the case were not considered at the ICJ hearing as revealed by a former Minister of Information of the Federation on Nigeria, Dr Walter Ofonagoro.[107] The former minister "wrote a history thesis on South-East Nigeria concerning the relationship between the Efik Chiefs and European emissaries and their relations with foreign powers before the 1885 Treaty with the British."[108] This position seems to find support in Nigerian media accounts. Some reporters for a major newspaper in Nigeria, *The Vanguard*, wrote in that regard:

> International relations experts, renowned historians, researchers and politicians told Vanguard in Lagos, last week, that contrary to the claims by the Cameroon and Nigerian legal teams that the first legal treaty on the Land and Maritime borders between Nigerian and Cameroon was the 1913 Anglo-German treaty, it was discovered that the limits of the Land and maritime boundaries between both countries went as far back as 1811 when the British made the treaty that went from the Lake Chad region down to the Atlantic ocean through the Rio Del Rey Estuary.[109]

The reporters further stated:

> Prof. Ofonagoro said that he has in his possession, 1822 documents which vested ownership of the Bakassi Peninsula to the Old Calabar Chiefs, by extension to Nigeria, and debunked claims that the 1913 Anglo-German treaty was the first recognised treaty on the land and maritime boundary between Nigeria and Cameroon.[110]

In the newspaper report, Professor Ofonagoro is quoted as saying:

> There were other treaties between Nigeria and Cameroon on the Land and Maritime boundaries, which were entered into in 1884, 1885 and 1886, all of which clearly demarcated the land and maritime border between Nigeria and Cameroon from the Lake Chad region down to the Akwa Yafe River, which was the land border from Akwa Yafe to Rio Del Rey estuary to the Atlantic Ocean … When the Germans got to Akwa Yafe River, they discovered that they could not gain a direct access to the sea because going toward West of Akwa Yafe River will take them straight to the Calabar

> Sea Port. The Calabar Sea Port was clearly outlined in the treaty. This was the main port of entry for the British merchants, and later missionaries, who were the first to establish sphere of influence in Nigeria.[111]

Professor Ofonagoro further stated that Cameroon concealed the fact of the existence of the old treaties because it wanted to deceive the Court. He insisted on advancing the application for review to counter the deceit, contending that the ICJ should not "allow a judgment that was obtained by fraud and concealment of fact to stand" as that would deal a terrible injustice to the people of Bakassi and a severe blow to the reputation of the ICJ, which the world expects to always uphold justice.[112]

The case for revision was also advanced on the grounds that the 1913 Anglo-German Treaty, which played a central role in the case,

> was neither ratified nor brought into fruition because of the outbreak of the First World War the following year. The territory of Bakassi remained in full occupation of the British and was not treated as part of the Mandate Territory of Southern Cameroons. Hence, the 1961 UN plebiscite on Southern Cameroons was never held there. British Occupation and Prescription passed on to Nigeria in 1960.[113]

Another fact that came to light subsequent to the Bakassi Decision was a document from the British Government on the status of the Bakassi Peninsula. On that, *The Vanguard* also reported as follows:

> There are evidence to show that in 1994 when a dispute erupted between Nigeria and Cameroon, Nigeria asked the British government to attest to the true status of Bakassi Peninsula, the British government replied to assert that the Peninsula belongs to Nigeria.[114]

The *Vanguard* reporters went on to make the interesting, if not disturbing, observation that "curiously that document was not tendered at the ICJ trial."[115]

The scholars that argued for revision in an open letter to the Nigerian president rounded off their submission by referencing the concepts of inter-temporal law and self-determination under international law, neither of which featured in the Court's consideration of the matter at trial. On inter-temporal law, the scholars noted that the ICJ referred to the principle in its judgment but it was not canvassed or discussed during trial: "It is a fact that neither the Parties nor the ICJ referred or commented on Inter Temporal Law in international law during the Court proceedings, so it was a new fact that emerged after the trial."[116] The scholars further stated that self-determination, which they argue has attained the status of *jus cogens* or peremptory norm of international law, should have played a role in the Court's determination: "In the Bakassi situation, compounded by Prescription, Occupation and Inter-temporal law, there cannot be disposition of territory without consulting the wishes of the people that are directly and intimately affected."[117]

Legitimate questions may be raised as to whether any of these facts or contentions constitute new facts under the criteria contained in Article 61 of the ICJ Statute. There would also be the uphill tasks of showing that the Court was not aware of them or that they would have been a decisive factor in the Court's decision. There is also the issue of absence of negligence in discovering the facts. For instance, the British statement on the status of the Bakassi Peninsula was in the possession of the Nigerian Government. If the government, out of its lack of due diligence or as part of its litigation strategy, failed or opted not to bring the information to the attention of the Court, it presents a formidable challenge to persuade the Court to use it as a basis for overturning the judgment. Similarly, if the Nigerian legal team allowed Cameroon's supposed concealment of information to go unchallenged during the proceedings, it is doubtful that they can rely on their own incompetence to impeach the resulting judgment ten years afterwards. The object of the revision procedure is not to provide the applicant a second chance to finesse its case and correct mistakes it should not have made in the original proceedings. It could also be said that some of these arguments or variations thereof were also canvassed before the ICJ during the initial proceedings, notably the purported invalidity of the Anglo-German Treaty, without success.[118]

Principles of equity

Nigeria probably would have been able to present a strong case based on equity. International tribunals may resort to equity as a basis not to disturb settled boundaries.[119] In such situations, where the result of the revision would be the disturbance of settled boundaries, the party seeking revision is likely to fail. In other words, equity would defeat the party that wants the judgment revised. Yet, equity can play a different role that is helpful to the party bringing the application. A close look at the role of equity in revision shows that it could instead have supported Nigeria's case, based on the history of the communities residing in the area and the impact a political transfer to another country would have on them. The equitable approach of the Permanent Court of Arbitration (PCA) in *Barbados v. Trinidad and Tobago*, decided a few years after the Bakassi Decision, provides some valuable insights.[120] The contention of one scholar on this subject of the central place occupied by equitable considerations in international boundary jurisprudence is quite pertinent:

> Equity can weigh for or against revision ... An emphasis on equity deters parties from asserting technical, doctrinal arguments, and requires them instead to challenge the fairness of the outcome based on sociocultural, political, or economic consequences such as the dislocation of traditional fishing grounds, the deprivation of access to the sea, and ethnic affiliation and national loyalties of resident populations.[121]

There is an abundance of facts to support a claim that the people of Bakassi dreaded the unwelcome consequences of being dislocated from their comfortable connection to Nigeria.[122] The Bakassi case was not simply about a physical space or resources contained in that area. It was also about human beings. There should be a marked distinction between cases where a State engages in a boundary dispute to protect its territory and assets and where it engages in a dispute that pertains to an inhabited territory.[123] It is not clear to what extent the Nigerian authorities took these factors into account in the decision not to seek revision.

On the other hand, it was also possible that the ICJ would have continued to be swayed by Cameroon's assurances of protection for the Bakassi residents, mindful of their ties to Nigeria and the desire to remain as Nigerians.[124] This undertaking has legal and political significance, as "the fishing rights of the local population and indeed those that traditionally have exercised fishing rights in the maritime area have become part and parcel of the obligations conferred on Cameroon by the Court."[125] These assurances were further amplified or fortified in the Greentree Agreement between Nigeria and Cameroon to implement the Bakassi Decision.[126] Seeking to defeat the legal implications of the assurances, the resulting judgment and subsequent agreement through a resort to equity might have met a brick wall of resistance from both Cameroon and the Court.

Conclusion

Successive Nigerian governments had the opportunity over the years to seek a revision of the 2002 judgment of the International Court of Justice awarding sovereign ownership over the Bakassi Peninsula to Cameroon. Each of the presidents in the period between 2002 and 2012, when the opportunity could have been exercised – Olusegun Obasanjo, Umar Yar'Adua, and Goodluck Jonathan – opted not to pursue that option. Their choice of action or inaction may have been justified, given all the facts at their disposal or factors they took into account. Yet, their decisions and actions are not necessarily unimpeachable. There was some basis, though not unassailable, for utilizing this once-in-a-lifetime opportunity for applying for a revision of the judgment.

Revision is a remedy that parties to a legal dispute use to change the original outcome in a dispute and turn things in their favor. The basis for seeking the remedy is tough and a high bar must be scaled to succeed. An applicant State inviting the ICJ to revise its judgment must show the discovery of new facts which are decisive enough to reverse the judgment, and further show that the absence of an earlier discovery of the facts was not due to its negligence. It is possible that Nigeria would not have met the threshold. It is also possible that Nigeria could have advanced a claim worth the attention of the Court. Apart from the legal implications, invoking the remedy probably would have applied pressure on Cameroon and secured more concessions from them in the post-judgment negotiations with Nigeria. Such concessions might have resulted in more favorable treatment to the residents of Bakassi, whether they chose to remain a part of Cameroon or reestablish their lives in another location within the territory of Nigeria. Since Nigeria had already commenced efforts to comply with the judgment through the Greentree Agreement, instituting revision proceedings would necessarily constitute or be construed as a ploy to use the remedy as a tool to evade or even delay compliance. In any case, under Article 61 (3) of the ICJ Statute, if Nigeria had not been in compliance with the judgment, any application for revision would have been rendered inadmissible.

Thus, looking back, one could still argue that pursuing the remedy would have been in Nigeria's interest, regardless of the eventual outcome in court.

Notes

1 I am deeply grateful for the excellent research and editorial assistance of TMSL students Kelechi Onwumere and Newton Tamayo and the resourcefulness of TMSL Law Library Associate Director, Danny Norris.

2 Philip C. Aka, "Human Rights in Nigeria's External Relations: Exigency, Methods, and Rebuttable Objections" (2015) 21 *Buff. Hum. Rts L. Rev.* 1, 5 fn 19; Aloysius P. Llamzon, "Jurisdiction and Compliance in Recent Decisions of the International Court of Justice" (2007) 18 *EJIL* 815, 835 ("Sovereignty over the Bakassi Peninsula and areas in the Lake Chad Basin was the source of this long-running territorial dispute between Nigeria and Cameroon"); Gbenga Oyebode, "Ownership and Control Issues regarding Oil, Gas and Hard Minerals in Areas of Disputed Borders: A West African Perspective" [1995] *Rocky Mtn. Min. L. Inst.* 2B (1995) (stating that ownership claims to the Bakassi Peninsula area did not come into serious manifestation until the early 1960s when Nigeria discovered and started exploiting oil in places near the peninsula, alerting both countries to the potential economic importance of the area and leading them to begin to assert ownership claims accordingly).

3 Mashood Issaka and Kapinga Yvette Ngandu, rapporteurs, "Pacific Settlement of Border Disputes: Lessons from the Bakassi Affair and the Greentree Agreement" (2008); www.ipinst.org/wp-content/uploads/publications/bakassipub.pdf; accessed January 9, 2016; 1, 2.

4 Ibid.

5 *Land and Maritime Boundary between Cameroon and Nigeria (Cameroon v. Nigeria, Equatorial Guinea intervening)* (Judgment) [2002] *ICJ Rep.* 303.

6 Gbenga Oduntan, "Maritime Pyrrhic Victories: Evaluation of the de facto Regime of Common Fishing Grounds Created in the Land and Maritime Boundary Case (Cameroon v. Nigeria)" (2006) 37 *J. Mar. L. & Com.* 425–426

> Several vocal sections of the Nigerian population including legal jurists, politicians and government officials have been arguing for outright rejection of the judgment of the Court especially as it relates to the Bakassi Peninsula, and quite ominously have been publicly proffering military solutions to the dispute.

Colin J. McMahon, "The United Nations Convention on the Law of International Territoriality" (2013) 21 *Willamette J. Int'l L. & Disp. Resol.* 155, 161–162.

7 See Soni Daniel, "FG Under Pressure to Reclaim Bakassi," *Vanguard*, September 25, 2012; www.vanguardngr.com/2012/09/fg-under-pressure-to-reclaim-bakassi/; accessed December 31, 2015; Editorial, "Reclaiming Bakassi Peninsula," *Vanguard*, August, 16, 2012; www.vanguardngr.com/2012/08/reclaiming-bakassi-peninsula; accessed December 31, 2015

> We are in full support of all efforts to ensure that the wrongs of our past leaders are corrected through the total reclamation of Bakassi Peninsula. We are happy with the House of Representatives, which has taken bold steps toward pushing the Federal Government to return to the ICJ for a re-visit of this shoddy verdict.

8 Kaiyan Homi Kaikobad, *Interpretation and Revision of International Boundary Decisions* (Cambridge: Cambridge University Press, 2007), 231 (citation omitted). See also Chester Brown, "The Cross-Fertilization of Principles Relating to Procedure and Remedies in the Jurisprudence of International Courts and Tribunals" (2008) 30 *Loy. L. A. Int'l & Comp. L. J.* 219, 224

> Revision is the power to reopen a decision or award in light of the discovery of new evidence that is likely to be a decisive factor. It can only be exercised when new, previously unknown, and relevant evidence is introduced, and the party claimed revision at the time of judgment. (Citations omitted)

9 For a valuable historical excursion, see Shabtai Rosenne, *Interpretation, Revision, and Other Recourse from International Judgments and Awards* (Boston: Martinus Nijhoff, 2007).

10 *Application for Revision and Interpretation of the Judgment of 24 February 1982 in the Case concerning the Continental Shelf (Tunisia/Libyan Arab Jamahiriya) (Tunisia v. Libyan Arab Jamahiriya)* (Judgment) [1985] *ICJ Rep.* 192; Rosenne (n. 8) 129 ("This was the first request for the revision of a judgment on the basis of Article 61 of the Statute before either the Permanent Court or the present International Court of Justice").

11 Kaikobad (n. 8) 4–7.

12 The architect of this particular scholarly effort was distinguished professor of international law Dr Christian Okeke of Golden Gate University in San Francisco, California. See n. 107 below.

13 Press Release, "Buhari: No Plan to Challenge Cameroon's Ownership of Bakassi Peninsula," *Premium Times*, July 29, 2015; www.premiumtimesng.com/news/headlines/187462-buhari-no-plan-to-challenge-cameroons-ownership-of-bakassi-peninsula.html; accessed January 9, 2016; Mohammed Momoh, "Buhari Puts Closure to Bakassi Dispute with Cameroon," *Africa Review*, July 30, 2015); www.africareview.com/News/Nigeria-puts-closure-to-Bakassi-dispute-with-Cameroon/-/979180/2814054/-/1vm76w/-/index.html; accessed January 9, 2016.

14 See Colter Paulson, "Compliance with Final Judgments of the International Court of Justice since 1987" [2004] *AJIL* 434.

15 Ibid. 457. For a discussion of the relative lack of hostilities that have attended boundary disputes in Africa, notwithstanding the fact that some of these boundaries were drawn by European colonial leaders, who often ignored ethnic and historical boundaries, see Joel H. Samuels, "Redrawing the Map: Lessons of Post-colonial Boundary Dispute Resolution in Africa, in

Africa," in Jeremy Levitt (ed.), *Mapping New Boundaries in International Law* (Oxford: Hart Publishing, 2008).

16 See e.g. Nejib Jibril, "The Binding Dilemma: From Bakassi to Badme –Making States Comply with Territorial Decisions of International Judicial Bodies" (2004) 19 *Am. U. Int'l L. Rev.* 633, 665.

17 Charles Riziki Majinge, "Emergence of New States in Africa and Territorial Dispute Resolution: The Role of the International Court of Justice" (2012) 13 *Melbourne Journal of International Law* 462, 494

> The fact that Nigeria has been keen to reassert its regional influence meant that it could not simply disregard the Court's decision and still maintain its claim to a leadership role in the region: as such, compliance with the Court's decision was also in its interests. Compliance with the decision can also be attributed to the growing international diplomatic pressure on Nigeria to accept and implement the Court's decision.
>
> (Citations omitted)

Steven R. Ratner, "Land Feuds and their Solutions: Finding International Law beyond the Tribunal Chamber" (2006) 100 *AJIL* 808, 816 (stating that "Nigeria's initial refusal to withdraw from the Bakassi Peninsula despite the ICJ's 2002 judgment awarding the area to Cameroon triggered intense UN diplomatic involvement before Nigeria began its evacuation in the summer of 2006"); Heather L. Jones, "Why Comply? An Analysis of Trends in Compliance with Judgments of the International Court of Justice since Nicaragua" (2012) 12 *Chicago-Kent Journal of International and Comparative Law* 1, 5–6.

18 Indeed, the relevance of the Bakassi judgment for future disputes cannot be overemphasized. David D. Caron and Pieter H.F. Bekker, "Land and Maritime Boundary between Cameroon and Nigeria" (2003) 97 *Am. J. Int'l L.* 387, 397 ("The Judgment also contains significant holdings potentially relevant to long-standing territorial disputes involving occupation of a contested region elsewhere in the world").

19 Kaikobad (n. 8) 239.

20 See Rosenne (n. 9) 11 (exploring arguments proffered for the introduction of the rule at the international level); P. Chandrasekhara Rao and Ph. Gautier (eds), *The Rules of the International Tribunal for the Law of the Sea: A Commentary* (Boston: Martinus Nijhoff, 2006).

21 Kaikobad (n. 8) 252, 257.

22 Ibid. 257.

23 Ibid.

24 W. Michael Reisman, *Nullity and Revision: The Review and Enforcement of International Judgments and Awards* (New Haven: Yale University Press, 1971) 226; But see Dr Karin Oellers-Frahm, "Book Review: *Interpretation, Revision and Other Recourses from International Judgments and Awards*" (2008) *EJIL* 623, 625 (arguing in favor of "an approach regarding the competence for revision as inherent power of any international court or tribunal due to its function to 'settle things right'").

25 Aaron Xavier Fellmeth, "Book Review: *Interpretation and Revision of International Boundary Decisions*" (2008) 102 *AJIL* 703, 706 (observing that

> without a constitutive power in its founding statute or the *compromis*, or without the express or implied consent of both parties, a tribunal generally lacks any power under international law to interpret or revise even its own decisions with binding force.

Kaikobad (n. 8) 252–253.

26 See Brown (n. 8) 225 (noting that the Iran–United States Claims Tribunal

> held that despite the absence of a power of revision in its Rules, an arbitral tribunal constituting a large number of disputes may have the power to reopen a case for new evidence if the original decision was induced by fraud.
>
> (Citation omitted)

27 *Land, Island and Frontier Dispute (El Salvador/Honduras: Nicaragua intervening)* (Application for Revision) [2003] *ICJ Rep.* 392, 400. The requirements are contained in Article 61 of the ICJ Statute.

28 Oellers-Frahm (n. 24) 624.

29 International Court of Justice, Document entitled "Application for revision of the Judgment of 26 February 2007 in the case concerning the Application of the Convention on the Prevention and Punishment of the Crime of Genocide (Bosnia and Herzegovina v. Serbia)," Statement by HE Judge Ronny Abraham, President of the International Court of Justice (March 9, 2017); www.icj-cij.org/presscom/files/6/19376.pdf; accessed May 5, 2017.

30 Ibid. For an excellent analysis of the ICJ's decision to reject the application, see Dapo Akande, "Applications for Revision of the International Court of Justice's Judgments: The Curious 'Case' for Revision of the Bosnian Genocide Judgment," EJIL Talk (March 13, 2017); www.ejiltalk.org/applications-for-revision-of-the-international-court-of-justice-judgments-the-curious-case-for-revision-of-the-bosnian-genocide-judgment/; accessed May 5, 2017.

31 Kaikobad (n. 8) 233.

32 For a historical discussion of nullity, especially in the context of municipal law, see Ronald J. Scalise Jr, "Rethinking the Doctrine of Nullity" (2014) 74 *La. L. Rev.* 663, 665–672. For further discussion of nullity and its possible application to the ICJ, see further Stephan Wittich, "Permissible Derogation from Mandatory Rules? The Problem of Party Status in the Genocide Case" (2007) 18 *EJIL* 591.

> No doubt it is a general principle of procedural law that a judicial decision which does not meet the essential conditions of its existence may be considered null and void. For instance, in the case concerning the Arbitral Award of July 31, 1989, the Court said that a decision rendered by a tribunal in excess of its jurisdiction might be a manifest breach of its competence or *excès de pouvoir*. That such a manifest *excès de pouvoir* may lead to the invalidity of a decision is generally recognized in arbitral practice. Some constituent treaties of arbitral tribunals even provide for annulment on the ground that there has been a serious departure from a fundamental rule of procedure. While to date such questions of invalidity have only been addressed in arbitral practice, it in theory could also arise in the context of judgments of the ICJ … In any event, it is fairly clear that absent any institutional framework or procedural devices for annulment, there is little or no room for a plea of nullity of judgments of the Court.
>
> (Ibid. 616–617, citations omitted)

33 See Fellmeth (n. 25) 704; See W. Michael Reisman, "Revision of the South West Africa Cases: An Analysis of the Grounds of Nullity in the Decision of July 18th, 1966 and Methods of Revision" (1966) 7 *VA. J. Int'l L.* 1, 12 [hereinafter Reisman, "South West Africa"] 16 ("Revision differs from nullity in that it proscribes unilateral denunciation and requires instead that the assertion of a defect vitiating the decision be brought to an impartial organ").

34 Reisman, see n. 24, 212 ("Interpretation and Revision overlap: both are means of amending an award when the seised tribunal deems that it should be amended").

35 Kaikobad (n. 8) 235.

36 Rosenne (n. 9) 1 ("It is commonplace that while a judgment of an international court is final, binding, and without appeal, circumstances can arise in which its finality can be questioned and its review can be required").

37 ICJ Statute Art. 60 ("The judgment is final and without appeal. In the event of dispute as to the meaning or scope of the judgment, the Court shall construe it upon the request of any party"); David M. Reilly and Sarita Ordone, "Effect of the Jurisprudence of the International Court of Justice on National Courts" (1995–1996) 28 *NYU J. Int'l Law & Pol.* 435, 438 ("The ICJ is both a trial court and a court of last resort. The court's judgments are final and cannot be appealed") (citation omitted).

38 *Genie-Lacayo v. Nicaragua*, Inter-American Court of Human Rights Series C. No. 45 6 (September 13, 1997).

39 Ibid. 9.

40 Thomas W. Walsh, "Substantive Review of ICSID Awards: Is the Desire for Accuracy Sufficient to Compromise Finality?" (2006) 24 *Berkeley J. Int'l L.* 444, 448 (stating that a party to a dispute under public international law may seek any of the three available remedies of interpretation, correction of minor errors and revision, adding that of all three options, only revision may lead to the reversal of an award).

41 *Argentina v. Chile* (Application for Revision and Subsidiary Interpretation of the Award of October 21, 1994) (1995) 113 *ILR* 194.

42 Ibid.
43 Ibid.
44 Ibid.
45 Ibid.
46 Timothy G. Nelson, "The Explosion and the Testimony: The WWI Sabotage Claims and an International Arbitral Tribunal's Power to Revise Its Own Awards" (2012) 23 *Am. Rev. Intl Arb.* 197–230 ("Commentators have often warned that untrammeled use of the revision procedure would undermine res judicata and confidence in the ICJ decision-making process") (citations omitted); Reisman (n. 24) 46–47.
47 Benjamin Klaftera, "International Commercial Arbitration as Appellate Review: NAFTA's Chapter 11, Exhaustion of Local Remedies and Res Judicata" (2006) 12 *U. C. Davis J. Int'l L. & Pol'y* 409, 430.
48 *Effect of Awards of Compensation Made by the United Nations Administrative Tribunal* (Advisory Opinion) [1954] *ICJ Rep.* 47, 53; Pedro J. Martinez-Fragaa and Harout Jack Samraaa, "The Role of Precedent in Defining Res Judicata in Investor–State Arbitration" (2012) 32 *N. J. Int'l L. & Bus.* 419, 423.
49 *Waste Management, Inc. v. United Mexican States* (Award on Jurisdiction, 2002) Case No. ARB(AF)/00/3 [39] (Waste Management, Inc.). See further Wittich (n. 32) 599–608.
50 Klaftera (n. 47) 431.
51 Reisman (n. 24) 44; Oellers-Frahm (n. 24) 623 (stating that "international adjudication is firmly linked to the maintenance of international peace and security so that the tension between *res iudicata* of a decision and any review procedure constitutes a very particular challenge").
52 Kaikobad (n. 8) 304–311.
53 Ibid.
54 Ibid.
55 Reisman (n. 24) 212.
56 Oellers-Frahm (n. 24) 623.
57 Nienke Grossman, "Legitimacy and International Adjudicative Bodies" (2009) 41 *Geo. Wash. Intl L. Rev.* 107, 151 ("The existence of another layer of review to prevent inconsistent decision making or to establish clear rules of law may affect whether a state authorizes or continues to authorize a particular tribunal or court to hear its disputes").
58 Reisman (n. 24) 44 (stating that "equating the granting of an award with the resolution of the underlying conflict [is] an identification that may be more wishful than real"); Maria Nudelman, "Who Owns the Scythian Gold? The Legal and Moral Implications of Ukraine and Crimea's Cultural Dispute" (2015) 38 *Fordham Int'l L. J.* 1261, 1291 (discussing a land dispute between Thailand and Cambodia and noting that despite the ICJ's decision in 1962 that the disputed area belonged to Cambodia, "between 1962 and 2011 there were recurrent violent protests and boundary disputes, even after the Thai government issued a statement reiterating its compliance with the ICJ judgment").
59 ICJ Statute Art. 59 ("The decision of the Court has no binding force except between the parties and in respect of that particular case").
60 Michael Ottolenghi and Peter Prows, "Res Judicata in the ICJ's Genocide Case: Implications for Other Courts and Tribunals?" (2009) 21 *Pace Int'l L. Rev.* 37, 53–54 (citation omitted).
61 Ibid. at 54 ("For the ICSID, by contrast, Article 53 refers to the various remedies of interpretation, revision, annulment, and referral to the ICJ, each of which could potentially undermine or overturn the binding nature of an award") (citation omitted).
62 Kaikobad (n. 8) 233.
63 Statute of the International Court of Justice, 15 UNCIO 35559 Stat. 1055 (1945) [hereinafter ICJ Statute]. A similar provision existed under the Statute of the Permanent Court of International Justice (PCIJ), the predecessor to the ICJ. See Reisman, "South West Africa" (n. 33); James Crawford, "'Dreamers of the Day': Australia and the International Court of Justice" (2013) 14 *Melbourne Journal of International Law* 520, 520–521 (highlighting the relationship between the ICJ, PCIJ, and their Statutes).
64 Nelson (n. 46) 221

> Other international judicial tribunals, including the European Court of Human Rights, European Court of Justice, and the tribunals dealing with human rights abuses in Yugoslavia, Rwanda and Sierra Leone, have similar revision procedures in their statutes each authorizing

revision only where decisive new facts emerge, but excluding facts overlooked through "negligence."

(Citations omitted)

But see Brown (n. 8) 224–225 (noting that the power of revision does not exist in the constitutive instrument of some tribunals).

65 Walsh (n. 40) 448 ("The standard of review for new facts is strict").
66 Reisman (n. 24) 209.
67 See Reisman, *South West Africa* (n. 33) 16.
68 Ibid. 17.
69 Kaikobad (n. 8) 236.
70 Ibid.
71 Reisman (n. 24) 209.
72 Ibid. 210.
73 Ibid.
74 *Application for Revision of the Judgment of 11 July 1996 in the Case Concerning Application of the Convention on the Prevention and Punishment of the Crime of Genocide (Bosnia and Herzegovina v. Yugoslavia), Preliminary Objections (Yugoslavia v. Bosnia and Herzegovina)* (Judgment) [2003] *ICJ Rep.* 7.
75 Richard Graving, "International Court of Justice Muddles Jurisdiction in Yugoslav Genocide Case" (2007) 15 *Tulsa J. Comp. & Int'l L.* 29, 55; Wittich (n. 32) 595

The Court stated that by basing its application for revision on its admission as a new member to the UN in 2000, Yugoslavia invoked facts that had occurred after the judgment had been given rather than relying on facts already existing in 1996.

76 *Application for Revision of the Judgment of 11 July 1996 in the Case Concerning Application of the Convention on the Prevention and Punishment of the Crime of Genocide (Bosnia and Herzegovina v. Yugoslavia), Preliminary Objections (Yugoslavia v. Bosnia and Herzegovina)* (Judgment) [2003] *ICJ Rep.* 30–32 [65]–[74].
77 Ibid. [67].
78 Ibid. [68].
79 *Venezuela Holdings B.V. and others v. Bolivarian Republic of Venezuela* (Decision on Revision, 2015) ICSID Case No. ARB/07/27 (Venezuela Holdings B.V.).
80 Kaikobad (n. 8) 267.
81 Ibid. 270–271.
82 Ibid.
83 Ibid. 277.
84 Ibid. 272.
85 *Battus Case*, IX Franco-Bulgarian Mixed Arbitral Tribunal, RDTAM, 284–286.
86 See notes 45–55 above and accompanying text.
87 ICJ Statute Art. 61(5).
88 Kaikobad (n. 7) 278.
89 [1985] *ICJ Reports* 192.
90 Ibid. 214.
91 *Lehigh Valley R.R. v. Germany* (1933) 8 *RIAA* 225, 458–460 (Mixed Claims Comm'n 1939). The earlier case was *Lehigh Valley Railroad Company (US v. Germany) (Sabotage Claims)* (1933) 8 *RIAA* 160, 190.
92 Nelson (n. 46) 225 ("one commentator notes that these claims, referred to as the *Sabotage Claims*, 'provide the prime, if not the only, example of such a fact'").
93 Ibid. at 197–198.
94 See Kaikobad (n. 8) 292–293.
95 See ibid. 293.
96 ICJ (n. 10) 207 ("Strictly speaking, once it is established that the request for revision fails to meet one of the conditions for admissibility, the Court is not required to go further and investigate whether the other conditions are fulfilled").
97 ICJ (n. 27) [411].
98 *McGinley and Egan v. United Kingdom*, Judgment (Revision) (App. no. 21824/93) 2000-I *ECHR* 321 [30].

99 Case 267/80 Rev. *Riseria Modenese Srl v. Council* [1985] *ECR* 3499 Judgment, 1985 *ECR* 3499.

100 Ibid. 3504 [10].

101 Fellmeth (n. 25) 703.

102 A part of the opposition was against the judgment itself while another component of the opposition was against the approach of the Nigerian Government in implementing the ICJ decision. Jesse Townsend, "Medellín Stands Alone: Common Law Nations Do Not Show a Shared Post-ratification Understanding of the ICJ" (2009) 34 *Yale Journal of International Law* 463–491; Paulson (n. 14) 450–451 ("The Nigerian national government is under tremendous internal political pressure not to respect the Judgment, especially with regard to Bakassi, as various large Nigerian groups have opposed it and called for war, if necessary") (citation omitted).

103 See Monticha Pakdeekong, "Who Owns the Preah Vihear Temple? A Thai Position" (2009) 2 *Journal of East Asia and International Law* 229–233 (discussing Thailand's registration of a protest and reservation of a right to seek revision if it discovered new facts in the future and stating that, decades after such steps were taken, the case that involved Thailand and Cambodia and which was decided in 1962 has not been brought to the attention of the Court again).

104 International Court of Justice, Malaysia requests a revision of the Judgment of May 23, 2008, in which the Court found, *inter alia*, that sovereignty over the island of Pedra Branca/Pulau Batu Puteh belongs to Singapore (February 3, 2017); www.icj-cij.org/docket/files/167/19344.pdf; accessed May 4, 2017.

105 Ibid.

106 Ibid.

107 Dr Chris N. Okeke, "Open Letter to Jonathan on Bakassi" (*Save Bakassi*, September 25, 2012); http://savebakassi.blogspot.com/2012/09/open-letter-to-jonathan-on-bakassi.html; accessed December 31, 2015.

108 Ibid.

109 Hugo Odiogor, Johnbosco Agbakwuru, Dotun Ibiwoye, Nkiruka Nnorum and Kunle Kalejaiye, "Bakassi Belongs to Nigeria – Fresh Facts Reveal," *Vanguard*, September 17, 2012; www.vanguardngr.com/2012/09/bakassi-belongs-to-nigeria-fresh-facts-reveal/; accessed December 31, 2015.

110 Ibid.

111 Ibid.

112 Ibid.

113 Odiogor (n. 109).

114 Ibid.

115 Ibid.

116 Okeke (n. 107).

117 Ibid.

118 Alberto Alvarez-Jimenez, "Boundary Agreements in the International Court of Justice's Case Law, 2000–2010" (2012) 3 *EJIL* 495:

> In its attempt to claim sovereignty over the peninsula, Nigeria argued that the [1913 British–German] agreement should be disregarded because it had to be approved by the German parliament according to the German law of the time, an approval that did not take place. The Court did not declare so. Instead of delving into German law to assess whether the agreement was valid, the Court looked at the parties' external behaviour regarding it. The Court found that Germany had stated that its domestic procedures had been followed, the UK had not raised the issue, and both parties had officially published the agreement. The agreement was then valid and constituted for the Court the fundamental ground for declaring that the peninsula belonged to Cameroon.
>
> (Ibid. 509, citations omitted)

119 See Fellmeth (n. 25) 705.

120 The PCA paid noticeable attention to arriving at an equitable outcome as it held:

> Within those constraints imposed by law, the Tribunal considers that it has both the right and the duty to exercise judicial discretion in order to achieve an equitable result. There will rarely, if ever, be a single line that is uniquely equitable. The Tribunal must exercise its judgment in order to decide upon a line that is, in its view, both equitable and as practically

> satisfactory as possible, while at the same time in keeping with the requirement of achieving a stable legal outcome. Certainty, equity, and stability are thus integral parts of the process of delimitation.
>
> (*Barbados v. Republic of Trinidad and Tobago* (2006) 45 *ILM* 800, 839 paras 240, 242 (Perm. Ct Arb. April 11, 2006))

121 Fellmeth (n. 25) 705–706.

122 See e.g. Yoram Rabin and Roy Peled, "Transfer of Sovereignty over Populated Territories from Israel to a Palestinian State: The International Law Perspective" (2008) 17 *Minnesota Journal of International Law* 59, 68 (discussing a lawsuit in Nigeria by Bakassi residents seeking to prevent the implementation of the ICJ decision).

123 See Andrew A. Rosen, "Economic and Cooperative Post-Colonial Borders: How Two Interpretations of Borders by the ICJ May Undermine the Relationship Between Uti Possidetis Juris and Democracy" (2006) 25 *Penn. St. Int'l L. Rev.* 207, 234–237 (for a criticism of the ICJ decision along these lines).

124 See Oduntan (n. 6) 427

> although the Court arrived at the drastic decision that the Bakassi territory ought to be handed over to Cameroon irrespective of the fact that the majority of the local population are Nigerian and considered themselves hostile toward the idea of becoming part of Cameroon, the Court took note of Cameroon's undertaking, given at the hearings, to "continue to afford protection to Nigerians living in the [Bakassi] peninsula and in the Lake Chad area."
>
> (Paragraph 318)

125 Ibid.

126 See Edwin E. Egede, "Bakassi: The Green Tree Agreement (GTA) and Section 12 of the Nigerian 1999 Constitution," *Daily Independent* (Nigeria, January 31, 2008) (proposing the establishment of a body to monitor compliance and ensure that Cameroon lived up to its obligations to Nigerian nationals remaining in Bakassi under the Greentree Agreement).

3 Resolution of international disputes through preventive diplomacy by the United Nations

Case study of the Cameroon v. Nigeria case

Bayo Ojo[1]

Introduction

Over the years, the United Nations has adopted several methods in resolving international disputes but several of these methods have proved ineffective in achieving lasting peace. The resolution of the land and maritime disputes between Nigeria and Cameroon through the assistance of the UN has helped to emphasize that shifting from the culture of reaction to one of prevention is not only a panacea for enduring peace but also highly cost-effective both in human and material terms.[2] Kofi Annan, former Secretary-General of the United Nations, had graphically articulated the importance of adopting a preventive approach to any dispute thus:

> In the early stages of a dispute, parties tend to be less polarized and more flexible and thus more inclined to settle their dispute peacefully than after violent conflict has become entrenched. Prevention also offers the best possible chance to address the root causes of a conflict, and not just its consequences, thus providing a real opportunity to sow the seeds of durable peace.[3]

The peculiar circumstances of the case concerning the land and maritime boundary between Nigeria and Cameroon and its progressive and peaceful resolution readily recommend it as a flagship for the present thinking in the UN and the international community that prevention is better than cure. It also shows that 'preventing potential conflict from crossing the threshold of violence requires early warning of situations with the potential for crisis, proper analysis, integrated preventive strategy, the political will and resources to implement such a strategy'.[4]

The case under reference is peculiar in many circumstances especially for the following reasons:

- It involves a massive and almost unprecedented claim for the determination of the entire land and maritime boundary between Nigeria and Cameroon, an area covering over 1,300 kilometres.
- It involves a claim for the sovereignty of the ostensibly oil-rich Bakassi Peninsula.
- The judgment, even though rendered in beautiful and appealing language characteristic of the International Court of Justice (ICJ), is highly prolix, tortuous and technical, which impedes easy comprehension.

Nigeria is the most populous black nation and it is said that one out of every four black men is a Nigerian.[5] Thus, any disobedience to the orders and declaration of the judgment leading to armed conflict would have spiralled refugee conflagration in the whole of sub-Saharan Africa and the rest of Africa. Nigeria could have easily chosen to disobey the judgment, following some precedents in the past, but willingly decided to implement the judgment, thus reinforcing one of her foreign policy objectives aimed at achieving peace in Africa, and the world at large.[6]

This chapter will focus on exploring the Bakassi dispute as a case study in the application of preventive diplomacy by the United Nations to prevent the escalation of a dispute.

United Nations and preventive diplomacy

The notion of preventive diplomacy has been traced back to Dag Hammarskjöld, who served as the second Secretary-General of the United Nations.[7] However, it appears to have been more clearly articulated in the Agenda for Peace, a report written in 1992 in the changing context of the end of the Cold War, by the then Secretary-General of the United Nations, Boutros Boutros-Ghali, which defined preventive diplomacy as 'action to prevent disputes from arising between parties, to prevent existing disputes from escalating into conflicts and to limit the spread of the latter when they occur'.[8] The Report mentioned that preventive diplomacy is most desirable and efficiently employed if it eases tensions before they result in conflict or, in the case where the conflict breaks out, it is utilized swiftly to contain such conflict and to seek to resolve its underlying causes.[9] In addition, the Report encouraged the United Nations to adopt a 'rich variety of complementary efforts' and pointed out that '[j]ust as no two regions or situations are the same, so the design of cooperative work and its division of labour must adapt to the realities of each case with flexibility and creativity'.[10] As we will see below as I discuss the preventive diplomacy efforts by the United Nations after the Bakassi Decision, this was an example of the flexible and creative tool of preventive diplomacy. In 2010, during the Nigeria's Presidency of the Security Council the Secretary-General was requested to submit a report that would make recommendations on how best to optimize the use of preventive diplomacy tools within the United Nations system and in cooperation with regional and sub-regional organizations and other actors.[11] The Report of the Secretary in response to this request was submitted in 2011 and also identifies other interesting case-studies of the use of preventive diplomacy in different parts of the world.[12]

Case concerning the land and maritime boundary between Cameroon and Nigeria (Bakassi)

This case was initiated by the Government of the Republic of Cameroon against the Federal Republic of Nigeria on 29 March 1994. It relates essentially to the question of sovereignty over the Bakassi Peninsula and the delimitation of the maritime boundary between the States, which had remained a partial one, and despite many attempts to complete it the two parties had been unable to do so. On 6 June 1994 an additional application was filed by Cameroon for determination of a dispute 'relating essentially to the question of sovereignty over a part of the territory of Cameroon in the area of Lake Chad'. It also requested the Court to 'specify definitely' the frontier between the two States from Lake Chad to the sea, and that the two applications be examined as a single case.

Nigeria raised a preliminary objection to the jurisdiction of the Court on eight grounds. This was promptly heard by the Court, and in its judgment of 11 June 1998 it dismissed the objection and assumed jurisdiction holding that Cameroon's requests were admissible. The eighth ground, which the Court held did not have an exclusively preliminary character, was reserved for disposition during the judgment on merits. After setting out the historical and geographical antecedents to the legal instruments, which the parties, subject to Nigeria's caveat, admitted were binding on them, the Court proceeded to consider the case under five broad divisions for ease of handling. The five broad areas were as follows: defining the boundary line in the Lake Chad area; determining the line from Lake Chad to the Bakassi Peninsula; defining the boundary in Bakassi and determination of sovereignty over the Peninsula; delimitation of the maritime boundary between the two States; and determining the issues of state responsibility raised by the parties.

The Court decided that the boundary between the Republic of Cameroon and the Federal Republic of Nigeria in the Lake Chad area had been delimited by the legal instruments that bind the parties, namely the Thomson–Marchand Declaration of 1929–1930, as incorporated in the Henderson–Fleuriau exchange of notes of 1933, and the line of the boundary following the coordinates set out in the judgment. Also, the Court decided that the land boundary between Cameroon and the Federal Republic of Nigeria is delimited from Lake Chad to the Bakassi Peninsula by relevant instruments binding on the parties,[13] and further, that the boundary between the Republic of Nigeria and Bakassi is delimited by Articles XVIII to XX of the Anglo-German Agreement of 11 March 1913. Thus, sovereignty over the Bakassi Peninsula lies with the Republic of Cameroon; the maritime boundary between the States follows a course and 'compromise line' jointly drawn on 4 April 1971 by the Heads of State of Cameroon and Nigeria on British Admiralty Chart No. 3433 (the Yaoundé II Declaration) and the line adopted in the Declaration signed by the parties via their Heads of State at Maroua on 1 June 1975 (Maroua Declaration), as corrected by Exchange Letters between them on 12 June and 17 July 1975, among others.[14]

With regard to the issues on State Responsibilities raised by the parties the Court held that each party was under an obligation expeditiously and without condition to withdraw its administration and its military and police forces from territories which fall within the sovereignty of Cameroon pursuant to points 1 and 3 of the judgment and of Nigeria pursuant to point 2 of the judgment respectively. It also unanimously rejected all other claims by the Republic of Cameroon and the Counterclaim of Federal Republic of Nigeria on State Responsibilities because there was not enough evidence to support these claims.[15]

It is believed that the judgment is a violation of the rights of Bakassi people to self-determination. Articles 1 and 55 of the United Nations Charter provide for the right to self-determination of all human beings. By the ICJ's judgment that sovereignty over Bakassi lies with Cameroon, the Court infringed on the right of the Bakassi people to self-determination by trying to make them Cameroonian citizens willy-nilly.[16] Further, the loss of Bakassi to Cameroon has endangered the multi-million Naira Export Processing Zone (EPZ).[17] The Calabar EPZ depends largely on this important segment, and it would only mean that the port belongs to Cameroon outright or Nigeria will have to pay charges for its usage.[18] There is also the danger of Nigeria losing 100 million barrels of oil deposit as well as four trillion cubic feet of gas deposits in the Peninsula. Nigerian oil companies have to leave the area and relinquish the oil wells to the Cameroonians. The implication is that the huge revenue from 'Bakassi oil' will be lost by Nigeria. Any nation striving to improve the lot of its people by adequately utilizing their sources of revenue will surely feel the severe impact of this type of judgment on its entire economy.[19]

The social implications of the ruling are that Nigerians who have lived in Bakassi all their lives have to face the sad reality of having to evacuate a region that is part and parcel of them. Most people living in that area have businesses located there and so leaving the area will mean detaching them from their source(s) of income. Moreover, all infrastructural facilities including hospitals, schools, recreational centres and so on that were originally put in place by the Nigerian Government would be forfeited, resulting in a fruitless effort and loss of income.

Another far-reaching implication of the judgment is the strategic or security implication for the Nigerian State. The victory of Cameroon will make the nation lose its eastern access to the Atlantic. This implies that without Cameroon's approval, Nigeria's naval ships cannot move freely to Southern Africa. This is certainly not in the interest of the Nigerian nation.[20]

Brief comments on the judgment

The above represents just a skeleton of the operative part of the judgment. The lead judgment alone runs into some 315 pages rendered in legal, geographical and land/survey technical language that hardly yields itself easily to comprehension by non-experts in relevant fields.

The bulky nature of the judgment is a function of the massive claims upon which the Court had to decide. The parties did not help matters either, as they filed repetitive claims and submissions in their Memorials and Counter-Memorials, written and oral submissions, equivocating and shifting grounds on the claims and the role of the Court. The Court noted this vacillating attitude of the parties in the following words:

> The questions upon which the parties differ is the nature of the task which the Court should undertake. The respective positions of the parties on this point changed somewhat in the course of the proceedings. Thus in its Additional Applications, Cameroon requested the Court to 'specify definitely' the frontier between (it) and the Federal Republic of Nigeria from Lake Chad to the sea. Then in its written pleadings and at the hearings, it requested the Court to confirm the course of the frontier as indicated in the delimitation instruments, emphasizing that, in requesting the court to specify definitely the frontier between Cameroon and Nigeria, it had not requested the Court itself to undertake a delimitation of the frontier.[21]

On the part of Nigeria, it first argued that there was no territorial dispute between the parties from Lake Chad to the Bakassi Peninsula at the preliminary objection stage. However, upon the dismissal of the objection, Nigeria subsequently indicated a number of specific locations on the land boundary which, in its view called for some form of consideration by the Court, either because the delimitation instruments themselves were 'defective' or because they had been applied by Cameroon in a way which was 'manifestly at variance' with the terms.[22]

The very technical nature of the case stems from the nature of the claims and the documents relied on by the parties. Most if not all the delimitation instruments defining areas of disputes are accompanied by annexure of maps and sketches. Again, each party also accompanied its Memorial and submissions with maps and sketches indicating the areas of claims by the respective party.

It is therefore not surprising that most of the decisions of the Court are followed by a clear list of maps, sketches and coordinates that sets out the contentious boundaries and lines with certainty and finality. In its detailed assessment of all the submissions and claims, the Court found itself relying and adopting the maps and sketches attached to one or the other of the parties as part and parcel of the judgment.

Another peculiar nature of the judgment is the declaration of state responsibility for and against each party. Thus while the Court found for Cameroon and gave sovereignty in its favour over settlements situated to the east of the frontier in the Lake Chad area and over Bakassi Peninsula, it equally found in favour of Nigeria in respect of some settlements along the boundary from Lake Chad to Bakassi Peninsula after careful interpretation of relevant delimitation instruments. Thus, each party was required, 'expeditiously and without condition to withdraw its administration and military and police forces from territories which fall within the sovereignty' of the other.[23]

The above clarification is necessary for a better understanding of the great task involved in the implementation of the judgment of the Court. Apart from the requirement of technical experts to interpret the judgment and transpose same to the ground and sea as the case may be, the length of delimitation and demarcation distance tasks not only human and material resources but equally time and space. This explains why, in spite of the prompt acceptance of the judgment by the parties and consistent implementation which commenced the same year, the implementation is still in progress, many after. It equally explains and clarifies the needed support of the UN and the political will commendably exhibited by the Presidents of the parties in undertaking to implement the judgment.

Implementation of the judgment

The anticipatory dispositions and summit

It is gratifying to note that the judgment delivered on 10 October 2002 by the ICJ met two willing parties. Nigeria's commitment to African brotherhood is already noted in its foreign policy objectives. On the part of Cameroon, it had already made undertaking to abide by the judgment of the Court even at the hearing stage of the case. This undertaking was noted and adopted by the Court in its judgment. According to the Court, it

> takes note of the commitment undertaken by the Republic of Cameroon at the hearings that 'faithful to its traditional policy of hospitality and tolerance' it will 'continue to afford protection to Nigerians living in the (Bakassi) Peninsula and in the Lake Chad area'.[24]

Even though the adoption of this undertaking was criticized by Judge Para-Araguren in his separate opinion[25] on the ground that neither of the parties requested for such a note to be taken especially in the operative part of the judgment, it shows the disposition of Cameroon to the friendly and peaceful implementation of the judgment.

Just about a month before the date fixed for the judgment, at the invitation of the Secretary-General of the United Nations, Mr Kofi Annan, President Paul Biya of Cameroon and President Olusegun Obasanjo of Nigeria met in Paris on 5 September 2002 to discuss the Bakassi Peninsula and other issues.

In the communiqué issued at the end of the meeting both Presidents agreed to respect and implement the decision of the ICJ on the Bakassi Peninsula and establish an implementation mechanism with the support of the United Nations. The two Presidents also agreed on the need for confidence-building measures, including the eventual demilitarization of the Peninsula with the possibility of international observers to monitor the withdrawal of troops, an early visit to Nigeria of President Biya and the avoidance of inflammatory statements or declarations on the Bakassi issue by either side.[26]

Thus before the judgment was handed down both the parties and the United Nations were already expectant of the delivery of an '8-year-old baby' with all preparations in place for implementation. The role of Mr Kofi Annan is especially commendable for his ability to identify the potential danger posed to Africa and the world in the event of non-implementation of the judgment and the foresight to take even anticipatory steps in preventive diplomacy.

Other implementation steps by the Secretary-General and the two Presidents

Shortly after the judgment, the two Presidents met again on 15 November 2002 at the invitation of the Secretary-General of the UN in Geneva. It is instructive that the first commitment of the two Presidents at this meeting was to acknowledge respect for their obligations under the United Nations Charter. On his part, the Secretary-General welcomed the Presidents' renewed commitment, 'as Heads of State of law-abiding countries, to renounce the use of force in their relations and pursue peaceful ways for the settlement of their boundary differences'.[27]

The two Presidents, apart from considering other confidence-building measures, also agreed to meet at summit level at the earliest possible opportunity to discuss defence and security issues of common concern. The high point of this meeting was the agreement of the two Presidents to ask the Secretary-General to establish a Mixed Commission of the two sides to be chaired by his Special Representative, Mr Ahmedou Ould Abdallah. The Mixed Commission was to consider ways of following up the ICJ ruling and moving the process forward. The Commission would meet in Abuja and Yaoundé on an alternate basis, the first meeting being scheduled for Yaoundé on 1 December 2002. The two Presidents further agreed to consider other areas of request for assistance by the UN and to meet again under the auspices of the Secretary-General to review the progress achieved.[28]

It is remarkable to note that, from then on, the UN through the Secretary-General and Observer Group continued to participate in and monitor the implementation of the judgment. This is in line with the reaffirmation of 'his personal commitment and that of the United Nations to continue to assist Cameroon and Nigeria in their efforts to settle their differences peacefully'.[29]

After some appreciable work was done by the Mixed Commission, the Secretary-General again invited the two Presidents for a third meeting to review the programme of implementation. Apparently elated by the report of a comprehensive work plan by the Commission up to 2005 and the peaceful and smooth withdrawal of civilian administration, military and police forces from the Lake Chad area, the Secretary-General 'emphasized that the program achieved so far had proved that neighboring states can with minimal United Nations support work together to prevent a border conflict and settle their differences peacefully'.[30] He reiterated his appeal to the international community to provide support within the context of preventive diplomacy, for the efforts being made by the two countries, in particular, by granting financial assistance for the demarcation process, as well as for the confidence-building measures such as the rehabilitation of Moutengene–Abakiliki interstate road, the reactivation of the Lake Chad Commission and other cross-border environmental projects.[31]

The two Presidents on their part resolved to continue their confidence-building commitments including exchange of ambassadors, opening of consulates along their common borders and the introduction of joint patrols of security forces. They also agreed to consider concluding a treaty of friendship and non-aggression between the two countries, and renewed their commitment to take appropriate measures to guarantee the security and welfare of the population affected by the Court's decision in areas under their respective sovereignty. In furtherance of their confidence-building commitments, President Obasanjo of Nigeria paid an official visit to President Biya of Cameroon between 28 and 29 July 2004. Issues of common interest relating to peaceful and prompt implementation of the judgment were discussed and agreed upon. This included an agreement to open discussion with a view to signing a non-aggression pact. At the end, President Obasanjo invited President Biya for a reciprocal visit, an invitation which was accepted. The fourth meeting of the two Presidents on the invitation of the Secretary-General took place on 11 May 2005 in Geneva. This meeting was significant for the agreement between the two countries to work out a new programme for the withdrawal of Nigerian troops from the Bakassi Peninsula as soon as possible.[32]

This understanding was the precursor for the popular Greentree Agreement, which set out in detail modalities for the withdrawal of Nigerian troops from the Bakassi Peninsula.

The Greentree Agreement

A separate agreement for the purpose of working out modalities for the withdrawal of Nigerian troops from the Bakassi Peninsula was not in the original concept of implementation of the judgment. From the outset all matters relating to the implementation of the judgment and attendant projects and activities were handed over to the Mixed Commission by the two Presidents. Accordingly, in the comprehensive work plan approved for the Commission by the two Heads of State the deadline for withdrawal and transfer of authority from the Peninsula was 15 September 2004. Pursuant to this arrangement the two Heads of Delegation to the Commission were empowered to meet and work out the modalities at the Commission's meeting of 18–19 August 2004. However, at the meeting of 21–22 October 2004, the Commission resolved to refer the issue to the two Heads of State and the Secretary-General 'as a result of divergence of views'.[33]

It was pursuant to this referral that the two Heads of State agreed to work out the requisite modalities leading to an agreement negotiated and signed by the two Presidents under the auspices of the Secretary-General at Greentree, United States on 12 June 2006. The Agreement was witnessed by the United Nations and the Federal Republic of Germany, the United States of America, the French Republic and the United Kingdom, generally referred to as the Witness States. In the main provisions of the Agreement Nigeria reaffirmed its recognition of the sovereignty of Cameroon over the Peninsula and undertook to withdraw its forces therefrom within 60 days of the date of signing the Agreement. The Secretary-General was empowered to extend same for a further period not exceeding a total of 30 days 'if exceptional circumstances so require'.[34] On the other hand, Cameroon guaranteed, in respect of Nigerian nationals living in the area, the exercise of the fundamental rights and freedoms enshrined in international human rights law, and in particular undertook to:

a not force them to leave the Zone or change their nationality;
b respect their culture, language and beliefs;
c respect their right to continue their agricultural and fishing activities;
d protect their property and their customary land rights;

e not levy in any discriminatory manner any taxes and other dues on Nigerian nationals living in the Zone; and
f take necessary measures to protect Nigerian nationals living in the Zone from any harassment or harm.[35]

The Agreement established a Follow-up Committee with the mandate to monitor its implementation with the assistance of the United Nations Observers of the Mixed Commission. The Follow-up Committee is composed of two representatives each from Cameroon, Nigeria and the United Nations, and one each from the Witness States.[36] While I was the head of the Nigerian representation with the former Inspector General of Police Mr Sunday Ehindero at the Committee, my colleague at the International Law Commission Professor Maurice Kamto was the head of that of Cameroon.

The Agreement created a special status for the Peninsula (Zone) to the intent that Cameroon shall allow Nigeria to keep its civil administration and police force necessary for the maintenance of law and order in the Zone for a non-renewable period of two years after the withdrawal of Nigerian forces. Similarly, Cameroon shall, following the transfer of authority to it, apply to the Zone a special transitional regime for a non-renewal period of five years. In the application of the special transitional regime, Cameroon shall:

a facilitate the exercise of the rights of Nigerian nationals living in the Zone and access by Nigerian civil authorities to the Nigerian population living in the Zone;
b not apply its customs or immigration laws to Nigerian nationals living in the Zone on their direct return from Nigeria for the purpose of exercising their activities;
c allow officers and uniformed personnel of the Nigerian police access to the Zone, in cooperation with the Cameroonian police, with the minimum of formalities when dealing with inquiries into crimes and offences or other incidents exclusively concerning Nigerian nationals; and
d allow innocent passage in the territorial waters of the Zone to civilian ships sailing under the Nigerian flag, consistent with the provisions of this Agreement, to the exclusion of Nigerian warships.[37]

In the spirit of *pacta sunt servanda* and the encouragement of the UN and the Witness Countries, Nigerian troops were successfully withdrawn from the Bakassi Peninsula on the 63rd day after the signing of the Agreement, i.e. on 14 August 2006. On that date, I handed over the territory in question to Professor Maurice Kamto of Cameroon in a solemn ceremony where the Nigerian national flag was lowered for the last time and that of Cameroon hoisted. It was indeed a very emotional moment for me. However, I took solace in the ecstasy of the success and the triumph of preventive diplomacy of the United Nations: the triumph of peace over war.

The Follow-up Committee and Observer Team

As set out in the Greentree Agreement and the mandate of the Cameroon–Nigeria Mixed Commission,[38] the Follow-up Committee and the Observer Team are to ensure the monitoring of the withdrawal and transfer of authority and also monitor the observance of the undertaking of either party in relation to the affected population. They are also to assess the conditions of the population and monitor the implementation of confidence-building measures, among others. The Follow-up Committee and the UN Observer Team of the

Cameroon–Nigeria Mixed Commission harmonized a unified visit each time a visit was to be made to the affected area. As at May 2008, the teams had made seven observer missions to the Bakassi Peninsula.

A look at the activities of this seventh mission will bring home the realities of the mission and the efficacy of preventive diplomacy and confidence-building in resolution of disputes of this nature. The detailed tasks of the mission were 'to collect information on the political, socio-economic and human rights situations of the affected population starting from the Zone area' and to check on the following outstanding issues:

- a The relationship between communities and the security agencies
- b Any more improvement on the provision of social amenities
- c The state of security on the provision of social amenities
- d The state of security on the Peninsula
- e Any places set aside for storage of fuel and whether cutting of wood for fuel is on the increase
- f State of passage of information to the authorities and population about the visit of the Observer Group
- g The state of use of *wee* in Mbenmong settlement
- h Inflation of wounds during fighting using cutlasses
- i Any incidence of attempted selling of ammunitions
- j The preparedness of the Zone towards final handover in August 2008.[39]

The report of this visit showed the grim situation of the people and their primordial concern and attachment to the Zone. For instance, in Komboa Muja II/Atabong East, it was reported that the Chief of the place appreciated the effort in providing a school in the area and a water storage tank. However, on the Group's suggestion that the natives should use alternatives to wood as a source of fuel, the Chief retorted that his ancestors had used firewood and therefore he would resist any effort that would try to dissuade him from using it.[40]

In Jabane/Abana, the Paramount Ruler lamented that the community had neither school nor health facilities as a result of the ICJ judgment, as all the facilities came to a halt after the judgment. He concluded that the youths were being unruly because of neglect. Another Chief was reported to have said that his people would never abandon their land and that they were ready to die for it. This underscores the undertaking of Cameroon not to disrupt the settled rights and lives of the local population.

In Kombo Bedimu/Ine Okoi, the report was more grim and touching as the Group was informed that the community had lost its Paramount Ruler to cholera caught from unsafe drinking water.[41]

In each case the members, particularly the Chairman of the Group, reassured the people of their safety and the readiness of the authorities to improve their lot, especially in the provision of social amenities, alongside other encouragement and assurances.

The Cameroon–Nigeria Mixed Commission

The Cameroon–Nigeria Mixed Commission (CNMC) is the central judgment implementation agency of the parties and the United Nations. It was set up at the second meeting of the two Presidents on the invitation of the Secretary-General on 15 November 2002 and held its first meeting in Yaoundé on 1 December 2002. It was chaired by the Special

Representative of the Secretary-General: Mr Ahmadou Ould Abdallah from its inception to 6 July 2007, General Lamine Cassé from 16 November 2007 to 14 March 2008 and by His Excellency Ambassador Said Djinnit from 20 June 2008 to 12 September 2014. He was succeeded by Mohammed Ibn Chambas, who is the current head of the Commission.[42]

The mandate of the Commission was clearly set out in the communiqué issued at the end of the meeting of 15 November 2002, and includes:

1. To consider all the implication of the decision, including the need to protect the right of the affected population in both countries;
2. To demarcate the land boundary between the two countries;
3. To make recommendations on additional confidence-building measures;
4. To hold on a regular basis meetings between local authorities, government officials and Heads of State;
5. To develop projects to promote joint economic ventures and cross-border cooperation;
6. To ensure the avoidance of inflammatory statements or declarations on Bakassi by either side;
7. To undertake troop withdrawal from relevant areas along the land boundary and eventual demilitarization of the Bakassi Peninsula with the possibility of international personnel to observe withdrawal; and
8. To work towards reactivation of the Lake Chad Basin Commission (LCBC).

The Commission has been meeting and working conscientiously and consistently pursuant to its demanding mandate. The Commission meets once every two months and held its 24th meeting in Abuja between 11 and 12 June 2009. The meetings of the Commission are still ongoing. The last was held in Abuja on 11 May 2007.

In the Herculean task of executing its mandate, the Commission adopted a comprehensive working plan and set up some sub-working groups, including:

- Sub-Commission on Demarcation of Land Boundary
- Sub-Commission on Affected Population
- Working Group on Withdrawal and Transfer of Authority on Land Boundary
- Working Group on Maritime Boundary
- Observer Personnel Group
- Joint Technical Team.

Through the instrumentality of these sub-working groups, the Commission has as at June 2009 completed the demarcation of the entire land boundary in the Lake Chad area, from Lake Chad to the sea and the maritime boundary, all in accordance with the highly technical specification of the ICJ judgment. The process of emplacement of pillars along the boundary has already commenced in January 2010.[43]

All in all, the Commission has creditably acquitted itself of its mandate in the physical demarcation of the land boundary between the parties, the withdrawal and transfer of authority from the Lake Chad area, the Bakassi Peninsula and along the land boundary, and in the confidence-building measures, has especially made provision of succour to a people caught in the maze of transfer of sovereignty of what they consider as their homeland. The members of the United Nations Security Council have commended the efforts of the Cameroon–Nigeria Mixed Commission in facilitating the performance of the obligations under the judgment of the International Court of Justice and the deliminating and demarcating of the boundary between Cameroon and Nigeria.[44] At a meeting of Heads of Delegations of the Mixed Commission in June 2016, the Special Representative of the United Nations Secretary-General for West Africa and the Sahel and Chairman of the Mixed Commission, Mr Mohamed Ibn Chambas, stated:

> The Cameroon–Nigeria Mixed Commission has distinguished itself as one of the finest, and most successful, examples of the United Nation's exercise of good offices and confidence building measures in the service of diplomacy: it has strengthened friendship and consensus between the two brotherly nations.[45]

The work of the Commission is still in progress and its meetings continue.[46] While the Mixed Commission has successfully completed the withdrawal and the transfer of authority in the Bakassi Peninsula and in the Lake Chad area, along the land boundary, it is still working on sections of the northernmost regions of the land boundary. The Mixed Commission's continuing field assessment of the terrain has been hindered by security breaches in the area and thus it is currently working on utilizing desktop demarcation rather than pillar emplacement projects. It is also working on cross-border development projects and other confidence-building initiatives to assist populations affected by the implementation of the ICJ decision so as to promote social cohesion.[47]

Other UN agencies involved in the implementation of the judgment

The Commission has also enjoyed the support of other United Nations agencies in the execution of its mandate. For instance, the United Nations Procurement Division helped to advertise all the demarcation contracts while the United Nations Office for Project Services was involved in the demarcation and pillar emplacement, which commenced in the first week of 2009. Similarly, the United Nations Institute for Training and Research is to help in capacity-building in the affected communities. However, it does appear that the surveyors involved in the demarcation appeared to have some concerns about the United Nations participation. In a paper prepared by two surveyors, one from Cameroon and the other from Nigeria, who were involved in the land boundary demarcation process of the Commission, the following concerns were expressed:

> UN involvement as a third party proved problematic. With no defined role in the case of dispute between the Parties, the United Nations was unable to prevent or mediate minor disagreements that threatened to prolong the field exercise. In addition, the UN cartographic consultant's *Specifications and Technical Guide* based on 'international standards' made the cost of the demarcation exercise prohibitive.[48]

The role of the Witness States

In the summary of Discussions and Modalities of Implementation annexed to the Greentree Agreement it was reiterated that:

> The presence and signature at the signing ceremony of Witness States representing key partners of the two parties is further evidence of the international community's

> interest in seeing the implementation of this agreement according to the time-frames contained in it.[49]

The Witness States not only witnessed the signing of the Greentree Agreement, but are participating in the monitoring of its implementation. They have one delegate each in the Follow-up Committee. They have also made some financial contributions to the work of the Cameroon–Nigeria Mixed Commission. Thus, apart from the US$3 million contributed by each of the parties to the United Nations Trust Fund for the Implementation Exercise, the United Kingdom has donated £1 million sterling while the European Union has contributed €4.4 million.

Conclusion

I have taken this long excursion into the basic dispute-resolution mechanisms of the UN and the judgment of the ICJ and its implementation so far to drive home the indisputable fact that together the world can achieve lasting and enduring peace through a unified action in preventive diplomacy and confidence-building. The personal commitment of Mr Kofi Anan, the then Secretary-General of the United Nations, in galvanizing the parties even in an anticipatory meeting before the judgment calls for particular acknowledgement. Special tribute must also be paid to former President Olusegun Obasanjo of Nigeria and President Paul Biya of Cameroon for their statesmanship, cooperation and unflinching commitment to the whole process. Without their buying into it, the United Nations would not have been able to make any headway.

The lesson of the judgment and its implementation to the world is that lasting world peace is not a mirage but is attainable, through a combination of political will on the part of feuding parties and the support of the United Nations and the international community as a whole. The judgment and its implementation is a study in the triumph of preventive diplomacy which is at the centre of the new thinking of the United Nations in dispute resolution. This is the only sure guarantee for other indices of peace and security, which, as we know it today, consists not only in the absence of armed conflict but also in the presence of social amenities and other entrenched rights in international law. Permit me to draw my last line in this regard from the book *The Quotable Kofi Annan*:

> We know that lasting peace requires a broader vision, encompassing education and literacy, health and nutrition, human rights and fundamental freedom. We know that we cannot be secure amidst starvation. We cannot build peace without alleviating poverty. We cannot build freedom on foundation of injustice.[50]

Certainly, the enduring peace that has persisted in all the regions from Lake Chad to the sea and the Bakassi Peninsula could not have been possible without the clear vision of the United Nations in cooperation with the parties in preventive diplomacy and confidence-building through the provision of the above irreducible minimum imperatives for lasting world peace.

Notes

1 The author is grateful to Dr Celestine Abugu and Mrs Ewuwuni Onnoghen-Theophilus for their assistance in researching this chapter.

2 See United Nations Department of Political Affairs: Prevention and Mediation, www.un.org/undpa/en/diplomacy-mediation.
3 *Common Destiny, New Resolve: Annual Report on the Work of the Organization, 2000* (New York: United Nations Department of Public Information, 2001), p. 13.
4 K.O. Annan, *Partnership for Global Community. Annual Report on the Work of the Organization, 1998* (New York: United Nations Department of Public Information, 1999), p. 9, para. 26.
5 Sola Odunfa, BBC *Focus on Africa* magazine.
6 Dr Samuel I. Odoh and David M.E. Nwogbaga, 'Theoretical Perspectives on Nigeria's Enforcement of the International Court of Justice's Verdict over Bakassi Peninsula', *International Affairs and Global Strategy*, ISSN 2224–574X (Paper) ISSN 2224–8951 (Online), Vol. 29, 2015. Available at www.iiste.org/Journals/index.php/IAGS/article/download/19665/20161, accessed 27 April 2017.
7 See Ban Ki-Moon, *Preventive Diplomacy: Delivering Results, Report of the Secretary-General* (a report dedicated to the memory of former Secretary-General Dag Hammarskjöld on the fiftieth anniversary of his death in 1961), S/2011/552, 26 August 2011. Available at www.un.org/undpa/sites/www.un.org.undpa/files/SG%20Report%20on%20Preventive%20Diplomacy.pdf.
8 Boutros Boutros-Ghali, *An Agenda for Peace: Preventive Diplomacy, Peacemaking and Peacekeeping* (New York: UN, 1992) A/47/277, 17 June 1992, para. 20. See also B.G. Ramcharan, *The International Law and Practice of Early-warning and Preventive Diplomacy: The Emerging Global Watch* (Boston: Martinus Nijhoff, 1991).
9 *Agenda for Peace*, para. 23.
10 Para. 62, ibid.
11 Statement by the President of the Security Council, S/PRST/2010/14, 16 July 2010.
12 *Preventive Diplomacy: Delivering Results, Report of the Secretary-General*, op. cit. pp. 2 and 14–17.
13 See Tanaka's chapter in this book (Chapter 6) for more discussion on this.
14 For further discussion of the delimitation of the maritime boundaries between the two States see Egede's chapter in this book (Chapter 7).
15 Para. 324 of ICJ judgment of 10 October 2002, www.icj-cij.org/en/case/94.
16 O.O. Okanga, 'Analysis of Judgement of the International Court of Justice' *The Nation Newspaper* Archives: Law (Nigeria 19 August 2008).
17 Y. Alhassan, *A Critique of the Mechanism for the Enforcement of International Court of Justice (ICJ) Judgment: A Case Study of Cameroon v. Nigeria*, at p. 19, LLM thesis, Ahmadu Bello University, Zaria, April 2014; available at http://kubanni.abu.edu.ng:8080/jspui/handle/123456789/7829; accessed 27 April 2017.
18 Ibid.
19 See Chapter 8 by Igiehon in this book on this.
20 A.I. Aghemelo and S. Ibhasebhor, 'Colonialism as a Source of Boundary Dispute and Conflict among African State: The World Court Judgement on the Bakassi Peninsula and its Implication' (2006) *Journal of Social Science* 13(3): 177–188. For more on the discussion on the implications of the decision on innocent passage of warships see Egede's chapter in this book (Chapter 7).
21 See ICJ judgment of 10 October 2002, p. 58, para. 77.
22 Ibid. para. 78.
23 Ibid. p. 150, para. 325.
24 Ibid. p. 452, para. 317.
25 See separate opinion of Judge Parra-Aranguren, especially paras. 2–5.
26 Brochure of the 24th Session of the Cameroon–Nigeria Mixed Commission held on 11–12 June 2009 at Transcorp Hilton, Abuja, p. 16. UN Secretary General, 'At the Secretary-General's Invitation, Presidents of Cameroon and Nigeria met in Paris to Discuss Bakassi Peninsula and Other Issues', SG/SM/8368-AFR/476 (United Nations, 5 September 2002), www.un.org/press/en/2002/sgsm8368.doc.htm; accessed 9 September 2017.
27 Ibid. p. 17.
28 Ibid.
29 Ibid.
30 Ibid. p. 26.
31 Ibid.
32 Ibid. p. 35.

33 Ibid. p. 33.
34 Article 1 and 2 of the Agreement.
35 Article 3.
36 Article 6 of the Agreement and the Modalities of Implementation.
37 See Article 4 of Annex 1 to the Agreement.
38 See the mandate as set out below under that subject.
39 See Tentative Plan for the Seventh Observation Mission to the Bakassi Peninsula, endorsed by General David Kattali, coordinator, UN Observer Team, Chairman Observer Group, dated 5 May 2008.
40 See Report of the Seventh CNMC Observer Group mission to the Bakassi Peninsula conducted from 10 to 16 May 2008, p. 5.
41 Ibid. pp. 5–6.
42 See the Brochure for the 24th session, op. cit and UN press release, SG/A/1505*–AFR/2964–BIO/4632* of 12 September 2014, www.un.org/press/en/2014/sga1505.doc.htm.
43 Ibid.
44 Security Council, 'Security Council Press Statement on Bakassi Peninsula Developments', SC/11094-AFR/2680 (United Nations, 15 August 2013); available at www.un.org/press/en/2013/sc11094.doc.htm; accessed 9 September 2017.
45 Meeting of Heads of Delegations of the Cameroon–Nigeria Mixed Commission (CNMC), Speech of Mr Mohamed Ibn Chambas, the Special Representative of the United Nations Secretary-General for West Africa and the Sahel and Chairman of the CNMC, June 2016; https://unowas.unmissions.org/sites/default/files/160606-_srsg_yaoudecnmc_eng.pdf.
46 See https://unowa.unmissions.org/cameroon-nigeria-mixed-commission?page=1.
47 See note 48 below.
48 Ali Toure and Sani M. Isa, 'Post-Conflict Demarcation of African Boundaries: The Cameroon–Nigeria Experience' in African Union Commission, *Delimitation and Demarcation of Boundaries in Africa: General Issues and Case Studies* (2013, Addis Ababa, African Union) at 190–202 at 201.
49 See Annex II to the Greentree Agreement.
50 Kofi Annan, *The Quotable Kofi Annan: Selections from Speeches and Statements from the Secretary General* (New York: United Nations, 1998), p. 11.

4 The ICJ decision on the Cameroon–Nigeria Bakassi dispute and issues arising

A Cameroonian perspective[1]

Nkwelle Ekaney

Introduction

The Bakassi Peninsula, rich in oil reserves and other natural resources and the long border between Cameroon and Nigeria stretching from Lake Chad to the Gulf of Guinea, may not have been considered as strategic territorial areas. However, the Peninsula, in particular, has been a contentious issue between Cameroon and Nigeria since the 1970s which resulted in escalating hostilities and armed conflicts in the early 1990s between both States.[2]

Cameroon initiated proceedings before the International Court of Justice (ICJ) on 29 March 1994, claiming sovereignty over the Bakassi Peninsula,[3] and in a separate additional application dated 6 June 1994 also claimed sovereignty over territory in the area of Lake Chad.[4] Cameroon also requested the Court to specify the course of the land and maritime boundary between the two countries. In its Counter-Memorial, Nigeria, *inter alia*, claimed sovereignty over the Bakassi Peninsula together with the disputed areas in Lake Chad.[5]

The Judgment of the Court of 10 October 2002 decided on the issues of sovereignty over the Bakassi Peninsula and in the disputed areas in the Lake Chad region. The Judgment was greatly contested by Nigeria. In order to encourage the peaceful implementation of aspects of the Judgment, President Paul Biya of Cameroon and President Olusegun Obasanjo of Nigeria requested the United Nations Secretary-General to establish a Cameroon–Nigeria Mixed Commission chaired by the Secretary-General's Special Representative for West Africa, Mr Ahmedou Ould-Abdallah, in order to consider 'ways of following up on the ICJ ruling and moving the process forward'.[6]

This chapter provides a Cameroonian perspective concerning aspects of the land and maritime boundary case between Cameroon and Nigeria, and provides the reaction to and a critique of the Court's Judgment. In this regard, it assesses the degree of implementation of the Judgment. It also explores post-conflict developments that have arisen following the ICJ ruling with a view to identifying whether they are continuing challenges in the implementation process.

Background

The origin of the Bakassi dispute predates the independence of either Party as sovereign States, and can be traced back to European colonial arrangements established in the late nineteenth and early twentieth centuries.[7] According to Anyu,[8] the Bakassi Peninsula conflict represents 'one of Africa's throwbacks to the colonial demarcation of the continent' that took place at the Berlin Colonial Conference of 1884–1885. In that Conference, the participating colonial powers partitioned Africa, largely without regard to social, political, cultural or ethnic affiliations[9] and also delimited maritime boundaries as part of this process.

The partition agreed at the Berlin Conference was effected through a series of agreements between the relevant colonial powers.[10] This included the 'Exchange of Notes' of 1885–1886,[11] which provided for the division of African Protectorates between Germany and Britain. This was followed by the conclusion of the Treaty of 1 July 1890,[12] and various interim agreements.[13] The final Anglo-German attempt to draw the boundary in the area resulted in the signing of the delimitation Agreement in London on 11 March 1913, which established the frontier between Cameroon and Nigeria from Yola to the Sea while regulating navigation on the Cross River.[14] Finally, the Obokwu Agreement of 12 April 1913 also settled the frontier demarcation between Cameroon and Nigeria from Yola to the Cross River.[15]

Of particular significance is Article XX of the Agreement of 11 March 1913, which provides, *inter alia* in relation to the Cameroon–Nigeria dispute that:

> Should the lower course of the Akwayafe so change its mouth as to transfer it to the Rio Del Rey, it is agreed that the area now known as the Bakassi Peninsula shall still remain German territory. The same condition applies to any portion now agreed to as being British which may be cut off in a similar way.

The fact that Article XX of the March 1913 Agreement declared the Bakassi Peninsula to be a German territory can logically be interpreted to mean that the Peninsula is Cameroonian.

The end of the First World War saw the transfer of German colonies to the Allies, followed by another division of French and British mandates in the area after the Milner–Simon Declaration of 10 July 1919 and Appended Declaration,[16] together with the Anglo-French Agreements of 29 December 1929 and 11 January 1930 respectively, which were ratified and embodied in a subsequent Exchange of Notes in 1931.[17] Maps attached to these instruments depicted the Bakassi Peninsula as remaining a part of the 'British Cameroons'.[18]

Following their independence, Cameroon and Nigeria commenced negotiations from 1963 to 1965 concerning the delimitation of their maritime boundary, which were suspended in 1965 following the eruption of the Nigerian civil war and subsequently resumed in 1970. The negotiations ultimately resulted in the conclusion of four important agreements: the Yaoundé I Agreement that established the Cameroon–Nigeria Joint Commission;[19] the Yaoundé II Declaration, signed on 4 April 1971, which demarcated a compromise boundary line between both States from the mouth of the Akwayafe River (Point 1) to a Point 12 southward and was drawn and signed on British Admiralty Chart No. 3433; the Lagos Declaration of 21 June 1971, which determined the exact coordinates of the April 1971 agreement and extended the 'Coker–Ngoh compromise line'[20] seaward; and finally, the Maroua Declaration, signed on 1 June 1975 by the Heads of State of Cameroon (Ahmadou Ahidjo) and Nigeria (Yakubu Gowon), through which the extension of the maritime boundary demarcation further seaward from Point 12 to Point G on the Admiralty Chart 3433 was agreed.[21] It is reported that Nigeria surrendered a tiny portion of its maritime territory to Cameroon as a consequence of this demarcation.[22]

In assessing the ramifications of the Yaoundé II and Maroua Declarations for both States, Ofonagoro asserts that the drawing of the 'Coker–Ngoh compromise line' through the Cross River estuary to the west of the Bakassi Peninsula effectively placed that zone within the territory of Cameroon.[23] Interestingly, following Nigeria's independence, the Bakassi Peninsula had also been recognised by that State as forming part of the territory of Cameroon in Diplomatic Note No. 570 dated 27 March 1962 (with an accompanying map) sent to the Cameroonian Government, which accepted the plebiscite results in Northern Cameroons and Southern Cameroons on 11 and 12 February 1961 respectively.[24] During the plebiscite organised in Southern Cameroons, of the 21 polling stations in the Bakassi Peninsula, 73 per cent of the zone's inhabitants voted to 'achieve independence by joining the independent Republic of Cameroun'.[25]

Since 1970, Cameroon and Nigeria had continued to attempt to settle the maritime boundary through a series of bilateral negotiations. This included negotiations carried out against the backdrop of the negotiation and conclusion of the 1982 United Nations Convention on the Law of the Sea (UNCLOS), to which both Cameroon and Nigeria became States Parties.[26] The Convention contains an internationally agreed framework of rules and principles governing the rights and obligations of States concerning the use of ocean space and resources. This includes rules on the determination of maritime zones and the delimitation of maritime boundaries where maritime zone entitlements overlap, including the Exclusive Economic Zone (EEZ) and Continental Shelf, together with rules concerning the exercise of various rights by States, balanced by adherence to certain obligations.[27] Both Cameroon and Nigeria had claimed an EEZ up to 200 nautical miles.

By 1994, the failure of these negotiations[28] led Cameroon to refer the land and maritime dispute with Nigeria to the ICJ. It should be pointed out that when the Cameroon–Nigeria negotiations began, a Nigerian initiative that had been accepted by both Parties had proposed the establishment of a Commission on Boundary Delimitation to determine a tri-point for the maritime boundary of all affected coastal States in the Gulf of Guinea.[29] Ultimately, however, the Nigerian proposal was never implemented. The mounting hostilities and strained relations between Cameroon and Nigeria that resulted in the proceedings before the ICJ from 1994 to 2002[30] also led to a segregation of interests of the coastal States in the area and, as shall be seen, the conclusion of separate bilateral agreements between Nigeria, Equatorial Guinea and Sao Tome and Principe respectively. This was the situation of boundary delimitation between Cameroon and Nigeria prior to the rendering of the Judgment of the ICJ, analysed in different chapters of this publication.

Reaction to the ICJ Judgment

The ICJ Judgment was welcomed by the Government of Cameroon, notwithstanding that the Court rejected the 'equitable method' of maritime boundary delimitation proposed by Cameroon in its arguments before the Court.[31] In contrast, the reaction in Nigeria to the Judgment was ferocious and the Government of Nigeria raised a number of objections to the Judgment.[32] Consequently, as Ariye correctly points out, the Judgment did not immediately end the dispute, and it was clear that both the Nigerian Government and the general public were reluctant to accept the findings of the Court concerning sovereignty over the Bakassi Peninsula and the disputed areas in the Lake Chad region.[33] More ominously, a number of senior Nigerian officials made statements that suggested Nigeria should consider using force in order regain the Bakassi Peninsula.[34] The reluctance of the Government of Nigeria to comply with the Court's Judgment was surprising given that it contradicted an earlier understanding reached between President Biya of Cameroon and President Obasanjo of Nigeria, in a meeting with the UN Secretary-General Kofi Annan prior to the 10 October 2002 Judgment, that they would respect the decision of the ICJ and establish implementation arrangements.[35] This position is confirmed by a UN press release to that effect, notwithstanding Nigeria's subsequent denial of the existence of any such entente.[36] Indeed, Llamzon observes that in an official government declaration following the Judgment, Nigeria appeared to accept aspects of the Judgment that it considered favourable and rejected those parts it felt were unsatisfactory.[37] Llamzon also observes that President Obasanjo's Government, *inter alia*, argued that since the Nigerian Constitution clearly defined all of the nation's land and territorial character, any amendments to the Constitution aimed at detaching the Bakassi Peninsula from Nigeria could only be carried out by both the Federal and State legislatures.[38] The anger and frustration of Nigeria were in sharp contrast to the caution expressed by Cameroon's Minister for Communication, Jacques Fame Ndongo, who appealed to Cameroonians to absorb Nigeria's reaction to the ruling with 'calm, dignity and serenity'.[39]

Besides the anger and frustration of the Nigerian Government and people, the Judgment was also criticised. Critics cite: (1) the non-ratification and non-registration of the Anglo-German Treaty of 1913[40] and its non-binding force, basing their arguments on Article 11 of the Vienna Convention on the Law of Treaties (VCLT),[41] the decision of the ICJ in the *North Sea Continental Shelf* cases (*Federal Republic of Germany v. Netherlands/Denmark*),[42] the *Nicaragua v. United States* case,[43] Article 80 of the 1969 VCLT, and Article 102(2) of the UN Charter;[44] (2) non-respect of legal principles[45] such as *nemo dat quod non habet* whereby Britain ceded Bakassi to Germany, contrary to a judicial precedence established in the *Island of Palmas* case (*Netherlands v. United States of America*),[46] and *pacta testis nec nocent nec prosunt*[47] which ought to have made the 1913 Anglo-German Agreement binding to the latter and not to Nigeria as a non-signatory;[48] (3) the Court's confirmation of the binding nature of the Maroua Declaration, mentioned earlier, the terms of which Nigeria ultimately rejected for reasons of its non-ratification, invoking Article 11 of the VCLT, the *North Sea Continental Shelf* cases, and *Nicaragua v. United States* case respectively; and (4) the fact that the ICJ ruling contravened the doctrine of precedent and the right of self-determination, as established by the *Frontier Dispute* case (*Burkina Faso v. Mali*,[49] and the 1975 *Western Sahara* case,[50] since it did not recognise the original title of the Kings, Chiefs and people of Old Calabar and relied instead on the 1913 Anglo-German Agreement.[51] It is argued that in the *Frontier Dispute* case,[52] the ICJ held, *inter alia* that *effectivités* should be given consideration, but failed to take a similar position in the Bakassi case. Thus the ceding of the Peninsula to Cameroon by the same Court is considered as infringing on the rights of the Bakassi people to self-determination by making them Cameroonian citizens.[53]

Supporters of the Judgment counter the criticisms of the ruling, noting that sovereignty and self-determination are mutually exclusive. As Armbruster explains,

> The principle of sovereignty excludes logically the right to self-determination. If international law guarantees the sovereignty of the existing states it cannot permit, at the same time, that this sovereignty be infringed under the title of the right to self-determination.[54]

In referring to the *Frontier Dispute* case between Burkina Faso and Mali cited by critics of the ICJ Judgment on the *Cameroon v. Nigeria* case, Tomuschat also contends that '*Uti possidetis* has … become the leading maxim for the territorial delimitation of Africa, relegating self-determination in that respect to an insignificant inferior place'.[55]

Indeed, it has been argued that while the application of the principle of *uti possidetis* can be traced to Spanish American juridical doctrine, it has also been applied to provide greater stability to the post-colonial African boundaries.[56] This helps to explain in part why Nigeria's claims to the Bakassi Peninsula on the basis of an 1884 colonial treaty of protection between Britain and the Kings and Chiefs of Old Calabar were rejected by the Court, given that that protection treaty was not concluded on the understanding that Old Calabar was part of Nigeria.[57] On the contrary, Nigeria as a geographical and political entity did not exist in 1884. Nor had it achieved the status of an independent State in 1913. As Franck again points out, African countries invoking the intangibility of boundaries inherited from colonialism at independence could continue to rely on the principle of *uti possidetis* 'as an absolute rule' for resolving boundary disputes.[58] This also explains why the Court argued that '*effectivités* cannot … have legal significance, for demonstrating a Nigerian title' over the Bakassi Peninsula,[59] in effect endorsing Cameroon's refutation of the existence of historical consolidation as a separate basis of legal title.[60]

In summary, while it was initially expected that the ICJ Judgment would rapidly be implemented by the affected Parties,[61] it became obvious that implementation would be difficult in light of the reaction by Nigeria coupled with the perception that the decision was incomplete, and in certain circumstances technically imperfect.[62]

Implementation of the Judgment and related issues

Mandate and role of the Cameroon–Nigeria Mixed Commission (CNMC)

Despite the perceived technical imperfection of the Judgment, Cameroon entered into negotiations with Nigeria as the Court had advised and requested the good offices of the UN Secretary-General prior to the Judgment of 10 October 2002. This approach was further applied after the Judgment to enable the Parties to develop an implementation plan that would facilitate a peaceful, comprehensive and lasting settlement of the dispute. In subsequent negotiations, it became clear that much was expected from the United Nations and its Secretary-General as neutral actors whom both States relied upon to ease tensions, resolve the conflict and reinvigorate their hitherto deteriorating relations. Following the ICJ ruling, several bilateral meetings initiated by the UN Secretary-General were held between Cameroon and Nigeria from which the latter requested for a UN Mixed Commission to be established to consider all possible implications of the ruling.

The mandate of the CNMC involved: (1) the demarcation of the land boundaries and delimitation of the maritime boundary between both States; (2) the withdrawal of civil administration, military and police forces and transfer of authority in relevant areas located along the boundary; (3) the eventual demilitarisation of the Peninsula; (4) the need to protect the rights of the affected populations in both States; (5) the development of projects intended to promote joint economic ventures and cross-border cooperation between the two States; and (6) the reactivation of the Lake Chad Basin Commission.[63]

At the outset, the CNMC's work plan that was initially agreed upon could not be implemented from 2003 to 2006 because of several Nigerian revisions of the work plan and that State's inability to respect the deadlines it had sought on several occasions.[64] These developments, in essence, delayed the implementation process and, invariably, the transfer of the Peninsula to Cameroon. However, by June 2006, the CNMC succeeded in ensuring the peaceful and orderly transfer of authority of some 40 villages in the Lake Chad area, together with the demarcation of some 460 km of land boundary.[65] In May 2007, the CNMC went on to finalise the conversion of the 1994 edition of British Admiralty Chart 3433 into WGS84 Datum and adopted the map, including accompanying geographical coordinates, thereby completing the maritime delimitation process between the two States.[66] The CNMC has subsequently made progress in the demarcation of the 1,700 km land border between Cameroon and Nigeria from Lake Chad to the Gulf of Guinea. This demarcation, which was unfortunately interrupted by the instability caused by the terrorist activities of Boko Haram in some sections of the land border of both States, will be resumed and completed as soon as international funding can be secured.[67] Additionally, negotiations carried out through the CNMC have resolved questions relating to the territorial sea, EEZ and the continental shelves of Cameroon and Nigeria, consistent with Articles 74(4) and 83(4) of UNCLOS.[68]

Cameroon–Nigeria unresolved Outer Continental Shelf (OCS) claims

It should be noted that the outer limits of the Continental Shelf entitlements of both States remain to be settled. It may be recalled in this regard that Article 76 of UNCLOS defines the legal Continental Shelf, and declares that all coastal States have a Continental Shelf that is co-extensive with the EEZ extending to a distance of 200 nm measured from the baseline (Article 76(1)).[69] This entitlement arises automatically for all coastal States, subject to the delimitation of boundaries between States in cases where their respective 200 nm EEZ/Continental Shelf entitlements overlap.

Article 76 also provides that States may be entitled to areas of Continental Shelf that extend beyond 200 nm – the extended Continental Shelf – where this can be demonstrated by reference to specific rules and criteria. Where the Continental Shelf extends beyond 200 nm from the baselines, a coastal State may delineate and establish the outer limits of its Continental Shelf up to the outer seaward limit permitted by Article 76 of the Convention.

Under Article 76(8) of the Convention, a coastal State is required to provide information on the outer limits of an extended Continental Shelf to the United Nations Commission on the Limits of the Continental Shelf (CLCS). The functions of the CLCS are stated in Annex II to the Convention, and concern the review of data and other material submitted.[70]

Following the examination of a Submission, the CLCS makes recommendations to the submitting State concerning the determination of the outer limits of the Continental Shelf. The outer limits of the Continental Shelf determined by the submitting State on the basis of recommendations of the CLCS are then deemed final and binding as a matter of international law.[71]

Nigeria has lodged a Submission concerning the outer limits of the Continental Shelf with the CLCS[72] and an amended Submission on 18 November 2016,[73] which was under examination at the time of writing. Cameroon has not yet lodged a Submission, but has provided preliminary information to the Commission concerning the potential area of Continental Shelf in respect of which Cameroon may seek to make a Submission to the CLCS at a future date.[74]

It is important to note that Article 9 of Annex II to UNCLOS provides that the actions of the CLCS shall not prejudice matters relating to the delimitation of boundaries between States with opposite or adjacent coasts. The CLCS has therefore adopted a practice, contained in Annex I to the Rules of Procedure, which is intended to prevent the consideration of a Submission covering a disputed area of Continental Shelf without the consent of the Parties in dispute.

Notwithstanding that Cameroon has not yet lodged a Submission, it is clear that there is a potential overlap between the area of Outer Continental Shelf covered by the Submission made by Nigeria, and the area identified by Cameroon in its preliminary information. Should Cameroon decide to lodge a Submission which confirms such a potential overlap, the CLCS would be required to give serious consideration to suspending or quarantining the ongoing examination of the Submission by Nigeria, subject to Cameroon consenting to the continued examination of the Submission

Of course, in the absence of any objections from other States in the Gulf of Guinea to the examination of the Submission, the CLCS will likely make recommendations concerning the establishment of the outer limits of the Continental Shelf of Nigeria, which would become final and binding once those recommended limits are accepted and applied by Nigeria to establish the outer limits, at which point the option of lodging objections to the CLCS would have ceased to be available to Cameroon or any other State.

Cameroon–Equatorial Guinea maritime delimitation negotiations

Although considerable progress has been made in demarcating the Cameroon–Nigerian land and maritime boundary, the opposite situation exists in respect of the delimitation of the Cameroon–Equatorial Guinea maritime boundary. It should be mentioned that prior to the 2002 ICJ Judgment in the *Cameroon v. Nigeria* case, Equatorial Guinea, *inter alia*, entered a declaration in accordance with UNCLOS Article 298(1)(a) stating its unwillingness to accept the procedures stipulated in Section 2 concerning disputes relating to the interpretation or application of Articles 15, 74 and 83 on maritime settlement of disputes. On 30 June 1999, it also requested permission to intervene as a non-party of its legal rights and interests that may be affected by the Court's decision in the area contested by Cameroon and Nigeria.

In effect, Equatorial Guinea was countering the 'Equitable Line' proposed by Cameroon by seeking to prevent the Court from delimiting a maritime boundary between Cameroon and Nigeria which extended to areas where it was also claiming rights and interests.[75] The ICJ refrained from including the maritime area where the legal rights of third States (Equatorial Guinea and possibly Sao Tome and Principe) may be affected.[76] The Court nevertheless recognised that 'North and East of Bioko the maritime rights of Cameroon and Equatorial Guinea have not yet been determined'.[77]

A major issue arising from the recognition by the ICJ of the unresolved boundary north and east of Bioko is the inability of both States to adopt a specific delimitation method to determine their respective maritime zones, including the Outer Continental Shelf. On this issue, both States seem not to have made tangible breakthroughs vis-à-vis the positions they held during the *Cameroon v. Nigeria* (*Equatorial Guinea Intervening*) case.

In this regard, Cameroon's position reflects its preference for an approach based on relevant circumstances that have to be taken into account in reaching an equitable maritime boundary delimitation.[78] This approach, *inter alia*, calls for

Equatorial Guinea's Bioko Island not to be granted full effect in the delimitation process, so as to prevent a 'radical and absolute cut-off of the projection of [Cameroon's] coastal front'.[79] On the other hand, the proposal for an equidistance or median line[80] favoured by Equatorial Guinea is unquestionably intended to give full effect to Bioko Island with little or no adjustment[81] based on relevant circumstances. How both principles can successfully be combined to reach an equitable maritime boundary delimitation result remains to be resolved by the two States. In view of the divergent positions of Cameroon and Equatorial Guinea and the Article 298 declaration made by Equatorial Guinea, the options open to Cameroon to advance the delimitation appear limited. Referral to the ICJ or ITLOS appears to be unavailable, leaving only conciliation under Annex V, Section 2 of UNCLOS. Article 298(1)(a)(i) requires States to engage in future negotiations of an agreement under UNCLOS Article 298(1)(a)(ii). However, Article 298(1)(a)(ii) places emphasis on 'mutual consent' as a condition for the Submission of the question to one of the procedures under Section 2.

Flowing from this contentious and non-resolved maritime issue has been Equatorial Guinea's objections to the Preliminary Information submitted by Cameroon to the CLCS in May 2009. Equatorial Guinea argues that the said preliminary information 'has no basis in law or fact'[82] and has also refused to give its consent[83] to any subsequent full Submission by Cameroon to the CLCS. Interestingly, Cameroon has not responded to the objections made by Equatorial Guinea. However, it can be argued that Equatorial Guinea's rejection of the legal and factual basis of the Cameroonian Preliminary Information remains problematic, given that there is no agreement between the Parties to underpin the negotiation of an OCS maritime boundary between the two States. Procedurally, Cameroon's Preliminary Information is not intended for consideration by the CLCS and does not, as far as international law is concerned, prevent its future Submission for the CLCS's consideration, pursuant to UNCLOS Article 76. Nor does such preliminary information prejudice the positions and alleged rights of any of the Parties, or even those of other affected States, since any overlapping claims in the Gulf of Guinea can only be negotiated by the Parties without assumptions or presumptions.

Nigeria–Equatorial Guinea–Sao Tome and Principe maritime boundary treaties

Emerging from the ICJ Judgment was the fact that the maritime delimitation effected by the Court between Cameroon and Nigeria from Point X southwards, which excluded maritime areas contested by Cameroon and Nigeria where the legal rights of third States such as Equatorial Guinea might be affected, left open the question of the determination of the final Cameroon–Nigeria–Equatorial Guinea common maritime boundary. Thus a lingering issue of considerable discomfort to Cameroon has been the series of treaties signed by three neighbouring States of Cameroon. The first of these treaties is the Nigerian–Equatorial Guinea Treaty of 23 September 2000, concerning their maritime boundary,[84] which does not take account of Cameroon's maritime rights and interests in the area. That is why Cameroon formally protested against the Treaty during the ICJ proceedings in a correspondence filed with the Registrar of the Court on 5 December 2000 and challenged that instrument's validity. Indeed, for Cameroon, the Treaty represents an arrangement between the concerned Parties only and cannot adversely affect its rights and interests as a non-participating State (*res inter dios acta*).[85]

The aforementioned instrument was complemented by a 'Unitisation Agreement' for the area, signed on 3 April 2002, where Nigeria and Equatorial Guinea have related oil interests.[86] It is interesting that the 'Unitisation Agreement' does not apply the strict equidistance method claimed by Equatorial Guinea in its maritime boundary negotiations with Cameroon. On the contrary, it takes into account circumstances such as relevant oil practice in the area and the difference in the length of coastlines.[87] The same equitable formula was adopted in the maritime boundary negotiations between Nigeria and Sao Tome and Principe, which resulted in the conclusion of a joint development agreement of the overlapping area of their EEZs.[88] Nigeria argued throughout these negotiations that special circumstances, particularly with regard to the immense differences in the size and population of the two States concerned, called for an equitable line rather than an equidistance one. While the 1999 Treaty between Equatorial Guinea and Sao Tome and Principe follows the equidistance method 'as a general criteria for an equitable boundary' not found in the Nigeria–Equatorial Guinea maritime boundary treaty,[89] it is clear that the absence of similar arrangements between the above three States and Cameroon is likely to affect any future agreement on a common Cameroon–Nigeria–Equatorial Guinea maritime boundary.

Assuming that the ongoing bilateral negotiations between Cameroon and Equatorial Guinea succeed in delimiting their common maritime boundary, it could also permit the final determination of the Cameroon–Nigeria–Equatorial Guinea boundary. However, this development arguably would ignore a legal reality relating to what Lathrop describes as 'known or presumed non-party third State's interests'[90] and the strategic economic interests that bind together Nigeria, Equatorial Guinea and Sao Tome and Principe. Should a Cameroon–Equatorial Guinea agreement be concluded, it would be interesting to know Equatorial Guinea's attitude towards its treaty obligations with Nigeria, or to predict the likely effects of a Cameroon–Nigeria–Equatorial Guinea maritime boundary arrangement on the interests of Sao Tome and Principe, which also has treaty obligations with both Nigeria and Equatorial Guinea.

Adoption of the Greentree Agreement

Although some of the maritime issues identified in the discussion of the dispute over the Bakassi Peninsula or ancillary to the dispute remain to be resolved, another major problem was how the ICJ Judgment would effectively be implemented, given Nigeria's objections to it, and the ICJ's limitations to enforce its judgments in the absence of 'good faith' on the part of any of the Parties. Admittedly, the intense diplomatic efforts undertaken by the UN Secretary-General Kofi Annan resulted in the historic Greentree Agreement of 12 June 2006 between Cameroon and Nigeria, which was also witnessed by Britain, France, Germany and the United States.[91]

The Agreement outlines the modalities for implementing the ICJ Judgment (Article 7). It provided, *inter alia*, for the withdrawal of Nigerian troops from the Bakassi Peninsula within 90 days and established a transition period of two years to enable a Cameroonian administration to replace the Nigerian administration. The Agreement also established a special arrangement permitting Nigerians living in the Peninsula to remain there for four years following Cameroon's complete take-over of the zone, including the option for them to take up residence after that if they so desired.[92]

Although the Greentree Agreement has comprehensively settled the dispute, it is interesting to consider whether the momentum created by the Agreement has been sustained by the interested Parties. The Greentree Agreement, has been described as 'a great achievement in conflict prevention, which practically reflected its cost-effectiveness when compared with the alternative of conflict resolution'.[93] In deciding to abide by the ICJ Judgment and withdraw Nigerian troops from the Bakassi Peninsula despite strong domestic opposition, President Obasanjo was expounding the dividends of a peaceful process of conflict resolution among African States. History would have judged him differently had he maintained his initial objections to the implementation of the ICJ Judgment.[94] This peaceful process of conflict resolution is affirmed by President Biya:

> [b]y opting for dialogue and negotiation, we have proved that resorting to force is not necessarily the best way to resolve disputes. Perhaps in this regard, the peaceful outcome of the Bakassi issue will set a precedent in our continent.[95]

It is therefore evident that the Treaty of Calabar of 14 August 2008 represents an important turning point in the relations between Cameroon and Nigeria.[96] Indeed, the successful adoption of the Greentree Agreement and the Treaty of Calabar, has eclipsed the myth that African States are incapable of brokering agreements among themselves, particularly where there exists sufficient political will. The obvious ramification of the final settlement of the Bakassi dispute is the peace dividend that will now allow more use by Cameroon and Nigeria of the resources spent on war purposes to be redirected to the economic, social and infrastructural development. The de-militarisation of the Peninsula in favour of major social projects such as education, health and other infrastructural developments will also provide an incentive for foreign investment in support of the development of economic activities in areas such as agriculture, fishing and oil exploration, particularly in view of the enormous resource potential of the zone.

Post-conflict developments and potential challenges

The Greentree Agreement, in Cameroon's view, also ushers in hopes for durable peace and economic prosperity between both States on condition that the desire for peace outweighs any procrastination for war. In her paper titled 'Comparative Perspectives: Territorial and Boundary Disputes in the Horn of Africa' Ruth Iyob, *inter alia*, makes the following recommendations aimed at normalising relations between the belligerents and the residents of any post-conflict territory:

- Protect the rights of cross-border residents: Pursue policies which would transform contested areas from barricades to bridges…
- Provide cross-border development incentives: Encourage communal interaction and economic exchanges and thereby turn what had been barricades into bridges…
- Acknowledge the unaddressed grievances that trigger territorial disputes: airing grievances rather than fanning fears could allow both ruling elites and grassroots actors to endorse pragmatic solutions that enhance shared benefits rather than zero-sum outcomes.[97]

What these recommendations convey in the case of the Bakassi Peninsula, as discussed below, is the fact that the Greentree Agreement also presents a challenge for Cameroon as the main protagonist and the Nigerian Government as an auxiliary actor to provide the political and security climate needed to promote sustainable economic development in the area, and build confidence among the Cameroonians and the Nigerian migrant community in order to promote intercultural dialogue between the residents and state actors on the one hand and residents and civil society proponents on the other hand.

Prioritising economic developments in the Peninsula

Subsequent to the complete withdrawal of Nigerian troops from the Bakassi Peninsula, feasibility studies on projects to offer basic services to the population of that area were launched by the Cameroonian Government in June 2006. In this connection the Cameroonian Government established a Coordination and Follow-up Committee for the implementation of Priority Projects in the Bakassi Peninsula on 27 August 2007. The Committee's responsibility is to propose to government a coherent global approach of priority projects to be realised, notably in the domains of road infrastructure, water and electricity, communication, post and telecommunications, urban development, as well as schools and health centres. This basic infrastructure is necessary for the development of important resources on the land, maritime areas and sub-soil which constitute part of Cameroonian territory, possessing huge quantities of these resources.

The establishment of the Coordination and Follow-up Committee was marked by the launching of an Emergency Programme in 2007 through which the Cameroonian Government engaged in the rehabilitation of the Mundemba–Isangele–Akwa road and the opening of the link between Isangele and Akwa 1 as well as the opening of roads in the periphery of the Peninsula. Important financial resources have since been mobilised for the construction of water points at Edema Mbassi, Ngosso and Barrack respectively. In the Idabato and Kombo Itindi Subdivisions, relay stations have been built to permit Cameroon Radio-Television (CRTV) signals in Mundemba and Ekondo Titi. Additionally, lodging at Akwa 1, Ngosso and Edema Mbassi, the introduction of ferry services at Kombo Abedimo, Idabato, Akwa 1, Mbenmong, Wanyo and Issobo, the rehabilitation of health centres at Akwa and the purchase of two engine ferries to facilitate transportation have been realised.[98]

The Public Investment Budget for the 2008 financial year provided more than 2.3 billion francs CFA (about US$4.7 million) for several social and economic infrastructures in the area, notably the rehabilitation of the Mundemba–Isangele–Akwa electrification and pipe-borne water projects, the construction of several classrooms for primary schools and the opening of secondary schools and health centres. By 2010, important projects already realised and amounting to over 12 billion francs CFA (about US$25 million) included the construction of government offices, residences for workers, markets, speed-boats for administrative authorities, water supply, generators for energy supply, social centres, women's empowerment centres and support to farmers' organisations.[99] To this amount should be added the 12 billion francs CFA (US$25 million) contributed by the Cameroon Government and its development partners, particularly the European Union through its European Development Fund and the French development agency from 2007 to 2009.[100] Another 2.5 billion francs CFA was approved for the construction of camps for fishermen and providing them with fishing gear, the construction of improved facilities for communal fish smoking, the extension of oil palm plantation, the construction of camps for workers, customs posts and community halls, and feasibility studies for the tarring of the Loum–Kumba–Ekondo–Titi–Mundemba–Isangele–Akwa road,[101] while 722 million francs CFA were allocated for development projects in 2016.[102]

During the 19th session of the Bakassi Project Follow-up Committee held in Yaoundé on 18 August 2016, the Chairperson of that Committee, Bertha Ndoh Bokata, reported that over 30.7 billion francs CFA (about US$63.9 million) had been spent on projects funded by the Cameroonian Government in the Bakassi Peninsula during the 2008–2016 period. She also announced that while a Committee has been working to repopulate the

Peninsula with Cameroonians, especially fishermen, a positive outcome of government's development projects and social cohesion policy has been the surge in voluntary naturalisation of Nigerians in the zone as Cameroonian citizens.[103] These important government initiatives will undoubtedly increase the population's development capacity and peaceful co-existence in the Peninsula.

However, other areas of intervention need to be reinforced through the government's Public Investment and Emergency Development budgets. These include the diversification of the monoculture form of agriculture, which is largely cassava farming, to include other food crops and especially protein-derived farming, which is a viable alternative to the fish tensions that exist between Nigerians and Cameroonians in the Peninsula. Although Article 126 of Law No. 94/01 of 20 January 1994 on fisheries bans unauthorised exports of fisheries resources from Cameroon, Nigerian fishermen continue to illegally export their fish to Nigeria rather than to sell the product in Cameroon because this is financially profitable, leading to confrontations between the two communities in 2014 which were quickly resolved by the local administration.[104] For example, in June 2014 a dispute between a Nigerian businessman and a Cameroonian tax collector led local officials to impose a curfew throughout the area.[105] The quick response by the Cameroonian Government to appoint a civilian tax collector in 2015 has de-escalated the reticence of Nigerians to pay taxes in the Peninsula. Yet to marry economic development to human development, the Government of Cameroon needs to carry out more important infrastructural development in the road, education, health, water, telecommunications and environment sectors. This will reduce the difficult socio-economic conditions of the Bakassi residents and encourage other Cameroonians and foreign investors, particularly in the infrastructure, hydrocarbons exploration and exploitation sectors, to accept working in the Peninsula.[106]

Fostering social cohesion among the residents in the Peninsula

A major sensitive political and socio-cultural issue arising from the ICJ Judgment relates to the concerns expressed by the Nigerian Government and public regarding the situation of Nigerians who wished to remain in the Bakassi Peninsula following the transfer of that zone to Cameroon in 2008. How, in particular, was the cohabitation of Cameroonians and Nigerian residents of the Peninsula to be managed in view of the reticence of many Nigerians to accept the transfer of the Peninsula to Cameroon and fears concerning the alleged overbearing attitude of Cameroonian gendarmes? It should be pointed out that the process of promoting social cohesion can be regarded as the transformation from social exclusion to social inclusion. In a post-conflict situation, this means residents should close the real or imagined divisions that may exist among them.

Article 3 of the Greentree Agreement stipulates:

1. Cameroon, after the transfer of authority to it by Nigeria, guarantees to Nigerian nationals living in the Bakassi Peninsula the exercise of the fundamental rights and freedoms enshrined in international human rights law and in other relevant provisions of international law.
2. In particular, Cameroon shall:
   - (a) not force Nigerian nationals living in the Bakassi Peninsula to leave the zone or to change their nationality;
   - (b) respect their culture, language and beliefs;
   - (c) respect their right to continue their agricultural and fishing activities;

(d) protect their property and their customary land rights;
(e) not levy in any discriminatory manner any taxes and other dues on Nigerian nationals living in the zone; and
(f) take every necessary measure to protect Nigerian nationals living in the zone from any harassment or harm.

This provision of the Agreement was inspired by Cameroon's commitment in March 2002 during the proceedings of the *Cameroon v. Nigeria* case that it will continue to afford protection to Nigerians living in the Bakassi Peninsula and in the Lake Chad area. Cameroon took this initiative pursuant to its customary policy of hospitality and tolerance[107] and as a confidence-building measure. This commitment, which was reaffirmed by President Biya following the conclusion of the Treaty of Calabar,[108] is undoubtedly intended to promote social cohesion among the mosaic of ethnic and cultural communities in the Peninsula and minimise the likelihood of inter-communal conflicts between these communities. Inter-communal conflicts are often triggered by polarised perceptions and experiences between the members of the community. Some of these perceptions easily transform into age-old stereotypes or prejudices born mostly out of ignorance, deep-seated animosity and veiled hidden agendas as well as intrinsic community values and external social stimuli. These factors are dynamic to the point where subsequent generations can translate negative dichotomies or skewed visions to converging symphonies or consensual vision.

Recent experiences in inter-community cohesion in the Bakassi Peninsula attest to the fact that young people, whether from Cameroonian or Nigerian origin, freely interact more with each other, especially in the areas of sports, fishing and education.[109] The younger inhabitants have quickly shifted from relationship to goals and from friendship to partnership. They are virtually abdicating from their parental myopia of colonial divide to a bigger picture of common indigenous bonding.[110] This newfound prism of communal liberalism resonates with the sociology of the Bakassi Peninsula as most of the languages or dialects in the Peninsula including the lingua franca called Pidgin enjoy wide mutual use between Cameroonians and Nigerians. One can also add the shared economic interests in both farming and fishing practices, the traditional African practice of trade by barter and the ongoing inter-marriages between the various ethnic groups. It can be argued that these indigenous practices serve as positive integrative factors that can build peace and prevent a re-escalation of violence in the Peninsula.[111] However, for this to be sustainable there is a need for the Cameroonian Government and foreign development partners to support non-state actors, in developing strategies in the areas of civic and gender-sensitive education, alternative farming methods and citizenship peace advocacy, as well as reinforcing the capacities of municipal or local government administrators whose capacity-deficiency has been compounded by decades of instability and protracted conflict. As discussed earlier, the Cameroonian Government is doing so much in infrastructural development in Bakassi. Yet for human capital development to have a durable impact in the Peninsula it would be necessary for the Cameroonian Government, in collaboration with some of the civil society organisations already working in the area, to design and implement special projects in the Bakassi Peninsula that can mitigate the socio-economic problems of the population and make cohabitation a reality.

This cohabitation was, initially, a tenuous one, given that a faction of Nigerian residents in the Peninsula were still not pleased with the ICJ verdict and had wrongly or rightly been accused of supporting external Nigerian actors and secessionist groups which in the recent past have been engaged in criminal activities such as piracy, armed robbery and the kidnapping and murder of Cameroonians in that zone. Indeed, between November 2007 and July 2016, more than 62 Cameroonians were murdered by unknown Nigerian gunmen in the Peninsula, while 10 other Cameroonians were kidnapped between October 2011 and July 2016 and only released following payments of ransom to the kidnappers.[112] These criminal activities could be interpreted as attempts by some neighbouring social and political movements to sabotage the peace process and, as will later be shown, the efforts being made by the Cameroonian Government to strengthen security and to promote economic development and social cohesion in the Peninsula.

Much more complex has been the attitude of the Nigerian community in the Peninsula, which has been reticent to use the Cameroonian currency (CFA franc) which is legal tender in Cameroon, rather than the Nigerian currency (naira). It is worth noting that the option given to Nigerian nationals in 2013 either to remain in Cameroon and respect Cameroonian laws or return to Nigeria has not been fully respected. While only 2,940 Nigerians moved to a new settlement in Akpabuyo, Calabar, Nigeria, a majority who chose to remain in the Peninsula maintain that they took that decision not because they wish to obtain Cameroonian nationality but primarily to remain near their ancestral shrines. These Nigerians hold the historical view that the Peninsula was part of the ancient kingdom of Calabar and tend to ignore the 1913 Anglo-German Treaty that formed the basis of the ICJ ruling.[113] Interestingly, the non-inclusion of Nigerians living in the Peninsula in the 'legal determination of the region's ownership' is criticised as a misjudgement on the part of the UN mediators of the dispute.[114] Contrary to this criticism, it is submitted that the principle of inviolability of African frontiers, derived from colonisation and reaffirmed in the 1964 OAU Cairo Resolution on Border Disputes Among African States,[115] makes the notion of inclusivity of Nigerians in deciding the destiny of the Peninsula inadmissible in international law. In essence, the Nigerian community is hiding behind the pre-colonial history of the Peninsula, apparently oblivious of post-colonial cartographic arrangements in vogue.

Notwithstanding, the Cameroonian and Nigerian Governments have focused attention on projects of common interests in line with the Greentree Agreement, particularly frontier development projects under construction such as the 383 km Bamenda–Mamfe–Ekok–Enugu road and the Kumba–Mamfe–Ekok–Enugu road. There are also studies of a project to construct a bridge over the Mayo Tiel and a Gamborou–Ngala–Kousseri road.[116] All these are part of the fulfilment of the menu of the Cameroon–Nigeria Mixed Commission and the Greentree Agreement.

Security and administration in the Peninsula

Following the ICJ Judgment and the adoption of the Greentree Agreement, the Cameroonian Government has placed security, safety and an effective administrative system in Bakassi Peninsula as one of its major priorities. As has been observed, the absence of security and effective administration in the zone for almost 12 years of armed conflict between Cameroon and Nigeria created a security vacuum that gave birth to criminal activities as mentioned earlier, including amphibious attacks on civilians and military forces and a general atmosphere of lawlessness. Indeed, people with questionable character and integrity, lured by the riches of the area[117] and determined to 'undermine the entire process of sustaining the peaceful settlement',[118] escaped to the zone aggravated by rebels in the Niger Delta.

The Government of Cameroon has created, in Ndian Division, nine Subdivisions, four of which are Maritime Subdivisions – Idabato, Isangele, Kombo Abedimo and Kombo

Itindi in the Bakassi Peninsula. These administrative units assist local government affairs of the areas. The government has also appointed civil servants representing several ministries in the Peninsula. In cooperation with District Officers administering each of the Subdivisions, special measures have been taken by Cameroonian defence forces to ensure that security and peace prevail in the Bakassi Peninsula so that the population can freely carry out their socio-economic activities without fear of any kind of victimisation. Accordingly, the government has set up the Rapid Intervention Battalion (BIR) which, in collaboration with the population and other forces of law and order, has been able to increase security in the zone.

Cross-border cooperation

The secession of hostilities and the withdrawal of the Nigerian military and administration from the Bakassi Peninsula and areas transferred to Cameroon in the Lake Chad region by the ICJ ruling have been followed by a sustained effort from both countries to continue building a strong foundation for peace, security and economic development. On 28 February 2012, Cameroon and Nigeria concluded in Abuja the Agreement Establishing the Cameroon–Nigeria Cross Border Security Committee.[119] The purpose of the Committee is to strengthen cooperation between the two countries in jointly fighting against all forms of transnational crimes and identification of areas of common interest.

In 2013, the first meeting was held in Yaoundé on 6, 7 and 8 November. The meeting underscored the need to give fresh impetus to cooperation between the two countries with respect to trans-border security in common borders. The meeting also highlighted the commitment of both governments to preserve the fraternal relations already existing between the two countries.

Three sub-committees were created in the meeting: Security Evaluation, Operation (preventive and repressive) and Related Activities. On border security evaluation, both Parties highlighted the need to share and protect the long maritime and land border of about 2,000 km, characterised by porosity, insufficient protection by the security forces of both States and a population of people with similar ethnicity and nationalities and strong socio-cultural ties, which makes it difficult to handle individual and group problems by the security forces of both States. Some maritime, land and air border threats were identified. In the maritime border areas, crimes such as maritime piracy; trafficking of drugs; human trafficking; trafficking in and proliferation of small arms and military ammunition; illegal fishing; incursion in territorial waters by bandits; destruction of oil facilities and siphoning of petroleum products; environmental degradation; kidnapping of persons and hostage-taking with demand for ransom; logging and illegal sale of wood; smuggling; illegal immigration and money laundering; terrorism; and organised crime, amongst others, were also identified.

The Committee's second meeting was held in Abuja from 8 to 11 July 2014 to evaluate the work of the respective sub-committees formed in the first meeting in Yaoundé. The third meeting of the Committee, held in Yaoundé from 18 to 20 February 2015, *inter alia* made some recommendations regarding sustained sensitisation and increased coordination on security and cross-border control operations between both States.

It is too early to assess the extent of the implementation of cooperation efforts so far in trans-border security. However, it is hoped that administrative bottlenecks, absence of effective coordination and sharing of information and inadequate financial resources will not stifle the Committee's mandate provided for in Article 3 of the Agreement.

While the peace and economic dividends of the Trans-Border Security Agreement remain to be seen, the willingness of both States to intensify cooperation in other areas is evidenced by the approval by their experts of a draft agreement, currently awaiting signature, on the management of protected areas shared between them on 11 November 2010. They also initialled another draft agreement on cross-border cooperation on hydrocarbons and decided to accelerate its signature and operationalisation.[120]

Conclusion: the way forward

This chapter has attempted to present a Cameroonian perspective concerning the Cameroon–Nigeria dispute over the Bakassi Peninsula and the issues arising from the ICJ Judgment in the *Cameroon v. Nigeria* case. In tracing the origin of the dispute, followed by several years of negotiations, it can be seen that the segregation of political, demographic and resources interests in the Gulf of Guinea prevented any chance of an early resolution of the maritime boundary dispute between the relevant States, Cameroon, Nigeria and Equatorial Guinea.

Although the territorial, sea and EEZ boundaries between Cameroon and Nigeria have now been settled, the issue of the Outer Continental Shelf of both States remains unresolved, as do the maritime zone claims between Cameroon and Equatorial Guinea resulting from disagreements on the specific delimitation formula(s) to adopt to reach an equitable solution.

Thanks to the untiring commitment and strong leadership shown by Presidents Biya and Obasanjo and subsequently emulated by Presidents Umaru Yar'Adua, Goodluck Jonathan and Muhammed Buhari of Nigeria, the good offices of the UN Secretary-General Kofi Annan and the commendable work undertaken by the CNMC, the implementation process is on course. Nevertheless, the implementation of the ICJ Judgment will require continuous monitoring and cooperation from both States for years to come. Indeed, the current development projects being undertaken in the Bakassi Peninsula respond to the Cameroonian Government's determination to improve the lives of the Cameroonian, Nigerian and other foreign inhabitants of that region, pursuant to the ICJ Judgment and the Greentree Agreement.

However, much remains to be done to overcome the problem of the inadequate infrastructure, remoteness and problems of accessibility to the Bakassi Peninsula due to poor roads linking Subdivisions and the mainland. Besides, lack of adequate water, electricity, health centres, telecommunications and security continue to slow down effective development in the Bakassi Peninsula. Solutions to some of these problems cannot be left to the Cameroonian Government alone. Nigeria also has the obligation, in accordance with the Greentree Agreement, to encourage Nigerians living in the Peninsula to respect Cameroonian sovereignty over the area. Additionally, Nigeria should closely monitor and eradicate criminal and other secessionist movements fighting for the so-called independence of the Peninsula and operating from the fringes of the zone. The involvement of international funding organisations and investment partners is crucial as well, in order to sustain ongoing and future development projects in the Peninsula.

The end of the conflict has established a new base in terms of diplomatic, political and economic dynamics given the tight historical and cultural links that the populations of both countries share. Moreover, the willingness of the Governments of Cameroon and Nigeria to cooperate to support a lasting peace through the use of legal and extra-legal mechanisms opens a positive chapter, given their past tumultuous relations. As President

Paul Biya of Cameroon intimated, only by respecting and implementing the ICJ ruling can the credibility of both States and of the United Nations, which brokered the peace settlement, be enhanced.[121]

Notes

1 The views expressed in this chapter are those of the author and do not necessarily reflect the position of the Cameroonian Government or institutions.
2 Jadesola E.T. Babatola, 'Nigeria–Cameroon Boundary Dispute: The Quest for Bakassi Peninsular' (2012) 4 *International Affairs and Global Strategy*, p. 89.
3 See *Land and Maritime Boundary between Cameroon and Nigeria Case (Cameroon v. Nigeria, Equatorial Guinea Intervening)* (Judgment) [2002] *ICJ Rep.* 303 paras 265–268.
4 Available at: www.icj-cij.org/docket/files/94/7203.pdf. Also see Cameroon's Memorial, www.icj-cij.org/docket/files/94/8595.pdf, accessed 16 February 2017.
5 See www.icj-cij.org/docket/files/94/8602.pdf, accessed 16 February 2017.
6 United Nations Office for West Africa, 'Cameroon–Nigeria Mixed Commission – Background' (April 2005), www.un.org/unowa. Ould-Abdallah was replaced in 2007 by Lamine Cissé and in 2008 by Saïd Djinnit.
7 E.C. Ariye, 'Nigeria, Cameroon and the Bakassi Territorial Dispute: The Triumph of Bilateralism' (2015) 38 *International Affairs and Global Strategy*, p. 25.
8 J. Ndumbe Anyu, 'The ICJ and Border-Conflict Resolution in Africa: The Bakassi Peninsula Conflict' (2007) 18 *Mediterranean Quarterly: A Journal of Global Issues* 3, p. 41.
9 Ieuan Griffiths, 'The Scramble for Africa: Inherited Political Boundaries' (1986), 152 *The Geographical Journal*, pp. 204–205.
10 For the Arrangements between Great Britain and Germany, see Ian Brownlie, *African Boundaries: A Legal and Diplomatic Encyclopaedia* (London: C. Hurst, 1979), pp. 553–557.
11 Ibid.
12 The Agreement between Great Britain and Germany respecting Zanzibar, Heligoland and the Spheres of Influence of the two Powers in Africa (signed 1 July 1890) BSP & Others 82/35, www.fco.gov.uk/en/treaties/search, accessed 16 February 2017.
13 Agreement between Great Britain respecting the Rio del Rey on the West Coast of Africa (signed 14 April 1893) BSP & Others 85/38); Agreement between Great Britain and Germany respecting Boundaries in Africa (signed 15 November 1893) 17 UKTS 1893; Agreement between Great Britain and Germany respecting the Boundary between British and German Territories from Yola to Lake Chad (signed 19 March 1906) 17 UKTS 1906; and the Exchange of Notes between the United Kingdom and Germany confirming Protocols defining Boundaries between British and German Territories in Africa: (1) Gorege to Lake Chad (Kofa 12 February 1907), (2) Uba to the Maio Tiel (11 March 1909) (signed 22 February–5 March 1909) 17 UKTS 1909, www.fco.gov.uk/en/treaties/search, accessed 16 February 2017.
14 See Brownlie, p. 556. In 2002 the ICJ ruled that these Agreements were valid and binding under international law, and relevant for the purposes of the Cameroon–Nigeria maritime delimitation. See *Cameroon v. Nigeria* (Judgment) [2002] *ICJ Rep.* 303, paras 265–268. For the text of the ICJ Judgment including Memorial, Counter-Memorial, Reply and Verbatim Records, see www.icj-cij.org, accessed 16 February 2017.
15 Francis Menjo Baye, 'The Implications of the Bakassi Conflict Resolution for Cameroon' (2010) 10 *African Journal of Conflict Resolution* 1, p. 19.
16 BFSP 116/817, www.fco.gov.uk/en/treaties/search, accessed 16 February 2017.
17 See Exchange of Notes between His Majesty's Government in the United Kingdom and the Governor of the French Cameroons respecting the Boundary between British and French Cameroons (9 January 1931) 34 UKTS 1931, www.fco.gov.uk/en/treaties/search, accessed 16 February 2017.
18 Nowa Omoigui, 'The Bakassi Story', www.dawodu.com/bakassi3.htm, accessed 16 February 2017.
19 Republic of Cameroon, Aide Memoire on the *Case Concerning the Land and Maritime Boundary between Cameroon and Nigeria (Cameroon v. Nigeria: Equatorial Guinea Intervening)* (English/French versions), Ministry of External Relations, Yaoundé, July 2002, p. 7.

20 Ibid., pp. 20–21.
21 Maroua Declaration of 1 June 1975, as supplemented by Exchange of Notes between the Cameroon and Nigeria Heads of State of 12 June 1975 and 17 July 1975, www.un.org/depts/los/LEGISLATIONANDTREATIES/PDFFILES/TREATIES/CMR-NGA1975MD.PDF, accessed 16 February 2017.
22 Baye, 'The Implications of the Bakassi Conflict Resolution for Cameroon' (2010) 10 *African Journal of Conflict Resolution* 1, p. 22.
23 Walter Ofonagoro, 'The Bakassi Sovereignty and International Politics', *Vanguard Nigerian Newspaper* (Lagos, 3 April 2013), www.vanguardngr.com/2012/09/the-bakassi-sovereignty-and-international-politics, accessed 16 February 2017.
24 Baye, 'Implications of the Bakassi Conflict for Cameroon' (2010) 10 *African Journal of Conflict Resolution* 1, pp. 19 and 21. In these plebiscites organised by the United Nations, Northern Cameroons decided to achieve independence by joining the Federal Republic of Nigeria, while Southern Cameroons decided to achieve independence by joining the independent Republic of Cameroon.
25 O.P. Olagunju, 'ICJ: Cameroun and Nigeria in View of the Bakassi' (2009) LLB thesis, University of Ibadan, p. 53.
26 Cameroon ratified the UNCLOS on 19 November 1985 and Nigeria on 14 August 1986. Cameroon adopted Law No. 2000/12 of 17 April 2000 on Maritime Areas of the Republic of Cameroon. Nigeria adopted the Exclusive Economic Zone Decree No. 28, of 5 October 1978, amended in 1998. Both States have seised the Commission on the Limits of the Continental Shelf (CLCS) for an extension of their Continental Shelves beyond the 200 miles of the EEZ under Article 77 of UNCLOS (see further below).
27 See Articles 74 and 83 of UNCLOS. Also see Egede's chapter in this book on the Bakassi case and the law of the sea (Chapter 7), which discusses these provisions vis-à-vis the Bakassi dispute.
28 Joint Communiqué, Third Session of the Cameroon–Nigeria Joint Meeting on Boundary Matters, Yaoundé (Cameroon), August 1993, pp. 11–13, www.google.fr/#q=Joint+Communiqu%C3%A9,+Third+Session+of+the+Cameroon-Nigeria+Joint+Meeting+on+Boundary+Matters,+Republic+of+Cameroon,+Ministry+of+External+Relations,+Yaound%C3%A9,+11–13+August+1993.&*&spf=63, accessed 16 February 2017.
29 Joint Communiqué of the First Working Session on Boundary Delimitation between Cameroon and Nigeria, Yaoundé (Cameroon), 29 August 1991, p. 4, www.google.fr/#q=Joint+Communiqu%C3%A9+of+the+First+Working+Session+on+Boundary+Delimitation+between+Cameroon+and+Nigeria,+Yaound%C3%A9+(Cameroon),+29+August+1991,++&*&spf=63, accessed 16 February 2017.
30 *Cameroon v. Nigeria*, www.icj-cij.org/docket/index.php?p1=3&p2=3&k=74&case=94&code=cn&p3=4, accessed 16 February 2017.
31 See Egede's chapter in this book on equitable principles/relevant circumstances as a methodology of maritime delimitation.
32 E.C. Ariye, 'Nigeria, Cameroon and the Bakassi Territorial Dispute Settlement: The Triumph of Bilateralism' (2015) 38 *International Affairs and Global Strategy*, p. 29.
33 Ibid.
34 Friends of the Earth (2003) 'Conflict, Corruption and Climate Change: George Bush's New Oil Agenda', cited by E.C. Ariye, 'Nigeria, Cameroon and the Bakassi Territorial Dispute: The Triumph of Bilateralism' (2015) 38 *International Affairs and Global Strategy*, p. 29.
35 Nicholas K. Tarlebbea and Sam Baroni, 'The Cameroon and Nigeria Negotiation Process over the Contested Oil Rich Bakassi Peninsula' (2010) 2 *Journal of Alternative Perspectives in the Social Sciences* I, p. 207.
36 UN Press Release 'Nigeria Defends Defiance of World Court Border Ruling' (10 September 2002) UN/Press SG/2344; Colter Paulson, 'Compliance with Final Judgments of the International Court of Justice since 1987' (2004) 98 *American Journal of International Law*, p. 450.
37 Aloysius P. Llamzon, 'Jurisdiction and Compliance in Recent Decisions of the International Court of Justice' (2008) 18 *European Journal of International Law* 5, p. 836 citing 'Cameroon; Bakassi: Why the ICJ Judgment is Unacceptable – Government', *Africa News Service* (Durham, North Carolina, 24 October 2002).
38 Ibid.

39 E.C. Ariye, 'Nigeria, Cameroon and the Bakassi Territorial Dispute Settlement: The Triumph of Bilateralism' (2015) 38 *International Affairs and Global Strategy*, 29, citing Cameroon Radio-Television (Yaoundé, 2002).

40 For examples see Bassey E. Ate, 'Nigeria and Cameroon', in Bassey E. Ate and Bola A. Akinterinwa (eds), *Nigeria and its Immediate Neighbours: Constraints and Prospects of Sub-Regional Security in the 1990s* (Lagos: Nigerian Institute of International Affairs, 1992), www.google.fr/#q=Bassey+E.+Ate,+%E2%80%98Nigeria+and+Cameroon%E2%80%99+in+Bassey+E.+Ate+and+B.A.+Akinterinwa+(eds),+Nigeria+and+its+Immediate+Neighbours:+Constraints+and+Prospects+of+Sub-Regional+Security+in+the+1990s+(Lagos,+Nigerian+Institute+of+International+Affairs+1992;&start=10&*&spf=108, accessed 3 March 2017; R. Akinjide, 'Bakassi, Whose Bakassi?' *West Africa News Magazine* (April 1994); Okanga Ogbu Okanga, 'Bakassi: Analysis of Judgment of the International Court of Justice', *The Nation* (19 August 2008) www.thenationonlineng.net/archive2/tblnews_Detail.php?id=59553, accessed 3 March 2017.

41 Vienna Convention on the Law of Treaties (adopted 23 May 1969, entered into force 27 January 1980) 1155 UNTS 331 (VCLT). Article 11 provides that 'the consent of a State to be bound by a treaty may be expressed by signature, exchange of instruments constituting a treaty, ratification, acceptance, approval or accession, or by any other means if so agreed'.

42 *North Sea Continental Cases*, www.icj-cij.org/docket/index.php?sum=295&code=cs2&p1=3&p2=3&case=52&k=cc&p3=5, accessed 3 March 2017. Here the ICJ ruled, *inter alia*, that Article 6 of the 1958 Continental Shelf Convention was not declaratory of existing or emergent rules of law and consequently the equidistance method of delimitation 'was not binding on the Federal Republic of Germany, which had not ratified the Convention'.

43 *Case Concerning the Military and Paramilitary Activities In and Against Nicaragua* (*Nicaragua v. United States of America*) (Merits) 1986, www.icj-cij.org/docket/?sum=367&p1=3&p2=3&case=70&p3=5, accessed 3 March 2017. The US contention that since Nicaragua did not deposit its instrument of ratification of the Protocol of signature of the Statute of the Permanent Court of International Justice (PCIJ), its declaration in 1929 failed to accept the PCIJ's compulsory jurisdiction as stipulated in Article 36(5) of the ICJ. Statute was rejected by the Court.

44 Article 80 of the VCLT provides that: 'Treaties shall, after their entry into force, be transmitted to the Secretariat of the United Nations for registration or filing and recording, as the case may be, and for publication.' Article 102(2) of the UN Charter stipulates that: 'No party to any treaty or international agreement which has not been registered in accordance with the provisions of paragraph 1 of this article, may invoke the treaty or agreement before any organ of the United Nations.'

45 See R. Akinjide, *Hallmark National Newspaper* (Lagos, 13 November 2002), cited in M.C. Anekwe, 'ICJ Ruling on Bakassi: Matters Arising', *Nigeria World* (27 December 2002), http://nigeriaworld.com/articles/2002/dec/273.html, accessed 3 March 2017; Okanga Ogbu Okanga, 'Bakassi: Analysis of the Judgment of the International Court of Justice', *The Nation* (19 August 2008), www.thenationonlineng.net/archive2/tblnews_Detail.php?id=59553. accessed 3 March 2017.

46 *Island of Las Palmas Case* (*Netherlands v. USA*), www.google.fr/#q=island+of+las+palmas+case&*&spf=108, accessed 3 March 2017.

47 It provides that 'treaties do not create either obligations or rights for third States without their consent'.

48 R. Akinjide, *Hallmark National Newspaper* (Lagos, 13 November 2002), cited in M.C. Anekwe, 'ICJ Ruling on Bakassi: Matters Arising', *Nigeria World* (27 December 2002), http://nigeriaworld.com/articles/2002/dec/273.html, accessed 3 March 2017.

49 *Frontier Dispute case: Burkina Faso v. Mali*, www.peaceau.org/uploads/burkina-faso-mali-1966.pdf, accessed 3 March 2017.

50 *Western Sahara* case (ICJ, 1975), www.icj-cij.org/docket/files/61/6195.pdf, accessed 3 March 2017. In this case, the Court recognised the local rulers' possession and title as superior to other forms of title.

51 Okanga Ogbu Okanga, 'Bakassi: Analysis of Judgment of the International Court of Justice', *The Nation* (19 August 2008), www.thenationonlineng.net/archive2/tb1news_Detail.php?id=5955.

52 *Frontier Dispute case*: *Burkina Faso v. Mali* (1966), www.peaceau.org/uploads/burkina-faso-mali-1966.pdf, accessed 3 March 2017.

53 Okanga Ogbu Okanga, 'Bakassi: Analysis of Judgment of the International Court of Justice', *The Nation* (19 August 2008) www.thenationonlineng.net/archive2/tblnews_Detail.php?id=5955.
54 H. Armbruster, 'Selbstbestimmungsrecht', in K. Strupp and H.-J. Schlochuer (eds), *Worterbuch des Volkerrechts III* (Berlin: De Gruyter, 1962), p. 250 at p. 253 cited by Dietrich Murswiek, 'The Issue of a Right of Secessionist – Reconsidered', in Christian Tomuschat (ed.), *Modern Law of Self-determination* (Dordrecht: Martinus Nijhoff, 1993), p. 23.
55 Christian Tomuschat, 'Secession and Self-determination', in Marcelo Kohen (ed.), *Secession: International Law Perspectives* (Cambridge: Cambridge University Press, 2006), p. 27.
56 *Burkina Faso v. Mali* (Judgment) [1986] *ICJ Rep.* 554, paras 20–26.
57 J.N. Aondongu, 'Law of the Sea and Nigeria–Cameroon Relations: The Bakassi Dispute Revisited', unpublished MSc, Department of Political Science, University of Nigeria Nsukka, http://repository.unn.edu.ng:8080/jspui/bitstream/123456789/743/1/JULUKU%20NATHAN%20AONDONGU.pdf, accessed 3 March 2017.
58 T.M. Franck, 'Post Modern Tribalism and the Right to Secession', in Catherine Brolmann, René Lefeber and Marjoleine Zieck (eds), *Peoples and Minorities in International Law* (Dordrecht: Martinus Nijhoff, 1993), pp. 9–10.
59 *Cameroon v. Nigeria* (Judgment) [2002] *ICJ Rep.* 303 para. 223.
60 Ibid.
61 Milano E. Papanicolopulu, 'Territorial Disputes and State Responsibility on Land and Sea', paper presented at Durham University during the 20th anniversary of the IBRU, 'The State of Sovereignty' (2009), pp. 1–3.
62 For the problematic issues associated with the Judgment, see, *inter alia*, J.G. Merrills, 'Land and Maritime Boundary Between Cameroon and Nigeria (Equatorial Guinea Intervening, Merits, Judgment of 10 October 2002)' (2002) 52 *ICLQ*, pp. 788–797; M. Mendelson, 'The Cameroon–Nigeria Case in the International Court of Justice: Some Territorial Sovereignty and Boundary Lessons' (2004) 75 *British Yearbook of International Law* 1, pp. 223–247.
63 Baye, 'The Implications of the Bakassi Conflict Resolution for Cameroon' (2010) 10 *African Journal of Conflict Resolution* 1, p. 24 (his footnote 9).
64 P. Konings, 'Settling Border Conflicts in Africa Peacefully: Lessons Learned from the Bakassi Dispute between Cameroon and Nigeria', in J. Abbink and M. de Bruijn (eds), *Law and Politics in Africa: Mediating Conflict and Reshaping the State* (Leiden: Brill, 2011), pp. 199–200.
65 UN Secretary-General Statement on Bakassi Peninsula, June 2006, www.un.org/sg/en/content/sg/statement/2006-06-12/secretary-generals-statement-bakassi-peninsula, accessed 8 March 2017.
66 Report of the 18th meeting of the UN–CNMC (5–6 April 2007); 5th Special Meeting (10–11 May 2007); and 19th Meeting of the CNMC (5–6 July 2007) which finalised the implementation of the ICJ's 2002 Judgment, www.cameroon-info.net/article/affaire-bakassi-la-frontiere-maritime-entre-le-cameroun-et-le-nigeria-definitivement-tracee-102117.html, accessed 8 March 2017.
67 Joint Communiqué of Cameroon–Nigeria Presidents, Yaoundé, 30 July 2015, para. 14; Joint Communiqué of Nigeria–Cameroon Presidents, Abuja, 4 May 2016, para. 15, www.google.fr/#q=See+Joint+Communiqu%C3%A9+of+Cameroon+Nigeria+Presidents,+Yaound%C3%A9,+30+July+2015,+&*&spf=63, accessed 8 March 2017.
68 These two Articles state that 'Where there is agreement in force between the States concerned, questions relating to the delimitation of the EEZ/continental shelf shall be determined in accordance with the provisions of that agreement'.
69 Article 76(1) provides:

> The continental shelf of a coastal State comprises the seabed and subsoil of the submarine areas that extend beyond its territorial sea throughout the natural prolongation of its land territory to the outer edge of the continental margin, or to a distance of 200 nautical miles from the baselines from which the breadth of the territorial sea is measured where the outer edge of the continental margin does not extend up to that distance.

70 See: Convention, Article 3, Annex II. *Commission on the Limits of the Continental Shelf.*
71 Article 76(8) provides:

> Information on the limits of the continental shelf beyond 200 nautical miles from the baselines from which the breadth of the territorial sea is measured shall be submitted by the

coastal State to the Commission on the Limits of the Continental Shelf set up under Annex II on the basis of equitable geographical representation. The Commission shall make recommendations to coastal States on matters related to the establishment of the outer limits of their continental shelf. The limits of the shelf established by a coastal State on the basis of these recommendations shall be final and binding.

72 See Executive Summary: A Submission of Data and Information on the Outer Limits of the Continental Shelf of the Federal Republic of Nigeria Pursuant to Part VI of Annex II to the United Nations Convention of the Law of the Sea, May 2009, www.un.org/depts/los/clcs_new/submissions_filesnga38_09/nga2009_executivesummary.pdf, accessed 8 March 2017.
73 For the amended Executive Summary see www.un.org/depts/los/clcs_new/submissions_files/nga38_09/nga2016_executivesummary.pdf, accessed 8 March 2017.
74 See Cameroon's 'Demande Préliminaire du Cameroun aux fins de l'extension des limites de son Plateau Continental', 11 May 2009, www.un.org/depts/los/clcs_new/submissions_files/preliminary/cmr2009informationpreliminaire.pdf, accessed 8 March 2017.
75 See Written Statement of Equatorial Guinea, pp. 1–2, paras 2–4, www.icj-cij.org/docket/files/94/8610.pdf, accessed 8 March 2017.
76 *Cameroon v. Nigeria* (Judgment) [2002] *ICJ Rep.* 303 paras 238, 307. See Chapter 7 in this book on the law of the sea for more details on this.
77 *Cameroon v. Nigeria* (Judgment) [2002] *ICJ Rep.* 303 para. 291.
78 *Cameroon v. Nigeria* (Judgment) [2002] *ICJ Rep.* 303 paras 272–273.
79 *Cameroon v. Nigeria* (Judgment) [2002] *ICJ Rep.* 303 para. 274.
80 *Cameroon v. Nigeria* (Judgment) [2002] *ICJ Rep.* 303 para. 284.
81 *Cameroon v. Nigeria*: Written Statement of the Republic of Equatorial Guinea (4 April 2001) paras 38 and 40, www.icj-cij.org/files/case-related/94/8610.pdf, accessed 11 September 2017.
82 See Note Verbale Ref. 090/C-1/10 dated 22 December 2009 from the Permanent Mission of Equatorial Guinea to the United Nations in New York, p. 1, www.un.org/depts/los/clcs_new/commission_preliminary.htm, accessed 11 September 2017.
83 Ibid., see Point 5 of Equatorial Guinea's Note Verbale.
84 Treaty between the Federal Republic of Nigeria and the Republic of Equatorial Guinea concerning their Maritime Boundary, signed on 23 September 2000, entered into force on 3 April 2002, www.un.org/depts/los/LEGISLATIONANDTREATIES/PDFFILES/TREATIES/NGA-GNQ2000MB.PDF, accessed 16 March 2017.
85 Written Observations of Cameroon, 4 July 2001, ICJ Pleadings, pp. 11–12, paras 27–32. In the letter filed with the Court's Registrar on 5 December, Cameroon argued that the treaty was a move to present a *faît accompli* before the Court; www.un.org/docket/files/94/8611, accessed 16 March 2017.
86 Treaty between Equatorial Guinea and Nigeria on Joint Exploration of Crude Oil, especially at the Zafiro–Ekanga Oil Field located at the maritime boundary of both countries ('Unitisation Agreement'), signed on 3 April 2002; www.un.org/depts/los/LEGISLATIONANDTREATIES/PDFFILES/TREATIES/GNQ-NGA2002ZE.PDF, accessed 16 March 2017.
87 Yoshifumi Tanaka, 'Reflections on Maritime Delimitation in the Cameroon/Nigeria Case' (2004) 53 *International and Comparative Law Quarterly*, p. 395.
88 Treaty between the Federal Republic of Nigeria and the Democratic Republic of Sao Tome and Principe on the Joint Development of Petroleum and other Resources in Respect of Areas of the EEZ of the two States (signed 21 February 2001), www.un.org/Depts/los/LEGISLATION ANDTREATIES/PDFFILES/TREATIES/STP-NGA2001.PDF, accessed 16 March 2017.
89 Treaty Regarding the Delimitation of the Maritime Boundary between the Republic of Equatorial Guinea and the Democratic Republic of Sao Tome and Principe (signed 26 June 1999), www.un.org/Depts/los/LEGISLATIONANDTREATIES/PDFFILES/TREATIES/GNQ-STP1999MB.PDF, accessed 16 March 2017.
90 C.G. Lathrop, 'Tripoint Issues in Maritime Delimitation', in D.A. Colson and R.W. Smith (eds), *International Maritime Boundaries* (Leiden: Brill and New York: American Society of International Law, 2005), p. 3307.
91 Baye, 'Implications of the Bakassi Conflict Resolution for Cameroon' (2010) 10 *African Journal of Conflict Resolution* 1, p. 11. For the Greentree Agreement, see www.peaceau.org/uploads/cn-agreement-12-06-2006.pdf, accessed 16 March 2017.
92 Ibid. p. 25.

93 UN Press Release, 'Cameroon, Nigeria Sign Agreement Ending Decades-Old Dispute' (12 June 2006), UN/Press AFR/1397; www.un.org/press/en/2006/afr1397.doc.htm.
94 Baye, 'Implications of the Bakassi Conflict Resolution for Cameroon' (2010) 10 *African Journal of Conflict Resolution* 1, p. 11.
95 President Biya's Message to the Nation on 21 August 2008, following the Treaty of Calabar, *Cameroon Tribune* (Yaoundé, 22 August 2008), p. 3.
96 The Treaty of Calabar 2008 is the Agreement transferring authority over the Bakassi Peninsula from Nigeria to Cameroon.
97 Ruth Iyob, 'Comparative Perspectives: Territorial and Boundary Disputes in the Horn of Africa', in Adam Lupel (ed.), *Pacific Settlement of Border Disputes: Lessons from Bakassi and the Greentree Agreement* (New York: International Peace Institute, 2008), pp. 33–34.
98 Interview by Martin Nkemnyu, *Cameroon Tribune* (Yaoundé, 18 August 2008), p. 4.
99 Emmanuel Kendemeh, 'Bakassi: Projects Worth CFAF 12 Billion Executed', *Cameroon Tribune* (Yaoundé, 15 March 2010).
100 Baye, 'The Implications of the Bakassi Conflict Resolution for Cameroon' (2010) 10 *African Journal of Conflict Resolution* 1, p. 31.
101 Kendemeh, 'Bakassi: Projects Worth CFAF 12 Billion Executed', *Cameroon Tribune* (Yaoundé, 15 March 2010).
102 George Mbella, 'Bakassi Reconstruction: FCFA 30.7 Billion Spent on Projects', *Cameroon Tribune* (Yaoundé, 19 August 2016), p. 3.
103 Ibid.
104 George Ngwane, 'Preventing Renewed Violence through Peace Building in the Bakassi Peninsula', p. 3, http://jimbicentral.typepad.com/files/preventing-renewed-violence-through-peace-building-in-the-bakassi-peninsula-cameroon.pdf, accessed 16 March 2017.
105 Ibid.
106 Ibid., p. 8.
107 *Cameroon v. Nigeria*, *ICJ Reports* 2002, p. 453, para. 318.
108 President Biya's Message to the Nation, *Cameroon Tribune* (Yaoundé, 22 August 2008), p. 3.
109 AFRICAphonie (Buea, 2013) *Bakassi Peace Letter*, p. 3, www.africaphonie.org/2010/11/bakassi-peace-letter-peace-through-culture.html, accessed 28 August 2017.
110 George Ngwane (2013), 'Building Social Cohesion through Culture in Conflict Context', www.gngwane.com/2013/06/building-social-cohesion-through-culture-in-conflict-context.html, accessed 24 March 2017.
111 Ibid.
112 'The Co-existence of Cameroonians and Nigerians within the Bakassi Peninsula', a special report from administrative sources in Mundemba, September 2016 (on file in the author's personal archives); A.N. Ngalim, 'African Boundary Conflicts and International Mediation: The Absence of Inclusivity in Mediating the Bakassi Peninsula Conflict', Working Paper No. 9, African Peacebuilding Network (APN) (September 2016), p. 10; and A. McGregor, 'Cameroon Rebels Threaten Security in Oil-Rich Gulf of Guinea' (November 2010) VIII *Terrorism Monitor* 43, 23, pp. 7–8.
113 George Ngwane (2015), 'Preventing Renewed Violence through Peace Building in the Bakassi Peninsula', p. 4, http://jimbicentral.typepad.com/files/preventing-renewed-violence-through-peace-building-in-the-bakassi-peninsula-cameroon.pdf, accessed 24 March 2017.
114 A.N. Ngalim, 'African Boundary Conflicts and International Mediation: The Absence of Inclusivity in Mediating the Bakassi Peninsula Conflict', Working Paper No. 9, African Peacebuilding Network (APN) (September 2016), p. 2.
115 OAU Resolution AHG/Res.16(1) of 21 July 1964.
116 See Joint Communiqué of Cameroon–Nigeria Presidents, Yaoundé, 30 July 2015, para. 13.
117 Andrew Sone Ewang, 'The Role of Legal and Extra-Legal Mechanisms in the Resolution of the Cameroon–Nigeria Bakassi Conflict', unpublished paper, University of Dschang, Cameroon, 2016, p. 20.
118 Baye, 'The Implications of the Bakassi Conflict for Cameroon' (2010) 10 *African Journal of Conflict Resolution* 1, p. 29.
119 Ministry of External Relations (Yaoundé, 4 August 2016).
120 See Joint Communiqué of Cameroon–Nigeria Presidents, Yaoundé, 30 July 2015, para. 15.
121 Baye, 'The Implications of the Bakassi Conflict for Cameroon' (2010) 10 *African Journal of Conflict Resolution* 1, p. 16.

5 The ICJ Bakassi Decision

The rights of the indigenous communities and populations in the Bakassi Peninsula

Hephzibah Egede

Introduction

Case background

This chapter appraises the 2002 judgment delivered by the International Court of Justice (ICJ) in the case of *Cameroon v. Nigeria*.[1] On 29 March 1994, the Republic of Cameroon filed an application at ICJ to institute proceedings against the Federal Republic of Nigeria. The key ground of the dispute bordered on the delimitation of the maritime boundaries between the two States and on the determination of which State had sovereignty over the Bakassi Peninsula. Cameroon filed an additional application seeking to extend the subject of the dispute to cover the question of the sovereignty over an area of the Lake Chad. The Court examined both matters 'as a whole in a single case'.[2] The Court held that permanent sovereignty over the disputed Bakassi Peninsula lay with Cameroon based on the boundary delimitation of the Anglo-German agreement of 11 March 1913. In furtherance of its decision, the Court required that Nigeria withdraw its administration and its armed forces (military and police) from the Bakassi Peninsula. With regard to the specified area of the Lake Chad, the Court found that this area fell within the sovereignty of Nigeria. It therefore required that Cameroon should expedite its withdrawal from this area.

In the course of the determination of the case, the Court took cognisance of the undertaking of the Cameroonian State to 'continue to afford protection to Nigerians living in the Bakassi Peninsula and in the Lake Chad area'.[3] The undertaking was predicated on a 'traditional policy of hospitality and tolerance'.[4] The Cameroonian undertaking (now enshrined in the Greentree Agreement[5]) deserves further consideration. This is because it deals with the important issue of how the rights of indigenous populations and their ancestral territories can be safeguarded.

To further explore this matter, the chapter is organised in the following manner. The first part provides the introduction and background of the case. The second part considers the meaning of indigeneity and indigenous peoples in international law and whether the peoples and communities within the Bakassi Peninsula can be regarded as indigenous communities. The third part evaluates the significance of the link between land and the cultural heritage of indigenous peoples and communities. In undertaking this discourse, it specifically considers whether this link between land and indigenous communities was fully considered by the ICJ, and by international institutions responsible for the implementation of the ICJ Cameroon/Nigeria judgment. The fourth part explores whether the resettlement of indigenous peoples as required by the Greentree Agreement[6] constitutes a forceful removal of indigenous peoples from their land and cultural heritage. It also addresses the role that an award of fair and just compensation can play in ensuring that the removal of indigenous peoples from their land is not in breach of international law. The fifth part appraises the relevance of free prior informed consent (FPIC) on matters impacting the rights of indigenous peoples in the Bakassi Peninsula. The sixth and final part provides the concluding remarks of the chapter.

Indigeneity and/or indigenousness of the peoples and communities in the Bakassi Peninsula

This section interrogates whether the communities living within the Bakassi Peninsula can be considered as indigenous peoples. In determining the status of the communities within the peninsula, it is necessary to consider how indigeneity and/or indigenousness are conceptualised under international law.

According to Merlan,[7] the term 'indigeneity' presupposes: 'a sphere of commonality among those who form a world collectivity of 'indigenous peoples' in contrast to their various others'.[8]

She further asserts that indigeneity can be characterised as belonging or a 'deeply felt processes of attachment'[9] between 'group and locality'.[10] Indigeneity therefore describes the sense of identification that an indigenous populace or a community feel towards one another as opposed to other groups outside their locality. To further understand this sense of attachment that indigenous people feel towards one another and their geographical locality, it is important to have a definitional understanding of 'indigenous peoples'.

It is generally accepted that there is no universal definition of the term 'indigenous peoples'.[11] The International Labour Organisation's (ILO) *Indigenous and Tribal Peoples Convention 1989*[12] (hereafter the ILO Convention 169) is considered as the key international treaty that provides a binding definition or characterisation of what is meant by the term 'indigenous peoples'.[13] Article 1(b) of the ILO Convention 169 refers to indigenous peoples as:

> peoples in independent countries who are regarded as indigenous on account of their descent from the populations which inhabited the country, or a geographical region to which the country belongs, at the time of conquest or colonisation or the establishment of present state boundaries and who, irrespective of their legal status, retain some or all of their own social, economic, cultural and political institutions.

It distinguishes tribal peoples in Article 1(a) as:

> tribal peoples in independent countries whose social, cultural and economic conditions distinguish them from other sections of the national community, and whose status is regulated wholly or partially by their own customs or traditions or by special laws or regulations.

Unlike the ILO Convention 169, the United Nations Declarations on the Rights of Indigenous Peoples 2007 (hereafter the UNDRIP)[14] does not provide a definition for indigenous peoples. A brief historical overview of the formulation of the UNDRIP is therefore required to provide some perspective on why the instrument does not provide a definition of the term 'indigenous peoples'.

During the proceedings of the Inter-Sessional Working Group,[15] which was mandated with the elaboration of a draft declaration providing rights for indigenous peoples, many States within the developing world felt that the definition of what groups could be defined as 'indigenous peoples' should be left to national legislative interpretation.[16] Although, representatives of indigenous peoples and some industrialised Western States rejected these States' position, the UNDRIP was drafted without a clear definition of the term 'indigenous peoples'.[17]

African States within the Inter-Sessional Working Group also questioned whether the term 'tribal peoples'[18] should be considered as interchangeable with the term 'indigenous peoples'.[19] They opined that Africans regardless of their ethnic or tribal identities should be considered as being indigenous to the countries that they belong to.[20] Asian States such as India, Pakistan and Indonesia also adopted the same position and argued that their national populations have 'inhabited their [countries] as at the time of colonization' and therefore did not require any further classification as indigenous peoples.[21] In classifying national populations as indigenous to the countries they inhabit, African and Asian States sought to curtail attempts by tribal peoples or indigenous peoples to use the concept of self-determination as a guise for secession.

Other States within the industrialised North, like Germany and Great Britain, also pressed for a distinction between the terms 'peoples' and 'indigenous peoples'. The call for the distinction between 'peoples' and 'indigenous peoples' was to assist in the determination on the groups of peoples that could be entitled to the right of self-determination.[22] These differing views on how indigenous peoples can be described partly explains why the UNDRIP did not provide a definition for the term 'indigenous peoples'.[23] However, the States within the Inter-Sessional Working Group did resolve that the right to self-determination (autonomy) could be accorded to indigenous peoples. However, this right to self-determination did not have attached to it the right of secession.[24]

Further attempts have been made to provide a working definition for the term 'indigenous peoples'. The Sub-Commission on the Prevention of Discrimination and Protection of Minorities at its 34th session provided some definitional context in its seminal *Study on the Problem of Discrimination against Indigenous Populations* (hereafter the Martinez Cobo Study).[25] Chapter 5[26] of the Martinez Cobo Study presents criteria that States and indigenous peoples have utilised to determine which groups fall under the classification of 'indigenous peoples'.

The Martinez Cobo Study states that:

> Indigenous communities, peoples and nations are those which, having a historical continuity with pre-invasion and pre-colonial societies that developed on their territories, consider themselves distinct from other sectors of the societies now prevailing on those territories, or parts of them. They form at present non-dominant sectors of society and are determined to preserve, develop and transmit to future generations their ancestral territories, and their ethnic identity, as the basis of their continued existence as peoples, in accordance with their own cultural patterns, social institutions and legal system.[27]

The Martinez Cobo Study and Article 1(b) of the ILO Convention 169 are the key international law documents that provide some definitional context on the groups that can be considered as indigenous peoples. Unlike the ILO Convention 169, the Martinez Cobo Study is non-binding, but its descriptors are frequently cited and are considered as 'a standard for discussion of the subject of indigenous peoples within the UN system'.[28] If the standards within the Martinez Cobo Study are applied to the *Cameroon/Nigeria* case, a determination will need to be undertaken on whether the populations within the Bakassi Peninsula can lay historic connection with the pre-colonial societies that existed in Bakassi prior to the countries that are now considered as Nigeria and Cameroon respectively.[29] Authoritative works[30] establish the historic connection that the present Bakassi communities have with pre-colonial societies, particularly the old Kingdom of Calabar, which is currently situated in Nigeria. In the advancement of its case before the ICJ, Nigeria aligned itself with this historical position. It referred to the 1884 Treaty of Protection between the Kingdom of Old Calabar and Great Britain, which affirmed that the peninsula belonged to the Old Calabar Kingdom. Nigeria therefore questioned whether the transfer of the peninsula under the 1913 Anglo-Germany agreement was valid, taking into consideration the pre-existing claims of the Old Calabar Kingdom over this region.[31] As expected, the ICJ transferred sovereignty over the peninsula to Cameroon based on Euro-centric jurisprudential concepts such as *uti possidetis*[32] and inter-temporal rules of expediency[33] (a further debate of these rules is beyond the scope of this chapter). In spite of the judicial transfer of the Bakassi Peninsula to Cameroon, the debate continues[34] on whether the ICJ judgment has stifled the ability of communities within the region to self-identify as indigenous peoples or communities. This point will be further considered in the next section of this chapter.

Apart from the definitional descriptions of 'indigenous peoples' set out in Article 1(b) of the ILO 169 and Chapter 5 of the Martinez Cobo Study, it is important to consider whether African regional treaties provide some discourse on indigenous peoples. As stressed earlier, African States treat indigeneity and indigenous peoples differently from other regions of the world. This is because the African historical colonial experience is viewed as being different from the 'aboriginality and foreign settler' experience of States such as Australia, New Zealand and Canada, which has helped to shape the discourse of indigeneity and indigenous peoples.[35] However, the African Commission on Human and Peoples Rights (hereafter the ACHPR) in its advisory opinion on the UNDRIP affirms that the concepts of indigeneity and indigenous peoples are well recognised concepts in African jurisprudence.[36]

The Working Group of Experts on Indigenous Populations/Communities (Working Group)[37] as constituted by the ACHPR also avows the existence of indigenous peoples within Africa. In affirming the existence of African indigenous communities, it is necessary to consider whether the Working Group's report[38] provides an African-centric definition on what it means to be an African indigenous population or community. This is important as there is no definition of 'indigenous peoples' within the African Charter on Human and Peoples' Rights (hereafter the African Charter).[39] The decision not to include a definition for African indigenous peoples within the African Charter appears to be deliberate. It was intended to avoid the 'difficult discussions'[40] that could have ensued in the future had a definition of 'indigenous peoples' been included in the text of the African Charter. According to Richard Kiwanuka,[41] this is not an uncommon practice in international law. He presents the example of the International Law Commission (hereafter the ILC), which states that the definition of a word is sometimes deliberately omitted from international documents to allow for explanatory flexibility.[42]

Although the definition for indigenous African peoples is not provided in the African Charter; the Working Group has provided explanatory descriptors on what it means to be an indigenous community in Africa. These descriptors are not meant to be treated as a wholesale definition of the term 'indigenous African peoples'. The decision of the Working Group not to provide a blanket definition of the term is similar to the position adopted by the ACHPR's Advisory Opinion on the UNDRIP. The ACHPR Advisory Opinion[43] states:

> a definition is not necessary or useful as there is no universally agreed definition of the term and no single definition can capture the characteristics of indigenous populations. Rather, it is much more relevant and constructive to try to bring out the main characteristics allowing the identification of the indigenous populations and communities in Africa.[44]

Chapter 4 of the Working Group's report lists in 4.1 the characteristics of indigenous peoples or populations:

> To summarize briefly the overall characteristics of the groups identifying themselves as indigenous peoples: their cultures and ways of life differ considerably from the dominant society and their cultures are under threat, in some cases to the extent of extinction. A key characteristic for most of them is that the survival of their particular way of life depends on access and rights to their traditional land and the natural resources thereon. They suffer from discrimination as they are being regarded as less developed and less advanced than other more dominant sectors of society. They often live in inaccessible regions, often geographically isolated and suffer from various forms of marginalisation, both politically and socially. They are subject to domination and exploitation within national political and economic structures that are commonly designed to reflect the interests and activities of the national majority. This discrimination, domination and marginalisation violates their human rights as peoples/ communities, threatens the continuation of their cultures and ways of life and prevents them from being able to genuinely participate in deciding on their own future and forms of development.[45]

In addition, the Working Group's report further asserts that pastoralists or agro-pastoralists can be deemed as possessing the characteristics of indigenous populations.[46] It is significant that the report includes fishermen in the definition of pastoralists and agro-pastoralists. On the face of it, this classification appears to be unconventional since pastoralism is normally viewed as animal husbandry. The categorisation may however not be out of place, since other works have classified indigenous groups such as the Yakut of Eurasia as 'fishing pastoralist communities'.[47] Founded on the Working Group's descriptors above, it is clear that the fishing communities within the Bakassi Peninsula can also be considered as indigenous to the peninsula. In addition, the ACHPR in the cases of *Social and Economic Rights Action Center and the Center for Economic and Social Rights v. Nigeria* (*Ogoni* decision)[48] and the *Center for Minority Development and Minority Rights Group International (on behalf of the Endorois Welfare Council) v. Kenya* (*Endorois* decision)[49] have also recognised that fishermen fall within pastoralist groups and can be classified as indigenous peoples.

An appraisal of paragraph 12 of the ACHPR's *Advisory Opinion on the Rights of Indigenous Peoples* also provides further grounds for classifying the communities within the Bakassi Peninsula as indigenous peoples. This paragraph outlines the core elements or characteristics of indigenous peoples. They include:

> (a) Self-identification (b) A special attachment to and the use of their traditional land whereby their ancestral land and territory have a fundamental importance for their collective physical and cultural survival as peoples and (c) A state of subjugation, marginalisation, dispossession, exclusion, or discrimination because these peoples have different cultures, ways of life or mode of production than the national hegemonic and dominant model.[50]

The groups within the Bakassi Peninsula, including those of Nigerian descent, appear to satisfy paragraph 12(a) and (b) above. This is because they self-identify and express a special attachment to the peninsula. They view the peninsula as their rightful ancestral land necessary for their physical and cultural survival as a community.[51] The fundamental question is whether they satisfy the third characteristic of indigenous peoples as set out paragraph 12(c). To answer this question, one needs to consider which national hegemonic and dominant model directly impacts on the rights of the Bakassi communities of Nigerian descent. Because of the ICJ judgment, the Bakassi Peninsula is now considered as part of the sovereign territory of Cameroon. There is therefore a basis to argue that Bakassites of Nigerian descent who self-identify with Bakassi as their ancestral home have become a dispossessed and marginalised people. This is because their culture and way of life now differs from the national Cameroonian hegemonic and dominant model. In fact, the wording of the Cameroonian undertaking and the Greentree Agreement[52] respectively accepts that the Bakassi communities of Nigerian descent are no longer considered as falling within the national hegemonic and dominant groups of people that can be identified as Cameroonian citizens.

To provide further context on whether the communities living within the Bakassi Peninsula prior to the ICJ decision can be considered as indigenous communities, it is necessary to provide a brief list of the groups of peoples that live within this locality. According to *Native Peoples of the World: An Encyclopaedia of Groups, Cultures and Contemporary Issues*,[53] the peninsula is home to several groups including the Annang, Efik, Efut and Ibibio peoples. Prior to the ICJ judgment which vested sovereignty of the Bakassi Peninsula to Cameroon, several of these groups would have characterised themselves as Bakassites indigenous communities of Nigerian descent.[54] Because of the ICJ judgment and the subsequent Greentree Agreement which implements the Court's decision, the Bakassi indigenes of Nigerian descent have been faced with the difficult choice of relocating to Nigeria or remaining as marginalised groups within a dominant national hegemonic model.

Based on indigeneity and their close cultural ties with the specific geographical location called the Bakassi Peninsula, some of these groups such as the Usakadet (Isangele) group[55] have chosen not to settle in Nigeria. While these groups consider themselves to be of Nigerian descent, they do not have close affinity or ties with the new regions or areas of Nigeria which have been provided for their resettlement.[56] Affinity and ties to ancestral land and territory are central to a better understanding of the concepts of indigeneity and indigenous communities. It is therefore necessary to consider how affinity and ties to land and territory are regarded under international law. This point will be further considered in the next section.

Indigenous ties and affinities to ancestral land: a case study of the Bakassi Peninsula

Allegiance to ancestral land is a core part of the identity of an indigenous population. Land and its resources are considered to be vital to the wellbeing and sustenance of indigenous communities.[57] The development of traditional knowledge and spiritual values in many indigenous communities is intricately connected with land and its resources. This is because land provides indigenous communities with a vast number of resources that can be utilised for spiritual and cultural rites. According to Sangha: 'Land provided people ceremonial objects, the sacred names, the kinship, and languages, demonstrating that diverse connections with land are central for well-being of Indigenous communities.'[58]

The ties between indigenous peoples and land are also firmly recognised in the UNDRIP framework and other international instruments.[59] Article 25 of the UNDRIP states:

> Indigenous peoples have the right to maintain and strengthen their distinctive spiritual relationship with their traditionally owned or otherwise occupied and used lands, territories, waters and coastal seas and other resources and to uphold their responsibilities to future generations in this regard.

The same right is recognised in Article 13 of the ILO Convention 169. While Article 22(1) of the African Charter affirms the cultural rights of peoples, it falls short of expressly affirming the spiritual or cultural link that African indigenous peoples and communities may have to land. The ACHPR in the landmark *Endorois* decision[60] has, however, broadly interpreted the cultural and property rights set out within the African Charter to include the right of indigenous groups to maintain spiritual and cultural ties and affinity with their ancestral land. The ACHPR found Kenya to be in violation of Articles 1, 8, 14, 17, 21 and 22 of the African Charter and recommended that the Kenyan State should 'Ensure that the Endorois community has unrestricted access to Lake Bogoria and surrounding sites for religious and cultural rites and for grazing their cattle'.[61]

Regrettably, the cultural and spiritual significance that indigenous communities attach to land and location appears to have been missed by the ICJ and the proponents of the Greentree Agreement. The failure to recognise these ties may be attributable to the fact that, at the time the case was decided, the UNDRIP had not been adopted. The ICJ, however, could have taken cognisance[62] of the ILO Convention 169 which was in force at the time of the decision of the Court (and also at the time of the entering into force of the Greentree Agreement). As earlier stressed, Article 13 of the ILO Convention 169 recognises and affirms the close ties between indigenous peoples and land. Perhaps the reason why the ILO Convention 169 was not brought to the attention of the Court is that Cameroon and Nigeria are not Parties to the Convention. This may explain why the ICJ had to obtain a state undertaking from Cameroon to protect the rights of the Bakassite communities of Nigerian descent in the peninsula.[63] Yet it is questionable whether the undertaking, which merely states that Cameroon will safeguard the interests of the communities based on its 'traditional policy of hospitality and tolerance', provides adequate protection for the Nigerian communities within the Bakassi Peninsula. It is therefore necessary to examine the status of undertakings or promises made by States under international law.

State undertakings under international law

Undertakings, acts or promises made by a State are normally described as 'unilateral in nature'.[64] A unilateral promise made by a State is not considered as a 'rare phenomenon'[65] under international law. Promises of this nature are frequently undertaken by States in their relationships with other States and entities. The ILC has made some attempt to codify the unilateral acts of state. This is set out in the *Guiding Principles Applicable to Unilateral Declarations Capable of Creating Legal Relations.*[66] Principle 1 of the guidelines sets out the framework as to when unilateral state declarations can be considered as creating binding legal relations. Principle 1 states that:

> Declarations publicly made and manifesting the will to be bound may have the effect of creating legal obligations. When the conditions for this are met, the binding character of such declarations is based on good faith; States concerned may then take them into consideration and rely on them; such States are entitled to require that such obligations be respected.

The ILC in its commentary on this principle explained that the principle was founded on the dicta in the *Nuclear Tests* case.[67] In taking judicial notice of Cameroonian undertaking, it is clear that the ICJ required that the undertaking will be legally binding on Cameroon. Yet, as the ILC points out in its commentary[68] on Principle 1 of its *Guiding Principles*, the legal effect of any state undertaking is still dependent on the intention of the State that makes the undertaking. The ILC referred to *Burkina Faso v. Republic of Mali*,[69] where the ICJ declined to hold as legally enforceable against the State of Mali a unilateral declaration which had been made by the Malian Head of State.[70] This raises an interesting point on the status of the undertaking provided to the ICJ by Cameroon's legal representatives in the Bakassi dispute. Is this undertaking legally enforceable against the Cameroonian State? This is particularly relevant when consideration is given to the fact that the undertaking was given, not directly to the indigenous communities, but to the Court. This calls into play the status of an undertaking given by a party to a court.

The English case of *Zipher Limited v. Markem Systems Limited*[71] highlights the uncertainty of the status of an undertaking provided to a court by a party, especially when it is not incorporated in a subsequent court order. The Court of Appeal held that an undertaking given by Zipher, that it would narrow its claim with respect to a particular patent, had not been committed into writing. It therefore constituted an 'an offer to give an undertaking' and could not be revived as a valid undertaking at the appeal stage. Unlike in the *Zipher* case, it can be argued that the undertaking provided by the Cameroonian State was legally binding since the Court had incorporated it into its final judgment.[72]

Article 94 of the United Nations Charter establishes the requirement for States to perform the obligations set out in an ICJ judgment. The Article states:

> if a party fails to perform the obligations incumbent upon it under a judgment rendered by the court under a judgment rendered by the court, the other party may have recourse to the Security Council, which may, if it deem necessary make recommendations or decide upon measures to be taken to give effect to the judgment.[73]

Apart from this state undertaking, Cameroon and Nigeria have also gone ahead to execute the Greentree Agreement, which imposes binding treaty obligations upon the States.

While the execution of the Greentree Agreement is a welcome development, there are still unanswered questions on whether the treaty provides the indigenous populations in the Bakassi region with comparable rights to those provided under international instruments such as the ILO Convention 169 and the UNDRIP. These questions will be further considered in subsequent sections of this chapter.

Greentree Treaty obligations and the rights of indigenous peoples to maintain close ties and links with ancestral land

The protagonists of the Greentree Agreement[74] would argue that the implementation of the agreement has made tremendous strides in ameliorating the adverse impact that the ICJ judgment could have had on indigenous communities within the Bakassi Peninsula. This is because Article 3 obligates Cameroon to guarantee to the Nigerian nationals living within the peninsula the fundamental rights and freedoms as enshrined in international human rights law and in other relevant provisions of international law. As discussed in the preceding section of this chapter, treaties such as the ILO Convention 169, which affirm the close ties between indigenous peoples and land, were already in force at the time the Greentree Agreement was executed. Accordingly, it is necessary to consider whether the rights set out in Article 3 of the Greentree Agreement sufficiently recognise and protect the right of indigenous peoples to maintain close ties with their ancestral lands.

Article 3(2) of the Greentree Agreement sets out the specific rights and freedoms that Cameroon is obliged to protect. It requires that Cameroon shall:

- (a) not force Nigerian nationals living in the Bakassi Peninsula to leave the Zone or to change their nationality;
- (b) respect their culture, language and beliefs;
- (c) respect their right to continue their agricultural and fishing activities;
- (d) protect their property and their customary land rights;
- (e) not levy in any discriminatory manner any taxes and other dues on Nigerian nationals living in the Zone; and
- (f) take every necessary measure to protect Nigerian nationals living in the Zone from any harassment or harm.

While these fundamental rights go some way in protecting the national and historical identity of Bakassi indigenous communities of Nigerian descent living within the peninsula, more could have been done within the treaty text to expressly affirm the close cultural and spiritual ties that indigenous communities have with ancestral land as recognised by international law. There is some allusion to these rights in Article 3(2)(b)(d) of the Greentree Agreement. These sub-articles require inter alia that Cameroon should recognise the culture of Nigerian nationals and protect their property and their customary lands. However, more could have been done to provide text in the treaty that expressly affirms the close ties that indigenous peoples have with their ancestral land. The failure of the Greentree Agreement to expressly affirm these close spiritual and cultural links to ancestral land may explain in part why the resettlement exercise appears not to have the full support of the communities concerned. The concerns of the communities are expressed this way:[75] 'How do you resettle a man from his ancestral home? How do you resettle his culture, his gods, his sense of community, his religion and his soul…?'[76]

In reality the ICJ judgment and the Greentree Agreement have provided the Bakassi indigenes of Nigerian descent with three stark options: (1) resettlement in Nigeria; (2) migrant status in the Bakassi Peninsula which is now part of Cameroon; or (3) adoption of Cameroonian citizenship. It is debatable whether any of these options is satisfactory to the affected communities. Those who have resettled in Nigeria feel they have been separated from the peninsula which they call their ancestral home. The fact that they are of Nigerian descent does not necessarily mean that they can self-identify with the other geographical locations in Nigeria. Those who have opted for migrant status in the Bakassi Peninsula complain of Cameroonian harassment and brutality,[77] while those who have adopted Cameroonian citizenship feel that they have been forced to change their identity to fit the dominant national majority. Regrettably, the attempt to peacefully resolve the boundary dispute between the two States has in turn disenfranchised the indigenous communities, especially as it relates to their right to maintain cultural and spiritual links with their ancestral land. The disenfranchisement of the Bakassi indigenous populations of Nigerian descent is evidenced in an ongoing resettlement exercise which will be considered in the following section of this chapter.

Relocation of Bakassi indigenous populations – forceful or peaceful removal from ancestral land?

International law recognises the right of indigenous peoples and individuals to belong to an indigenous community or nation. In furtherance of this right, international law prohibits the forceful removal of indigenous peoples from the land or territories. Several international law instruments[78] enshrine the prohibition against the forceful removal of indigenous communities from the land. Chief among these instruments is the UNDRIP 2007. Article 10 of the UNDRIP[79] states that:

> Indigenous peoples shall not be forcibly removed from their lands or territories. No relocation shall take place without the free, prior and informed consent of the indigenous peoples concerned and after agreement on just and fair compensation and, where possible, with the option of return.

The prohibition against forceful removal of land is connected with the right of self-determination. While the right to self-determination does not include the right to secede,[80] it is an established human right recognised in core human rights treaties such as Article 1 of the International Covenant on Economic, Social and Cultural Rights 1966 (ICESCR)[81] and Article 20 of the African Charter. It is debatable whether the African Charter has a comparable provision like Article 10 of the UNDRIP with regard to the prohibition of forceful removal of indigenous peoples from their territories. However, ACHPR jurisprudence[82] has provided a purposive interpretation of the Charter that is broad enough to recognise the prohibition of forceful removal of indigenous peoples from their lands and territories.

Further, at the national level, domestic courts in Sub-Saharan Africa have also taken a progressive approach in interpreting national constitutions in favour of the prohibition against forcible removal of indigenous peoples from land. In the landmark case of *Sesana v. AG of the Republic of Botswana*,[83] the High Court of Botswana found in favour of the San indigenous communities that they had been forcibly removed from their ancestral home contrary to the provisions of the Botswana constitution and international law standards.

In the early case of *Amodu Tijani v. The Secretary, Southern Provinces*,[84] the Privy Council also acknowledged the validity of native title over land. It recognised that if land under native title was transferred, compensation must be paid to the members of the community through their recognised representatives.[85] What is significant about this case is that it pre-dates the international instruments such as the ILO Convention 169 and the UNDRIP that enshrine the rights of indigenous peoples and populations, including the prohibition of the forceful removal from ancestral land. The *Tijani* case is also symbolic, since it addresses the rights of indigenous communities residing in Nigeria (one of the state Parties in the Bakassi proceedings). The *Tijani* and *Sesana* decisions as well as African Commission jurisprudence suggest that judicial recognition has been provided for the prohibition against the forceful removal of indigenous African populations from their land. Before a further evaluation is undertaken on whether the Greentree Agreement enunciates this position, it is necessary to consider what is meant by forceful removal of land.

The Committee on Economic, Social and Cultural Rights (hereafter the CESR) in its general comment[86] provides a working definition of what constitutes forceful removal or forced eviction of land. It states that this is 'the permanent or temporary removal against their will of individuals, families and/or communities from the homes and/or land which they occupy, without the provision of, and access to, appropriate forms of legal or other protection'.

What constitutes provision or access to appropriate forms of legal or other protection has been given further meaning in treaty instruments. For instance Article 16 of the ILO Convention 169 requires that where relocation of indigenous peoples is deemed necessary, it can only be undertaken where the free and informed consent of the peoples has been obtained or, where this is not possible, it should be done 'following appropriate procedures established by national laws and regulations, including public inquiries where appropriate, which provide the opportunity for effective representation of the peoples concerned'.[87]

Equally Article 10 of the UNDRIP requires that free prior informed consent (FPIC) must be obtained. Both instruments require that the State must provide just and fair compensation to the dispossessed peoples and where possible give them the option to return to their land.

An examination of the Greentree Agreement establishes that the norm of the prohibition of forceful eviction from ancestral line is embodied in Article 3(2) (a) of the Agreement. This Article requires the Cameroonian State not to 'force Nigerian nationals living in the Bakassi Peninsula to leave the zone or to change their nationality'. However, it is debatable whether Article 3(2) (a) of the agreement is as wide ranging as the rights set out in Article 10 of the UNDRIP and in Article 16 of the ILO Convention 169. This is because it is silent on the requirements of free prior informed consent, the award of appropriate compensation and the possible return of Bakassi indigenous populations to their ancestral homes.

Again, the argument that may be raised against these rights as set out in the UNDRIP and the ILO Convention 169 is that the former instrument is non-binding whereas the latter has only been ratified to date by one African state party (the Central Republic of Africa). Notwithstanding these limitations, as earlier discussed, national case law,[88] Privy Council decisions[89] and ACHPR[90] jurisprudence suggest that adequate compensation must be provided to indigenous communities if a resettlement exercise is to be considered as lawful and not contrary to the prohibition against forceful eviction from land. It is instructive that the Greentree Agreement does not expressly provide a clear framework for compensating the Bakassi indigenes who have been resettled in Nigeria as part of the implementation of the ICJ judgment.

Compensating displaced indigenous communities

Ordinarily, compensation is to be claimed from the party dispossessing another party of rights in land. This raises an interesting question with regard to the displacement and resettlement of Bakassi indigenes from their ancestral land in the Bakassi Peninsula. The question is: which State should be required to pay compensation? Should it be Cameroon or Nigeria? The Greentree Agreement is silent on this point. It does, however, require in Article 3(2)(d) that Cameroon should protect the property and customary land rights of the indigenous Bakassi population of Nigerian descent. This raises an interesting question on whether the protection of property and customary land rights extends to an award of appropriate compensation when indigenous populations are dispossessed of land. Regrettably, the ACHPR could not address this issue when a communication was filed before it by the Bakweri indigenous community[91] against the Cameroonian State. The failure of the African Commission to address this substantive issue was due to procedural concerns with regard to the non-exhaustion of judicial remedies at the national level. Had the Commission determined this claim, it may have provided further perspective on how the displacement of indigenous communities from ancestral land in Cameroon should be treated and whether the Cameroonian State was obligated to pay compensation under the African Charter and other international instruments. However, the *Endorois*[92] *and Ogoni*[93] decisions, which deal with the claims of indigenous communities within Kenya and Nigeria respectively, suggest that the ACHPR would be disposed to grant compensation when indigenous peoples are dispossessed of their homeland. The same position has also been adopted by some African national courts, as can be seen in the *Sesana*[94] decision.

Unlike these cases, it appears that no compensation has been paid out by Cameroon to date to the indigenous Bakassi populations who have been displaced or have had to resettle in Nigeria.[95] Instead, it is Nigeria which has had to bear the financial burden of resettling displaced Bakassi indigenes in other settlements within Nigeria.[96] Cameroon may assert that it is not required to pay compensation to the Bakassi indigenes of Nigerian descent because of the fact that the 'displacement' of the Bakassi indigenes of Nigerian descent and the subsequent resettlement exercise of these indigenes is in accordance with the ICJ judgment and the Greentree Agreement. Even so, the Office of the High Commissioner, United Nations Human Rights,[97] asserts that evictions carried out in pursuance of a court decision or legislation must comply with international standards. These standards under international law require that compensation should be paid where indigenous peoples are displaced from their land.

As earlier stated, Nigeria appears to be the state party that has had to bear the financial burden of resettling the Bakassi indigenes of Nigerian descent after their displacement from the Bakassi Peninsula. It is debatable whether the Nigerian funding of this resettlement exercise amounts to compensation for the displaced indigenous peoples. A recent call for the *Resettlement and Compensation of the Bakassi People*, which is before the Nigerian Senate, indicates that Nigerian Government is yet to undertake a proper valuation of its loss of Bakassi or work out what is a 'just and perpetual compensation to Cross River State'.[98] It is instructive that this call for the 'just and perpetual compensation' refers to Cross River State, a component State of the Nigerian federation, and not to the displaced Bakassi indigenes. This raises an interesting question on whether the component States of

Nigeria, where the resettlement exercise has taken place, adequately represent the interest of the Bakassi indigenes. If the answer is in the affirmative, it may explain why compensation payments should be made to these States instead of directly to the Bakassi indigenous communities.

The Privy Council decision in the *Amodu Tijani* decision[99] provides the judicial position on this issue by requiring that compensation made to a titular community head is to be done in a representative capacity and for the benefit of the community at large. While rights under Native Title laws in Nigeria have now been subsumed and replaced by customary rights of occupancy as prescribed by the Nigerian Land Use Act 1978,[100] this does not imply that the Act has completely divested communities of traditional rights to land.[101] Accordingly, the component States in Nigeria and relevant local authorities involved in the resettlement exercise are required to judiciously administer, on behalf of the Bakassi community, any compensation received from the federal government. Apart from the call to compensate the affected communities, the Nigerian Senate further resolved that the Federal Government of Nigeria should 'As a matter of urgency, properly resettle the Bakassi people through a participatory and properly negotiated Resettlement Program'.[102]

This is a significant development as it provides some evidence of an African State's recognition of the concept of FPIC. This final point will now be further evaluated.

The role of free prior informed consent (FPIC) in the furtherance of the rights of indigenous populations in the Bakassi Peninsula

This section begins by providing some definitional context of the term 'free, prior informed consent (FPIC)' in international law. The concept of FPIC has its origin in medical law and, under this specialism, FPIC has assumed hard law status in domestic and international law.[103]

With regard to the rights of indigenous peoples, FPIC has been authoritatively defined as 'a consultative process whereby a potentially affected community engages in an open and informed dialogue with individuals or other persons interested in pursuing activities in the area or areas traditionally used by the affected communities'.[104] Unlike medical law, there is some debate on whether the FPIC of indigenous peoples has assumed hard law status in international and domestic law. This is due to the non-binding nature of the UNDRIP which extensively refers to the principle throughout its text.[105] The FPIC principle does, however, have binding treaty status in the ILO Convention 169,[106] which requires that relocation of peoples from their land can only be done when free and informed consent has been obtained. Unfortunately, as earlier stressed, the ILO Convention 169 has very limited application in the Sub-Saharan African region owing to the fact that the Central African Republic is the only State that has ratified the document to date.[107]

The non-binding nature of the UNDRIP and the limited applicability of the ILO Convention 1969 may explain why there is still some uncertainty as to whether the relocation of indigenous peoples from the ancestral land is subject to FPIC. Different perspectives obtain on the current status of the FPIC. Some assert that the principle as enunciated in the UNDRIP is now 'established principle of international law'.[108] To assume the status of customary international law, a rule must reflect state practice and the necessary opinion juris.[109] Unlike medical law and clinical research, where there is wide state practice to suggest the FPIC has attained customary international law status, the same cannot be said about the status of the concept under the indigenous rights regime. This is why other works[110] do not necessarily subscribe to the position that the concept of FPIC has assumed customary law status as it pertains to the rights of indigenous peoples. Even so, these works accept that: 'at a minimum States must engage in good faith consultations with indigenous peoples prior to the exploration or exploitation of resources within their lands or actions that would impact their traditionally used resources'.[111]

With regard to the role FPIC should play in matters relating to the indigenous populations in the Bakassi population, a further appraisal of the African Charter is necessary. It is instructive that the African Charter which sets out binding treaty rights for African peoples does not expressly impose an FPIC obligation when communities are relocated from their ancestral lands. For instance, no mention of the FPIC is contained in Article 22(2) of the African Charter, which grants the rights of lawful recovery of property and the grant of adequate compensation to dispossessed people where there has been a spoliation of their wealth and natural resources.

In offering dispossessed peoples the right to recover property and to seek adequate compensation, the African Charter aligns itself with the provisions of other international rules that deal with the rights of indigenous peoples. However, unlike the clear wording set out in the UNDRIP and ILO 169, the African Charter does not address the concern of whether the relocation or resettlement of indigenous African populations should be subject to FPIC. This uncertainty on whether the FPIC principle applies to the relocation of African indigenous populations in the African Charter framework may explain why the Greentree Agreement between Cameroon and Nigeria did not embody the principle within its text.[112]

In spite of the fact that the African Charter does not expressly provide for the FPIC principle within its text, the ACHPR in its 51st Ordinary session has affirmed the role that this principle should play in natural governance matters that affect indigenous communities in Africa. The ACHPR states that 'necessary measures must be taken by the State to ensure participation, including the free, prior and informed consent of communities, in decision making related to natural resources governance'.[113]

In addition the recent jurisprudence from the African Commission, including cases such as *Endorois*[114] establish the growing recognition of the application of the principle of FPIC in matters relating to African indigenous communities. Likewise, in a 2010 resolution,[115] the ACHPR denounced the failure of the World Heritage Committee (hereafter the WHC) to consult the Endorois community before including Lake Bogoria in the World Heritage List. The Commission in this resolution also linked the concept of FPIC with the right of development, as enshrined in Article 22 of the African Charter.

These recent developments confirm the evolving role of the FPIC in Africa, particularly as it relates to natural resource governance decisions that affect indigenous African communities. It is therefore a matter of concern that the FPIC has played little or no role in the activities of the Cameroon–Nigeria Mixed Commission (hereafter the CNMC)[116] which has oversight over the implementation of the Greentree Agreement. It is questionable whether the CNMC in its oversight over the recent relocation of indigenous populations of Nigerian descent took into account the FPIC requirement during the resettlement process. Indeed, the current composition of the CNMC confirms the non-participation of indigenous communities in its decision-making process. The Joint Communiqué establishing the CNMC[117] shows that it is headed by the special envoy to the United Nations Secretary-General and is composed of a delegation of officers from both the Nigerian and Cameroonian states.[118] What is significant is that the delegations of both States are chosen by the States and it is unclear whether the indigenous populations had any say on how the CNMC was constituted.

This is an unsatisfactory state of affairs. While both States are to be commended for accepting the outcome of the ICJ judgment and for taking the necessary steps to implement it, it is disappointing that the ICJ judgment has been implemented with so little regard to the FPIC principle. This chapter recommends that there is still a window of opportunity for the CNMC to apply the FPIC principle in its ongoing work on matters relating to the implementation of the ICJ judgment. On its website the CNMC states[119] that it is working with a UN Support Team and other partners 'on socio-economic projects in the border areas, for populations that have been affected by the demarcation process'.

It is yet to be seen whether representatives of the affected populations have been or will be afforded the right to actively participate in the decision-making process regarding these socio-economic projects. To avoid the situation that obtained in the WHC's work in Lake Bogoria,[120] this chapter recommends that the ACHPR should pass a resolution requiring the CNMC to apply the FPIC principle in the formulation and execution of socio-economic projects for the communities that have been affected by the Cameroon/Nigerian boundary demarcation process. In addition, Cameroon and Nigeria should be pressed upon to comply with the ACHPR's 2012 resolution[121] on the utilisation of the FPIC principle in natural resource governance decisions.

As the Bakassi Peninsula and areas of the Lake Chad are reportedly oil-rich regions, the exploitation of natural resources in these regions will undeniably be a test case to see if African States are truly committed to the concept of FPIC in natural resource governance. Oil and gas exploitation in these regions will further provide a case study for ascertaining whether international oil and gas companies (hereafter IOCs) and other companies within the extractive energy sector are complying with the concept of FPIC in their operational activities in the Sub-Saharan African region.[122] As earlier stressed, while much of the work of the CNMC has already been completed, there is still scope within the ACHPR framework to ensure the participation of indigenous communities in natural resource exploitation in the Bakassi Peninsula and Lake Chad regions.

Conclusion

The implementation of the ICJ judgment on the Bakassi dispute through the Greentree Treaty framework has been applauded as a good example of the peaceful resolution of boundary disputes between African sovereign States. This chapter considers whether the rights of the affected indigenous communities and populations within the Bakassi Peninsula were adequately protected under the Greentree treaty regime and by the subsequent work undertaken by the CNMC in the implementation of the ICJ judgment on the Cameroon/Nigeria dispute. The rights regime provided by Article 3 of the Greentree Agreement was considered in light of other rules in international law that safeguard the rights of indigenous peoples. The chapter also considered jurisprudence from the ACHPR and African domestic courts which provide a purposive and progressive interpretation of the African Charter and the domestic laws of African States. The chapter concludes with recommendations for the more active application of the FPIC principle in matters regarding indigenous communities that have been affected by the ICJ judgment and the ensuing activities of the CNMC under the Greentree Agreement framework.

Notes

1 *Land and Maritime Boundary between Cameroon and Nigeria (Cameroon v. Nigeria: Equatorial Guinea Intervening)* (hereafter the *Cameroon/Nigeria* case) *Judgment of 10 October 2002*, available at www.icj-cij.org/docket/index.php?p1=3&p2=3&k=74&case=94&code=cn&p3=4 (accessed 1 June 2017).
2 *Case Concerning Land and Maritime Boundary between Cameroon and Nigeria (Cameroon v. Nigeria) Summary of the Judgement* (hereafter the *Cameroon/Nigeria* case), available at www.icj-cij.org/docket/index.php?sum=496&code=cn&p1=3&p2=3&case=94&k=74&p3=5 (accessed 1 June 2017).
3 See *Cameroon/Nigeria* case (note 1) para. 317. It is unclear whether Nigeria provided the same undertaking with regard to Cameroonians living within the Lake Chad region.
4 Ibid.
5 *Greentree Agreement between The Republic of Cameroon and The Federal Republic of Nigeria Concerning the Modalities of Withdrawal and Transfer of Authority in The Bakassi Peninsula*, text transmitted to the Security Council by the Secretary-General on 20 June 2006 (S/2006/419).
6 Ibid.
7 F. Merlan, 'Indigeneity: Global and Local' (2009) 50(3) *Current Anthropology* 303.
8 Ibid.
9 Ibid. 304.
10 Ibid.
11 B. Mortenson, 'The Self-Government and the Overall Framework concerning Greenland', in V. Ulfbeck and A. Mollman (eds), *Responsibilities and Liabilities for Commercial Activity in the Arctic: The Example of Greenland* (London: Routledge, 2016) 15; J. Summers, *Peoples and International Law* (Leiden: Martinus Nijhoff, 2014, second revised edition) 261.
12 ILO C169 *Indigenous and Tribal Peoples Convention 1989*, adopted in Geneva 26 June 1989.
13 S. Saugestad, *The Inconvenient Indigenous: Remote Area Development in Botswana, Donor Assistance and the First People of Kalahari* (Uppsala: Nordic African Institute, 2001) 44.
14 *UN Declaration on the Rights of Indigenous Peoples* (UNDRIP), G.A. Res. 61/295, Annex, UN Doc. A/RES/61/295 (13 September 2007).
15 *The Inter-Sessional Working Group on the Draft Declaration* established in 1995 in accordance with the Commission on Human Rights Resolution 1995/32 and Economic and Social Council Resolution 1995/32.
16 J. Summers (note 11), 261.
17 See further discussions in D. Sambo Dorough, 'Reflections on the UN Declaration on the Rights of Indigenous Peoples: An Arctic Perspective', in S. Allen and A. Xanthaki (eds), *Reflections on the UN Declaration on the Rights of Indigenous Peoples* (Oxford: Hart Publishing, 2011); and I. Shin and K. Buttery, 'Indigenous Belonging: A Commentary on Membership and Identity in the United Nations Declaration on the Rights of Indigenous People', unpublished paper, Paper 49, University of York, 2013, available at http://digitalcommons.osgoode.yorku.ca/all_papers/49.
18 As stated above, the ILO Convention 169 (see note 12) provides a definition for this term.
19 K. Maranga, *Indigenous Peoples and the Roles of Cultures, Law and Globalisation: Comparing the Americas, Asia-Pacific and Africa* (Boca Raton, FL: Universal Publishers, 2013) 7–8.
20 Ibid. 8.
21 J. Summers (note 11) at 261.
22 Ibid. 258.
23 Ibid. 262.
24 Ibid. 257–258.
25 *Study of the Problem of Discrimination against Indigenous Populations: Final Report Submitted by the Special Rapporteur, Mr José Martínez Cobo*, E/CN.4/Sub.2/1982/2/Add.6.
26 Ibid.
27 Ibid.
28 S. James Anaya, *Indigenous Peoples in International Law* (Oxford: Oxford University Press, 2004) 63.
29 See a further discourse on the link between the pre-colonial era and the Bakassi Peninsula in J. Babatola, 'Nigerian–Cameroon Boundary Dispute: The Quest for Bakassi Penisular' (2012) 4 *International Affairs and Global Strategy* 81.

30 See, for example, E. Ike-Idogu, 'Historicizing and Contextualizing the Discourse on African International Law and a Concise Overview of the Pacific Settlement of the Cameroon–Nigeria Bakassi Peninsula Dispute' (2008) 7(1) *African and Asian Studies* 89–90; M. van der Linden, *The Acquisition of Africa (1870–1914): The Nature of International Law* (Leiden: Brill, 2016) 252–260.
31 See *Cameroon/Nigeria* case (note 1) at paras 194 and 201.
32 See a detailed discussion of this rule in G. Oduntan, *International Law and Boundary Disputes in Africa* (London: Routledge, 2015), Chapter 16 in particular.
33 M. van der Linden (note 30).
34 E. Milano, *Unlawful Territorial Situations in International Law: Reconciling Effectiveness, Legality and Legitimacy* (Leiden: Martinus Nijhoff, 2006) 78, 79.
35 *Advisory Opinion of the African Commission on Human and Peoples' Rights on the United Nations Declaration on the Rights of Indigenous Peoples* at p. 4, www.achpr.org/files/special-mechanisms/indigenous-populations/un_advisory_opinion_idp_eng.pdf (accessed 17 May 2017). See also further discussions in H. Egede and E.E. Egede, 'The Force of the Community in the Niger Delta of Nigeria: Propositions for New Oil and Gas Legal and Contractual Arrangements' (2016) 25 *Tulane Journal of International and Comparative Law* 61.
36 Ibid.
37 Working Group on Indigenous Populations/Communities in Africa AFR. COMMISSION HUM. & PEOPLES' RHTS pursuant to the adoption of Resolution 51 at the 28th Ordinary Session (Cotonou, Benin – 23 October to 6 November 2000). The legal basis for the existence of the Working Group of Experts is premised on Article 45 of the African Charter on Human and Peoples' Rights, which sets out the legal framework for the African Commission's 'promotion and protection mandates'.
38 Report of the African Commission's Working Group of Experts on Indigenous Populations/ Communities (DOC/OS(XXXIV)/345).
39 *The African Charter on Human and Peoples' Rights* (hereafter the African Charter), adopted 27 June 1981, OAU Doc. CAB/LEG/67/3 rev. 5, 21 ILM 58 (1982), entered into force 21 October 1986.
40 11 Rapporteur's Report, OAU Doc. CM/I 149 (XXXVII), Ann. 1, at 4, para. 13 (1981), quoted in N.S. Rembe, *Africa and Regional Protection of Human Rights – A Study of the African Charter on Human and Peoples' Rights: Its Effectiveness and Impact on the African States* (Rome: Leoni Editore, 1985) at 112.
41 R. Kiwanuka, 'The Meaning of "People" in the African Charter' (1988) 82 *American Journal of International Law* 80 at 82.
42 Ibid.
43 See the Advisory Opinion of the African Commission on Human and Peoples' Rights on the United Nations Declaration on the Rights of Indigenous Peoples adopted by The African Commission on Human and Peoples' Rights at its 41st Ordinary Session Held in May 2007 in Accra, Ghana 2007.
44 Ibid. at paragraph 10, p. 3.
45 Report of the African Commission's Working Group of Experts on Indigenous Populations/ Communities (note 37) 60–61.
46 The report classifies the Ogoni community, comprising of farmers and fishermen, as pastoralists, ibid. at 9.
47 A. Harcourt, *Human Biogeography* (Berkeley: University of California Press, 2012) 198.
48 *Ogoni* decision, Communication 155/96, Afr. Comm'n HPR, 55, 58.
49 *Endorois* decision, Communication 76/03, Afr. Comm'n HPR, 267.
50 Ibid. at paragraph 12, p. 4. The advisory opinion also distinguishes the defining characteristics of African indigenous communities from other groups in other jurisdictions in Australia and Canada. This is because it does not validate the concept of 'first inhabitants' in determining indigeneity.
51 O. Edet, *Bakassi Peninsula: The Untold Story of a People Betrayed* (Singapore: Partridge Publishing, 2015), especially Chapter 2.
52 See *Cameroon/Nigeria* case (note 1) at para. 317. See also Article 3 of the Greentree Agreement note 5) 2.
53 S. Danver, *Native Peoples of the World: An Encyclopaedia of Groups, Cultures and Contemporary Issues* (London: Routledge, 2013) 583.

54 O. Edet (note 51) Chapter 13.
55 Described in Danver's work (note 53) as Ifut (Efut). See also I. Miller, 'Cuban Abakua Chants: Examining New Linguistic and Historical Evidence for the African Diaspora' (2005) 48(1) *African Studies Review* at 40.
56 See Chapter 13 of Edet's work (note 51 above) for a further account of the plight of the Usakadet (Isangele) community, who have refused to resettle in Nigeria as per the terms of the UNOWA's Greentree Agreement. Their refusal to resettle in Nigeria arises out of the deep cultural ties and links that they have with the Bakassi Peninsula, which they view as their ancestral home.
57 D. Posey, *Cultural and Spiritual Values of Biodiversity* (London and Nairobi: UNEP, 1999), discussed in K. Sangha, A. Le Brocque, R. Constanza and Y. Cadet-James, 'Ecosystems and Indigenous Wellbeing: An Integrated Framework' (2015) 4 *Global Ecology and Conservation* 197.
58 Shagnha et al., ibid. at 200; see also J. Altman, 'Economic Development and Indigenous Australia: Contestations over Property, Institutions and Ideology' (2004) *Australian Journal of Agricultural Resources and Economics* 513.
59 See, for example, Article 25 of the UNDRIP (note 14); Article 13 ILO 169 (note 12).
60 *Endorois* decision (note 49).
61 See recommendation 1(b) of the ACHPR's communication in the *Endorois* decision (note 49).
62 Article 37 of the ILO Constitution authorises the International Court of Justice to adjudicate on any question or dispute relating to the interpretation of the ILO constitution or subsequent ILO conventions. See the Constitution of the International Labour Organisation (as amended), adopted by the Peace Conference in April of 1919.
63 *Cameroon/Nigeria* case (note 1) para. 317.
64 C. Eikhart, *Promises of States under International Law* (London: Bloomsbury, 2012) 1.
65 Ibid.
66 *ICL Guiding Principles Applicable to Unilateral Declarations of States Capable of Creating Legal Relations, with Commentaries thereto 2006*, text adopted by the ILC in its 58th Session in 2006, and submitted to the General Assembly as a part of the Commission's report covering the work of that session, UN Doc. A/61/10/2006, available at http://legal.un.org/ilc/texts/instruments/english/commentaries/9_9_2006.pdf (accessed 7 June 2017).
67 *Nuclear Tests (Australia v. France; New Zealand v. France)*, Judgments dated 20 December 1974, *ICJ Reports* 1974, pp. 267–268, paras 43 and 46 and pp. 472–473, paras 46 and 49.
68 *ILC Guiding Principles* (note 66) 370.
69 *Case Concerning the Frontier Dispute* case: *Burkina Faso v. Republic of Mali*, Judgment of 22 December 1986, *ICJ Reports* 1986, p. 573, para. 39.
70 Ibid.
71 [2009] FSR 14, [2009] *CP Rep*. 23, [2009] EWCA Civ. 44 (2009) 32(4) IPD 32026.
72 See *Cameroon/Nigeria* case (note 1) para. 317.
73 The Charter of the United Nations was signed on 26 June 1945, in San Francisco, at the conclusion of the United Nations Conference on International Organisation, and came into force on 24 October 1945.
74 The preamble of the Greentree Agreement states that it was formulated to enable the two States to 'peacefully implement the judgment of the International Court of Justice'.
75 See E. Osagie, 'Weep Not for Bakassi', *Daily Sun Newspapers* (29 August 2008), narrated in I. Urua Adiakod, *The Untold Story and the Politics of Bakassi Handover: A Compendium of Politics, Ekid History and African Traditional Religion* (Bloomington, IN: Xlbris Corporation, 2012) 66.
76 Ibid.
77 Danver (note 53) at 583.
78 See, for example, the ILO Convention 169 (note 12) and UNDRIP 2007 (note 14).
79 UNDRIP 2007 (note 14).
80 K. Engle, 'On Fragile Architecture: The UN Declaration on the Rights of Indigenous Peoples in the Context of Human Rights' (2011) 22(1) *European Journal of International Law* 141 at 147.
81 *International Covenant on Economic, Social and Cultural Rights (ICESCR)*, adopted and opened for signature, ratification and accession by General Assembly Resolution 2200A (XXI) of 16 December 1966, entered into force 3 January 1976.

82 See again the *Endorois* case (note 49) and *The Centre on Housing Rights and Evictions v. The Sudan, Communication Nos. 279/03 & 296/05, African Commission on Human and Peoples' Rights* (2009).

83 *Sesana and Others v. Attorney-General* (2006) *AHRLR* 183 (BwHC 2006).

84 *Amodu Tijani v. The Secretary, Southern Provinces* (1921) 2 *AC* 403–404.

85 See A. Mason, 'The Rights of Indigenous Peoples in Lands Once Part of the Old Dominions of the Crown' (1997) 46(4) *International and Comparative Quarterly* 812 at 816, where it was pointed out that the 'rights of indigenous peoples in Southern Nigeria so recognized were held to be a burden to which the Sovereign's ultimate title to land was subject'.

86 Committee on Economic, Social and Cultural Rights, *General Comment No. 7 (1997) on the Right to Adequate Housing: Forced Evictions* (New York and Geneva: United Nations, 2014).

87 ILO Convention 169 (note 12).

88 *Sesana and Others v. Attorney-General* (note 83).

89 *Amodu Tijani v. The Secretary, Southern Provinces* (note 84).

90 *Endorois* decision (note 49) and *Ogoni* decision (note 48).

91 African Commission on Human and Peoples' Rights (ACPHR) 260/02: *Bakweri Land Claims Committee/Cameroon*, 36th Ordinary Session, 23 November–7 December 2004, Dakar, Senegal.

92 *Endorois* decision (note 49).

93 *Ogoni* decision (note 48).

94 *Sesana* decision (note 83).

95 This does not imply that Cameroon has not improved the living conditions of the Bakassi indigenes of Nigerian descent who have chosen to remain in Bakassi. Yet there are reported skirmishes between Cameroon state agents and Bakassi indigenes of Nigerian descent regarding tax collection. See VOA Africa, 'Cameroon Takes Control of Disputed Bakassi', 14 August 2013, available at www.voanews.com/a/cameroon-takes-control-of-disputed-bakassi-territory/1729687.html (accessed 7 June 2017).

96 To ensure that the resettlement exercise is executed in line with international standards, Nigeria constituted a Presidential Committee on the Resettlement of the Displaced Persons of Bakassi. It is reported that the Nigerian Government released over nine billion naira between 2006 and 2015 for the purpose of resettling the displaced people from Bakassi and building homes for them. See Economic Confidential, 'FG May Probe N9bn Bakassi Resettlement Fund', available at https://economicconfidential.com/news/national-news/fg-may-probe-n9bn-bakassi-resettlement-fund/ (accessed 31 May 2017).

97 *UN Habitat for a Better Urban Future*, Office of the High Commissioner, United Nations Human Rights Fact Sheet No. 25/Rev. 1 (New York and Geneva: United Nations, 2014) 5. Although the focus is on national courts, the same standards will apply to the implementation of judicial decisions of international courts.

98 See the Announcement of the Senate Federal Republic of Nigeria Committee on Appropriations, National Assembly Complex No. 63, dated 28 February 2017, at 1024–1027, which calls for the proper resettlement and compensation of the Bakassi people, available at www.nassnig.org/document/download/8460 (accessed 31 May 2017).

99 *Amodu Tijani* decision (note 84).

100 Land Use Act 1978, Cap 20, Laws of the Federation of Nigeria, 1990.

101 *Adole v. Gwar* (2008) 11 *NWLR* (PT 1099) 562.

102 Announcement of the Senate, Federal Republic of Nigeria, Committee on Appropriations (note 98) at 1207.

103 See further discussion on this point in *Rabi Abdullahi v. Pfizer Inc.* 562 F.3d 163 (2d Cir. 2009) 30 January 2009 in Oceana Editorial Board (ed.), *American International Law Cases 2009* (Oxford: Oxford University Press, 2010) 13–21.

104 D. Macgraw and L. Baker, 'Globalisation, Communities and Human Rights: Community Based Property Rights and Prior Informed Consent' (2007) 35 *Denver Journal of International Law and Policy* 413 at 421. See also A. Perrault, K. Herbertson and O.J. Lynch, 'Partnerships for Success in Protected Areas: The Public Interest and Local Community Rights to Prior Informed Consent (PIC)' 19 *Georgetown International Environmental Law Review* 475–542; and R. Goodland, 'Free, Prior and Informed Consent and the World Bank Group', (2004) 4 *Sustainable Development Law & Policy* 66.

105 See Articles 10, 11(2), 19, 28, 29 and 32 of the UNDRIP 2007 (note 14).
106 See Articles 6 and 16 of the ILO Convention 169 (note 12).
107 See M. Ssenyonjo, *The African Regional Human Rights System: 30 Years after the African Charter on Human and Peoples Rights* (Leiden: Martinus Nijhoff, 2012) 198.
108 B. Tobin, *Indigenous Peoples, Customary Law and Human Rights: Why Living Law Matters* (London: Routledge, 2014) 48.
109 See *North Sea Continental Shelf (Ger./Neth./Den.), Judgment*, 1969 *ICJ Rep*. 3, 61–63,77, 83 (20 February 1969).
110 T. Ward, 'The Right to Free, Prior, and Informed Consent: Indigenous Peoples' Participation Rights within International Law' (2011) 10 *Northwestern University Journal of International Human Rights* 54.
111 Ibid.
112 See for example, Article 3 of the Greentree Agreement, which is meant to safeguard the rights of the indigenous populations of Nigerian descent in the peninsula.
113 African Commission on Human and Peoples' Rights (ACPHR), *Resolution on a Human Rights-Based Approach to Natural Resources Governance*, 51st Ordinary Session held from 18 April to 2 May 2012 in Banjul, The Gambia.
114 *Endorois* decision (note 49).
115 African Commission on Human and Peoples' Rights (ACPHR), *Resolution on the Protection of Indigenous Peoples' Rights in the Context of the World Heritage Convention and the Designation of Lake Bogoria as a World Heritage Site*, 50th Ordinary Session held from 24 October to 5 November 2011 in Banjul, The Gambia.
116 See the Joint Communiqué Establishing the Cameroon–Nigeria Mixed Commission (CNMC) of 15 November 2002, available at https://unowa.unmissions.org/thirty-second-session-cameroon-nigeria-mixed-commission (accessed 1 June 2017).
117 Ibid.
118 Ibid.
119 See *Activities of the Cameroon–Nigeria Mixed Commission*, available at https://unowas.unmissions.org/cameroon-nigeria-mixed-commission (accessed 7 June 2017).
120 ACPHR, *Resolution on the Protection of Indigenous Peoples' Rights in the Context of the World Heritage Convention and the Designation of Lake Bogoria as a World Heritage Site* (note 115).
121 ACPHR, *Resolution on a Human Rights-Based Approach to Natural Resources Governance* (note 113).
122 E. Greenspan, 'Free, Prior, and Informed Consent in Africa: An Emerging Standard for Extractive Industry Projects', Oxfam America Research Backgrounder series (2014), www.oxfamamerica.org/publications/fpic-in-africa, pp. 27–34.

6 Bakassi Decision

International law and the acquisition of sovereignty over land territory

Yoshifumi Tanaka

Introduction

Given that territory is the fundamental element of States, clarification of rules applicable to acquisition of sovereignty over territory should be an important issue in international law.[1] An essential issue on this subject concerns a vacillation between title and *effectivités*.[2] Indeed, the opposition between the two elements constitutes a key issue in the *Cameroon/Nigeria* case of 2002.[3] In this case, Cameroon asked the ICJ to adjudge and declare, *inter alia*, that sovereignty over the Bakassi Peninsula is Cameroonian.[4] In this regard, Cameroon claimed that the Anglo-German Agreement of 11 March 1913 (hereafter the 1913 Anglo-German Agreement) fixed the course of the boundary between the Parties in the area of the Bakassi Peninsula, placing the latter on the German side of the boundary; and that when Cameroon and Nigeria acceded to independence, this boundary became that between the two countries, successor States to the colonial powers and bound by the principle of *uti possidetis*.[5] However, Nigeria argued that title to the Bakassi Peninsula lay in 1913 with the Kings and Chiefs of Old Calabar and that, in 1913, Great Britain was unable to pass title to Bakassi because it had no title to pass (*nemo dat quod non habet*).[6] It then contended that the sovereignty over the Bakassi Peninsula is vested in Nigeria.[7] In support of its view, Nigeria invoked multiple elements of *effectivités*, such as long occupation by Nigeria and by Nigerian nationals constituting an historical consolidation of title, peaceful possession by Nigeria and manifestations of sovereignty by Nigeria.[8] Thus, the *Cameroon/Nigeria* dispute is characterised by the confrontation between title claimed by Cameroon and *effectivités* claimed by Nigeria. The *Cameroon/Nigeria* judgment provides an insight into the relationship between title and *effectivités* in the international law of acquisition of territory. This chapter thus aims to examine the *Cameroon/Nigeria* judgment focusing particularly on sovereignty over the Bakassi Peninsula since this is at the heart of the territorial dispute in the *Cameroon/Nigeria* case.[9]

Framework for analysis: three paradigms concerning acquisition of territory

Before turning to an examination of the *Cameroon/Nigeria* judgment, it is necessary to consider paradigms with regard to acquisition of sovereignty over territory. This issue is of particular importance since a framework for analysis of particular territorial disputes differs according to the paradigms adopted by international courts and tribunals. In a broad perspective, three paradigms can be identified.

The traditional paradigm

According to the traditional paradigm inspired by Roman law,[10] acquisition of sovereignty over territory can be made on the basis of several modes. Traditionally five modes have been distinguished: cession, occupation, accretion, subjugation and prescription.[11] These modes can be divided into two categories according to whether the title they give is derived from the title of a prior owner-State or not: derivative mode and original modes.[12] A derivative mode of acquisition is cession which means the transfer of sovereignty over State territory by the owner-State to another State. Original modes contain occupation, accretion, subjugation and prescription.[13] Despite frequent reference in the standard textbooks of international law, the traditional modes have not been applied by international courts and tribunals.[14] This judicial reticence is not without reason.

Under the traditional paradigm, the modes of acquiring territory are *a priori* fixed and title to territory is to be established on the basis of one of the modes. In reality, however, the issue of acquisition of territory is so complicated that it cannot always be ascribed to any mode of acquisition.[15] It is not infrequent that neither claim of the parties in dispute can meet requirements of any modes. In this case, the traditional paradigm is hard to apply.[16] Furthermore, it is possible that more than one State may engage in various activities in the same place. In this case, it is difficult to judge the relative strength of competing claims over territory under the traditional paradigm. In particular, it is problematic that those modes afford no solution to territorial disputes where the parties in dispute rely on different modes.[17] Added to these difficulties is that the distinction of each mode is not always clear-cut. This is particularly true with regard to occupation and prescription. As a matter of theory, occupation concerns the acquisition of *terra nullius* by a State in an effective manner, while acquisitive prescription refers to the acquisition of territory not *terra nullius* by effective control. Yet, more often than not, the status of the disputed area at the relevant time remains obscure and, thus, the distinction of the two modes is difficult to make.[18]

Moreover, the traditional paradigm seems to presuppose that title to territory can be established instantly at a certain moment. This may apply to cession and subjugation. However, title to territory cannot always be instantly established by one act only. Normally title to territory is to be gradually consolidated through various activities over time. Even if title to territory was established, situations surrounding the territory may change over time. Accordingly, a gap may arise between title (law) and fact (*effectivités*). Under the traditional paradigm, however, there is no mechanism to address the difference between law and fact.

In summary, the traditional paradigm is so static that it cannot take account of time elements, i.e. changing situation over time, in the process of acquisition of territory.[19] It may be said that this is an essential deficiency with the traditional paradigm. In fact, the traditional paradigm was not echoed by the ICJ in the *Cameroon/Nigeria* case.

The Island of Palmas paradigm

In 1928, Max Huber, the sole arbitrator in the *Island of Palmas* case, presented a novel paradigm with regard to acquisition of territory. The essence of this paradigm can be seen in the following statement:

> As regards the question which of different legal systems prevailing at successive periods is to be applied in a particular case (the so-called intertemporal law), a distinction must

> be made between the creation of rights and the existence of rights. The same principle which subjects the act creative of a right to the law in force at the time the right arises, demands that the existence of the right, in other words its continued manifestation, shall follow the conditions required by *the evolution of law*.[20]

In light of its strong impact on the subsequent jurisprudence concerning territorial disputes, the formula presented by Max Huber can be called the Island of Palmas paradigm.[21] This paradigm is evolutionary in the sense that title to territory must be maintained through continuous and peaceful display of sovereignty.[22] The Island of Palmas paradigm relies on the idea that territorial sovereignty is accompanied with the obligation to assure human activities at all points the minimum of protection of which international law is the guardian.[23] It contrasts with the traditional paradigm at least in three respects.[24]

First, as noted, under the traditional paradigm, title to territory is to be established at the moment when a State fulfilled requirements of one of the modes of acquisition of territory. Under the Island of Palmas paradigm, however, acquisition of territory is regarded as a *process* and title must be maintained by 'continuous and peaceful display'[25] or 'continuous and prolonged manifestation' of sovereignty.[26]

Second, under the Island of Palmas paradigm, modes of acquisition of territory are not *a priori* fixed. What is of importance under this paradigm is a 'continuous and peaceful display' of territorial sovereignty, not a particular mode of acquiring territory.

Third, under the traditional paradigm, title is absolute in the sense that if one State acquires title over territory, the other State has no title over the same territory at all. In contrast, under the Island of Palmas paradigm, title is *relative* in the sense that acquisition of territory is determined by relative strength of the titles invoked by each party.[27] It follows that territory belongs to the State which invoked a *better* title than that invoked by another State.[28] Title to territory under the Island of Palmas paradigm is also relative since the strength of legal title required to acquire territory varies according to geographical and political circumstances surrounding the territory.[29] Although this paradigm has had a strong impact in subsequent cases,[30] such as the *Manquiers and Ecrehos*[31] and *Rann of Kutch* cases,[32] the ICJ, in the *Cameroon/Nigeria* case, did not rely on this paradigm.

The Burkina Faso/Mali paradigm

As will be seen, the ICJ in the *Cameroon/Nigeria* case relied on the paradigm expounded in the *Frontier Dispute* case between Burkina Faso and Mali:[33]

> Where the act corresponds exactly to law, where effective administration is additional to the *uti possidetis juris*, the only role of *effectivité* is to confirm the exercise of the right derived from a legal title. Where the act does not correspond to the law, where the territory which is the subject of the dispute is effectively administered by a State other than the one possessing the legal title, preference should be given to the holder of the title. In the event that the *effectivité* does not co-exist with any legal title, it must invariably be taken into consideration. Finally, there are cases where the legal title is not capable of showing exactly the territorial expanse to which it relates. The *effectivités* can then play an essential role in showing how the title is interpreted in practice.[34]

The *dictum* of the Court can be called the 'Burkina Faso/Mali paradigm'.[35] In general, the paradigm contains four elements:[36]

1 Where the *effectivités* correspond to the legal title, the role of *effectivités* is to confirm the exercise of the right derived from the legal title.
2 Where the *effectivités* do not correspond to the legal title, the title prevails over the *effectivités.*
3 Where the *effectivités* exist but no legal title exists, the *effectivités* must be taken into consideration.
4 Where the legal title exists but it cannot show exactly the scope of the territorial expanse to which it relates, the scope is identified on the basis of the *effectivités.*

Later on, this paradigm has provided a key legal framework in the jurisprudence of ICJ concerning territorial disputes. In addition to the *Cameroon/Nigeria* case, this paradigm was reflected in subsequent cases before the ICJ, such as the 1996 *El Salvador/Honduras* (1992),[37] *Indonesia/Malaysia* (2002),[38] the *Benin/Niger* (2005),[39] *Nicaragua/Honduras*[40] and the *Nicaragua/Colombia* (2012) cases.[41] The chapter now seeks to examine the *Cameroon/Nigeria* judgment focusing particularly on the application of the Burkina Faso/ Mali paradigm.

Legal title: the validity of the Anglo-German Agreement of 11 March 1913

The first issue to be considered is whether legal title of Cameroon to the Bakassi Peninsula derives from the 1913 Anglo-German Agreement. In approaching this issue, the 1884 Treaty of Protection signed by Great Britain and the Kings and Chiefs of Old Calabar must be examined. Under this Treaty, Great Britain undertook to extend its protection to these Kings and Chiefs.[42] According to Nigeria, however, the Treaty did not transfer sovereignty to Britain over the territories of the Kings and Chiefs of Old Calabar, but only conferred certain limited rights on Great Britain. Therefore, Nigeria argued that Articles XVIII to XXII of the 1913 Anglo-German Agreement are invalid on the grounds of inconsistency with the principle *nemo dat quod non habet.*[43]

In this regard, the ICJ observed that in sub-Saharan Africa, 'treaties of protection' were entered into not with States, but with important indigenous rulers exercising local rule over identifiable areas of territory. Here the Court referred to *dictum* in the *Island of Palmas* case, which stated that such a treaty

> is not an agreement between equals; it is rather a form of internal organisation of a colonial territory, on the basis of autonomy of the natives ... And thus suzerainty over the native States becomes the basis of territorial sovereignty as towards other members of the community of nations.[44]

The ICJ also referred to the *Western Sahara* Advisory Opinion, which stated that:

> [T]he State practice of the relevant period indicates that territories inhabited by tribes or peoples having a social and political organization were not regarded as *terrae nullius.* It shows that in the case of such territories the acquisition of sovereignty was not generally considered as effected unilaterally through 'occupation' of *terra nullius*

> by original title but through agreements concluded with local rulers ... such agreements with local rulers ... were regarded as derivative roots of title, and not original titles obtained by occupation of *terrae nullius*.[45]

On the basis of the *dicta*, the Court ruled that:

> Even if this mode of acquisition does not reflect current international law, the principle of intertemporal law requires that the legal consequences of the treaties concluded at that time in the Niger delta be given effect today, in the present dispute.[46]

According to the Court, the choice of a protectorate treaty by Great Britain was a question of the preferred manner of rule and, from the outset Britain regarded itself as administering the territories comprised in the 1884 Treaty, not just protecting them.[47] In this regard, there is no evidence of any protest in 1913 by the Kings and Chiefs of Old Calabar, nor any action by them to pass territory to Nigeria as it emerged to independence in 1960. The Court thus concluded that, under the law at the time, Great Britain was in a position in 1913 to determine its boundaries with Germany in respect of Nigeria, including in the southern section.[48]

Yet the Court's interpretation of the 1884 Treaty seems to leave some room for discussion. Articles 1 and 2 of the Treaty provide as follows:

> Article 1. Her Majesty the Queen of Great Britain and Ireland &c, in compliance with the request of the Kings, Chiefs, and people of Old Calabar, hereby undertakes to extend to them, and to the territory under their authority and jurisdiction, her gracious favour an protection.
>
> Article 2. The Kings and Chiefs of Old Calabar agree and promise to refrain from entering into any correspondence, Agreement, or Treaty with any foreign nation or Power, except with the knowledge and sanction of Her Britannic Majesty's Government.[49]

Taken literally, these provisions contain no reference to a transfer of territorial sovereignty.[50] Therefore, it seems debatable whether these provisions provide any cession of territory. In this regard, Judge Koroma took the view that the 1884 Treaty did not involve any cession or transfer of territory since Great Britain undertook only to extend 'her gracious favour and protection' to the Kings, Chiefs and people of Old Calabar.[51] Judge Mbaye also considered that: 'In sub-Saharan Africa, the sole purpose of the *protectorates* which resulted from the colonial treaties was to create a system of indirect administration.'[52] In this connection, the Court stressed the absence of a characteristic of an international protectorate: that is, ongoing meetings and discussion between the protecting Power and the Rulers of the Protectorate, in the present case.[53] Yet some doubts might be raised regarding whether the Court's view is *ex post facto* legitimisation of colonisation of territory concerned.[54] Indeed, the validity of the Court's interpretation on the 1884 Treaty was also questioned by Judges Rezek,[55] Al-Khasawneh[56] and Judge ad hoc Ajibola.[57]

The further issue to be considered in this context concerns the treatment of the southern sector of the boundary as defined by the 1913 Anglo-German Agreement in the period 1913 to 1960.[58] After examination of the practice concerning mandate of the League of Nations and trusteeship under the United Nations, the Court held that Bakassi was comprised within British Cameroon for the entire period from 1922 until 1961 and that the boundary between Bakassi and Nigeria remained an international boundary.[59] Related to this, the Court stressed the fact that the frontier line of the Southern Cameroon under British trusteeship including Bakassi was acknowledged by Nigeria when it voted in favour of General Assembly Resolution 1608 (XV), which both terminated the Trusteeship and approved the results of the plebiscite.[60] According to the Court, the common understanding of where title lay in Bakassi continued through until the late 1970s[61] and it is also reflected by the geographic pattern of the oil concessions granted by the two parties up to 1991.[62] In light of above consideration, the Court found that Nigeria accepted that it recognised Cameroonian sovereignty over the Bakassi Peninsula.[63] It is notable that recognition of Nigeria was considered as a key element in acknowledging Cameroonian sovereignty in the Bakassi Peninsula. In conclusion, the Court ruled that the 1913 Anglo-German Agreement was valid and applicable in its entirety.[64]

Effectivités: examination of basis of title to Bakassi advanced by Nigeria

An historical consolidation of title

The next issue to be examined concerns Nigeria's claims to Bakassi on the basis of *effectivités*. In this regard, Nigeria claimed three bases of its title over the Bakassi Peninsula: an historical consolidation of title, peaceful possession by Nigeria, and manifestation of sovereignty by Nigeria together with acquiescence by Cameroon. Among those elements, an historical consolidation of title merits particular consideration.

The concept of an historic consolidation, articulated in the 1951 *Norwegian Fisheries* case,[65] was formulated by Charles de Visscher as follows:

> The fundamental interest of the stability of territorial situations from the point of view of order and peace explains the place that consolidation by historic title holds in international law and the suppleness with which the principle is applied ... Proven long use, which is its foundation, merely represents a complex of interests and relations which in themselves have the effect of attaching a territory or an expanse of sea to a given State. It is these interests and relations, varying from one case to another, and not the passage of a fixed term, unknown in any event to international law, that are taken into direct account by the judge to decide *in concreto* on the existence or non-existence of a consolidation by historic title.[66]

While the concept of historical consolidation needs careful consideration,[67] it seems possible to consider that this concept is essentially characterised by three elements which are closely interlinked: time, effectivity and recognition. According to the concept of historical consolidation, effective possession consolidated by the passage of time, along with acquiescence or absence of opposition by other States, creates legal title to territory.[68]

Nigeria relied on the concept of historical consolidation as a basis of title to both the Lake Chad areas and to the Bakassi Peninsula. Concerning historical consolidation of title to the Lake Chad areas, Nigeria cited five elements: (1) the attitude and affiliations of the population of Darak and the other Lake Chad villages, (2) the existence of historical links with Nigeria in the area, (3) the exercise of authority by the traditional Chiefs, (4) the long settlement of Nigerian nationals in the area, and (5) the peaceful administration of the disputed villages by the Federal Government of Nigeria and the State of Borno.[69] Nigeria further contended that Cameroon acquiesced in the peaceful exercise of Nigerian sovereignty over the disputed areas and that that acquiescence constitutes a major element in the process of historical consolidation of title.[70]

However, the ICJ refused to accept the notion of historic consolidation as a basis of legal title for four reasons:[71]

1 The notion of historical consolidation has never been used as a basis of title in territorial disputes.
2 The theory of historical consolidation is highly controversial and cannot replace the established modes of acquisition of title under international law.
3 Nothing in the *Fisheries* judgment suggests that the 'historical consolidation' allows land occupation to prevail over an established treaty title.
4 The facts and circumstances put forward by Nigeria with respect to the Lake Chad villages concern a period of some 20 years. Yet this is far too short, even according to the theory of historic consolidation.

According to the Court, since Cameroon held the legal title to the Lake Chad area,[72] an issue to be examined is whether Cameroon acquiesced in the establishment of a change in treaty title.[73] In this regard, the Court held that there was no acquiescence by Cameroon in the abandonment of its title in the area in favour of Nigeria.[74] By referring to the Burkina Faso/Mali paradigm, the Court confirmed that where the *effectivités* does not correspond to the legal title, the title prevails over the *effectivités*.[75] It follows that Cameroon's title prevails over the *effectivités* claimed by Nigeria, regardless of the validity of historical consolidation. Here we can find a clear application of the Burkina Faso/Mali paradigm.

Historical consolidation of Nigeria's title is also at issue in relation to the Bakassi Peninsula. In this regard, Nigeria presented evidence of various State activities, together with acquiescence, to support its historical consolidation of title as a basis of title to Bakassi Peninsula.[76] Here the ICJ recalled that at the time of Nigeria's accession to independence, there was no Nigerian title capable of being confirmed subsequently by long occupation and that, on the date of its independence, Cameroon succeeded to title over Bakassi as established by the 1913 Anglo-German Agreement. The Court thus concluded that:

> [I]nvocation of historical consolidation cannot in any event vest title to Bakassi in Nigeria, where its 'occupation' of the peninsula is adverse to Cameroon's prior treaty title and where, moreover, the possession has been for a limited period.[77]

However, the Court's view was questioned by Judge Koroma. According to the learned judge, 'historical consolidation, if supported by the requisite evidence, can be a sound and valid means of establishing territorial title in international law'.[78] Likewise, Judge Ajibola stated that the argument of Nigeria based on its historical consolidation and *effectivités* is sound.[79]

Despite dissent of the two judges, as noted, the majority opinion of the ICJ did not accept the Nigeria's claim over the Bakassi Peninsula on the basis of the concept of historical consolidation. In this regard, three reasons merit particular highlighting. The first is the absence of acquiescence by Cameroon in the abandonment of its title in the area in favour of Nigeria. Given that acquiescence or toleration of the opponent party is a key element of the concept of historical consolidation,[80] the lack of acquiescence of Cameroon can be said to be an important reason to reject historical consolidation of title advanced by Nigeria. Second, as explained earlier, the Court acknowledged that Nigeria clearly and publicly recognised Cameroon title to Bakassi. Third, the passage of time is another key element of the concept of historical consolidation. In this regard, it is notable that the ICJ considered that a period of some 20 years is inadequate to establish title through historical consolidation.

Conflict between title and *effectivités*

Nigeria advocated many activities in Bakassi as proof of settled Nigerian administration and of acts in exercise of sovereign authority. These acts include: the establishment of schools, the provision of health facilities and some tax collection.[81] However, the Court observed that: '[I]n none of these cases were the acts referred to acts *contra legem*; those precedents are therefore not relevant'.[82] By referring to the *Frontier Dispute* case again,[83] the Court explicitly ruled that: '[W]here there is a conflict between title and *effectivités*, preference will be given to the former'.[84] According to the Court, the more relevant legal question was whether the conduct of Cameroon, as the title holder, can be viewed as an acquiescence in the loss of the treaty title that it inherited upon independence. Reviewing conduct of Cameroon, the Court ruled that there is no evidence to indicate acquiescence by Cameroon in abandonment of its title in favour of Nigeria.[85] The Court thus concluded that sovereignty over the Bakassi Peninsula lies with Cameroon.[86]

Impact of the Bakassi Decision on maritime delimitation

As land boundaries indicate a starting point for maritime boundaries between States with adjacent coasts, the Court's decision on the Bakassi Peninsula inevitably affects upon maritime delimitation between Cameroon and Nigeria.[87] Conversely, a maritime boundary might also affect the territorial sovereignty over land. The Court, in the *Cameroon/Nigeria* case, ruled that the maritime boundary up to Point G was already fixed by the Maroua Declaration as well as the Yaoundé II Declaration.[88] It is of particular interest to note that these Declarations were also used for determining the sovereignty over the Bakassi Peninsula. In this regard, the Court held that: 'Cameroon and Nigeria participated from 1971 to 1975 in the negotiations leading to the Yaoundé, Kano and Maroua Declarations, *with the maritime line clearly being predicated upon Cameroon's title to Bakassi.*'[89]

The above passage seems to imply that if the existence of a maritime boundary was supported by relevant documents, the location of the existing maritime boundary might be a factor to be taken into account in determining the sovereignty over territory. However, this is not true in a case where there is no existing maritime boundary.[90] In any case, as the sovereignty of Cameroon over the Bakassi Peninsula relies primarily on the 1913 Anglo-German Agreement, it can be said that the Declarations relating to maritime boundary played only a modest role with regard to territorial dispute over the Peninsula.

Evaluation: change and continuity of the international law of acquisition of territory

Variable meaning of title and effectivités

The *Cameroon/Nigeria* judgment can be regarded as a clear example with regard to the application of the Burkina Faso/Mali paradigm. However, care must be taken in noting that the concepts of title and *effectivités* under the paradigm may be used in different senses in different cases.

First, originally the concept of 'title' in the *Frontier Dispute* case referred to the ground on which the implementation of the principle of *uti possidetis* is grounded.[91] As discussed earlier, however, the 'title' of Cameroon to the Bakassi Peninsula does not relate to the principle of *uti possidetis*, but title derived from a treaty.[92] Therefore, the meaning of title in the *Cameroon/Nigeria* case differs from that presented in the *Frontier Dispute* case. Likewise, in the 2002 *Indonesia/Malaysia* case, the application of the principle of *uti possidetis* was not at issue and the parties based their titles on legal instruments.[93] On the other hand, in the 1996 *Land, Island and Maritime Frontier Dispute* case between El Salvador and Honduras, the Chamber of the ICJ focused on title on which the implementation of the principle of *uti possidetis* is grounded.[94] In the 2005 *Benin/Niger* case, legal titles of the parties in dispute to the River Mekrou sector were determined on the basis of the principle of *uti possidetis.*[95] In these two cases, the concept of legal title was used in the original sense. By the same token, the ICJ, in the 2007 *Honduras/Nicaragua* case, examined title involving the application of the principle of *uti possidetis.*[96] In the 2012 *Nicaragua/Colombia* case, however, it seems that both treaty and the principle of *uti possidetis* were examined as a source of title of the parties.[97]

Second, the concept of *effectivités* in the *Frontier Dispute* case referred to the conduct of the administrative authorities as proof of the effective exercise of territorial jurisdiction in the disputed region during the colonial period (colonial *effectivités*).[98] However, *effectivités* with regard to the Bakassi Peninsula relate to activities of Nigeria itself after independence (post-colonial *effectivités*). The same is equally true in the 2002 *Indonesia/Malaysia* case. While the ICJ ruled that Malaysia has title to Ligitan and Sipadan on the basis of the *effectivités*, the *effectivités* concerned activities by Malaysia in its own name and as successor State of Great Britain.[99] In the 2005 *Benin/Niger* case, however, the Chamber of the ICJ examined *effectivités* exercised by local colonial authorities in the sector of the River Niger.[100] In the 1996 *Land, Island and Maritime Frontier Dispute* case, the Chamber of the ICJ considered both colonial and post-independence *effectivités.*[101] The same is equally true in the 2007 *Honduras/Nicaragua* case.[102]

In summary, the judicial practice shows that if the Burkina Faso/Mali paradigm is applied, the concept of legal title may be used independent of the principle of *uti possidetis.* Further, the concept of *effectivités* may include both acts of colonial authorities and acts of States after their independence. In this sense, the scope of the concepts of title and *effectivités* under the Burkina Faso/Mali paradigm can be said to be expanded through practice of the ICJ. In consequence, it may be said that theoretically the Burkina Faso/Mali paradigm can cover all situations, independent of the implementation of the principle of *uti possidetis.*

Static characteristics of the Burkina Faso/Mali paradigm

The Burkina Faso/Mali paradigm differs from the traditional paradigm in that the former is not subject to *a priori* fixed modes of acquisition of territory. Even so, it cannot pass unnoticed that the Burkina Faso/Mali paradigm has a commonality with the traditional paradigm. Under the Burkina Faso/Mali paradigm, where title of one party was established, the title prevails over *effectivités*. Thus, time is fixed at the moment when title was established and *effectivités* which are contrary to the title, i.e. *effectivités contra legem*, do not affect the rights of the holder of the title. By the same token, in principle, acts of the party after establishing its title to territory do not affect the existence of its rights. To this extent, the Burkina Faso/Mali paradigm is also thought to be static.[103]

The static nature of the Burkina Faso/Mali paradigm is demonstrated by the rejection of the concept of historical consolidation in the *Cameroon/Nigeria* judgment. According to the ICJ, once title of a party was established, there is no scope to accept historical consolidation of title advanced by another party. In this regard, the *Cameroon/Nigeria* judgment shows a clear contrast with the 1998 *Eritrea/Yemen* arbitration (the First Phase)[104] and the 2002 *Eritrea/Ethiopia* decision.[105] In fact, the Arbitral Tribunal, in the *Eritrea/Yemen* arbitration, explicitly referred to the concept of a gradual consolidation of title named by Charles de Visscher when assessing various factors intended to show not only physical activity and conduct, but also repute, and the opinions and attitudes of other governments.[106] In this regard, the Arbitral Tribunal linked the concept of gradual consolidation of title to the Island of Palmas paradigm which is characterised by 'the continuous and peaceful display of the functions of state within a given region'.[107] In the 2002 *Eritrea/Ethiopia* decision, both parties agreed that the whole of the boundary between them was covered by three treaties: the 1900 Treaty (the central sector), the 1902 Treaty (the western sector), and the 1908 Treaty (the eastern sector).[108] According to the Eritrea–Ethiopia Boundary Commission, however, its role is not limited to identification of the boundary based on the Treaties. The Commission thus examined the subsequent conduct of the parties with a view to determining whether any such conduct required it to adjust the boundary based on the relevant Treaty. After examination of conduct of the parties relevant to the exercise of sovereign authority, i.e. *effectivités*, the Commission adjusted the 1900 Treaty line in the Belesa and Endeli projections that are part of the central sector.[109] Accordingly, the Treaty boundary was modified in light of *effectivités* conducted after the conclusion of the Treaty.[110]

In contrast, according to the Burkina Faso/Mali paradigm, changing situation after the establishment of title does not affect the process of acquisition of sovereignty over territory. In the *Cameroon/Nigeria* case, it is submitted that the number of Nigerian nationals living in the Bakassi Peninsula has grown considerably.[111] Under the Burkina Faso/Mali paradigm, however, 'these facts of themselves do not establish Nigerian title over Bakassi territory; nor can they serve as an element in a claim for historical consolidation'.[112] Here a tension between law and fact may arise.[113] There is a concern that the tension makes it difficult to implement the judgment of the Court.[114] In this regard, the Court took note of the commitment undertaken by Cameroon at the hearing that 'faithful to its traditional policy of hospitality and tolerance', it would 'continue to afford protection to Nigerians living in the [Bakassi] Peninsula and in the Lake Chad area'.[115] Yet this is a matter of policy, and further consideration must be given to the question how it is possible to address the tension between law and fact in international law of acquisition of territory. In considering this issue, as will be seen next, the approach taken by the ICJ in the 2008 *Malaysia/Singapore* case deserves serious consideration.[116]

Passing of sovereignty in the 2008 Malaysia/Singapore *case*

The central issue in the *Malaysia/Singapore* dispute related to sovereignty over the Pedra Branca/Pulau Batu Puteh. While Singapore argued that the legal status of Pedra Branca was that of *terra nullius*,[117] Malaysia maintained that it had an original title to Pedra Branca of long standing.[118] In this regard, the Court held that in 1844 Pedra Branca was under the sovereignty over the Sultan of Johor, i.e. a predecessor of Malaysia.[119] It follows that Singapore's *effectivités* do not correspond to Malaysia's original title over Pedra Branca. In this case, according to the Burkina Faso/Mali paradigm, preference is to be given to Malaysia.

Nonetheless, the ICJ moved on to examine the question whether Malaysia has retained sovereignty over Pedra Branca following 1844 or whether the sovereignty has since passed to Singapore.[120] In considering this issue, the ICJ gave much weight on the 1953 correspondence as an evidence to show that Johor understood that it did not have sovereignty over Pedra Branca.[121] It further ruled that multiple actions of Singapore can be seen as conduct *à titre de souverain*.[122] In the view of the Court, the relevant facts reflect 'a convergent evolution' of the positions of the parties concerning title to Pedra Branca. The Court thus found that by 1980 sovereignty over Pedra Branca had passed to Singapore.[123]

The *Malaysia/Singapore* judgment shows a sharp contrast with the *Cameroon/Nigeria* judgment in at least three respects. The first point pertains to the non-application of the Burkina Faso/Mali paradigm. Unlike the *Cameroon/Nigeria* judgment, the ICJ in the *Malaysia/Singapore* judgment made no reference to this paradigm at all. Second, the Court accepted original title of Malaysia to Pedra Branca on the basis of the display of sovereignty. To this extent, the Court's approach in the *Malaysia/Singapore* judgment seems to be in the line with the Island of Palmas paradigm.[124] Third, when considering passing of sovereignty over Pedra Branca from Malaysia to Singapore, notably the Court referred to the concept of an 'evolving views of the authorities',[125] 'evolving understanding shared by the Parties'[126] or a 'convergent evolution of the position of the Parties'.[127] The Court thus examined whether a series of facts and events reflected a convergent evolution of the positions of the parties regarding title to Pedra Branca. This is a novel approach that is unknown to precedents of the ICJ jurisprudence. As the ICJ observed, the Johor authorities and their successors took no action at all on Pedra Branca from June 1850 for the whole of the following century or more,[128] while Singapore performed a series of acts. Accordingly, there is a gap between law and fact with regard to Pedra Branca. It may be said that the Court filled the gap by referring to the concept of 'convergent evolution of the position of the Parties'. On the other hand, caution is needed with regard to the Court's approach in at least two respects.

First, among multiple factors taken into account, the Court seemed to place much weight on acquiescence.[129] Given that passing of sovereignty cannot be easily presumed,[130] however, the concept of an 'evolving understanding shared by the Parties' or a 'convergent evolution of the position of the Parties' requires careful consideration.

Second, the Court's approach may entail the risk of encouraging *effectivités contra legem*. If this is the case, this approach might contribute to threaten the stability of territory. In any case the *Malaysia/Singapore* judgment seems to suggest that the Burkina Faso/Mali paradigm is not the sole one applicable to territorial disputes in the jurisprudence of ICJ.

Conclusions

The above consideration seems to reveal the following conclusions.

First, the *Cameroon/Nigeria* case can be considered as a clear example concerning the application of the Burkina Faso/Mali paradigm. However, it must be noted that the concepts of title and *effectivités* in this case differ from those in the *Frontier Dispute* case. In fact, unlike the *Frontier Dispute* case, title in the *Cameroon/Nigeria* case does not rest on the implementation of the principle of *uti possidetis* and *effectivités* in the present case concerns the post-colonial conduct of Nigeria.

Second, on the basis of the Burkina Faso/Mali paradigm, the Court ruled that title of Nigeria prevails over the *effectivités* advanced by Nigeria. It may be said that this paradigm places much weight on the safeguard of the title holder, stressing the stability of sovereignty over territory.

Third, under the Burkina Faso/Mali paradigm, the role of subsequent conduct of the parties in dispute is modest where title of a party was already established. Subsequent conduct which is contrary to title does not affect acquisition of sovereignty over territory since such conduct is regarded as act *contra legem*. In this sense, it is argued that the Burkina Faso/Mali paradigm is static by nature. As situations surrounding territory may change with the passage of time, however, a gap may arise between law and fact. Here an issue arises how it is possible to address the tension between law and fact and between stability and change. Given that a significant gap between law and fact may be a source of destabilising sovereignty over territory, this issue needs further consideration in theory and practice.

Fourth, unlike the *Cameroon/Nigeria* case, the ICJ in the *Malaysia/Singapore* dispute determined the case on the basis of the subsequent conduct of the parties. According to this approach, the establishment of original title alone is inadequate and title must be maintained through subsequent practice. It appears that this approach has an affinity with the Island of Palmas paradigm.

Fifth, an essential issue of the international law of acquisition of territory relates to the reconciliation between the requirement of stability and that of change. While stability of territory based on title requires the maintenance of the status quo, *effectivités* stress the reality of governance of territory by taking account of changing situations in international relations. Since the tension between stability and change derives from passage of time, the consideration of time elements becomes the key issue in the law. While the antithesis between stability and change is a fundamental issue underlying international law in general, the reconciliation between the two elements should also be a particularly important issue in international law of acquisition of territory.

Notes

1 P. Reuter, *Droit international public* (Paris: PUF, 1993, seventh edition), 25–26.

2 According to Jennings, '[t]he primary meaning of "title" is the vestitive facts which the law recognises as creating a right'; R.Y. Jennings, *The Acquisition of Territory in International Law* (Manchester: Manchester University Press, 1963) 4. Strictly speaking, the term 'title' has two meanings: title as evidence which may establish the existence of a right (title-proof) and title as the actual source of that right (title-source). *Frontier Dispute* (Burkina Faso/Republic of Mali), Judgment of 22 December 1986 [1986] *ICJ Rep.* 554, 564, para. 18; G. Distefano, 'The Conceptualization (Construction) of Territorial Title in the Light of the International Court of Justice Case Law' (2006) 19 *Leiden Journal of International Law* 1041, 1045. See also G. Distefano, 'La notion de titre juridique et les différends territoriaux dans l'ordre international'

(1995) 99 *RGDIP* 335–366; by the same writer, *L'ordre international entre légalité et effectivité: le titre juridique dans le contentieux territorial* (Paris: PUF, 2002) 393 *et seq.*

3 *Land and Maritime Boundary between Cameroon and Nigeria (Cameroon v. Nigeria: Equatorial Guinea intervening)* (hereafter the *Cameroon/Nigeria* case), Judgment of 10 October 2002 [2002] *ICJ Rep.* 303.

4 Ibid., 399, para. 193.

5 Ibid., 400, para. 194.

6 Ibid.

7 Ibid., 327, para. 27.

8 Ibid., 412, para. 218.

9 Originally the proceedings initiated by Cameroon in March 1994 concerned a dispute over the Bakassi Peninsula, together with the maritime boundary between Cameroon and Nigeria. J.G. Merrills, 'Land and Maritime Boundary between Cameroon and Nigeria (*Cameroon v. Nigeria: Equatorial Guinea Intervening*), Merits Judgment of 10 October 2002' (2003) 52 *ICLQ* 788, 788; M. Mendelson, 'The Cameroon–Nigeria Case in the International Court of Justice: Some Territorial Sovereignty and Boundary Delimitation Issues' (2004) 75 *BYIL* 223, 223. At the same time, this chapter also discusses sovereignty over the Lake Chad areas when examining historical consolidation.

10 P. Malanczuk, *Akehurst's Modern Introduction to International Law* (London: Routledge, 1997, seventh edition) 147; A. Clapham, *Brierly's Law of Nations* (Oxford: Oxford University Press, 2012, seventh edition) 169; M.N. Shaw, *International Law* (Cambridge: Cambridge University Press, 2014, seventh edition) 358.

11 R.Y. Jennings and A. Watts, *Oppenheim's International Law, ninth edition, Vol. 1, Peace*, Parts 2 to 4 (Oxford: Oxford University Press, 1996) 679. These modes are mentioned by many of the standard textbooks, including: Jennings, *supra* note 2, 6–7; I. Brownlie, *Principles on Public International Law* (Oxford: Oxford University Press, 2008, seventh edition) 127; Shaw, *supra* note 10, 358; J. Crawford, *Brownlie's Principles on Public International Law* (Oxford: Oxford University Press, 2012, eighth edition) 220; Clapham, *supra* note 10, 169.

12 Jennings and Watts, *supra* note 11, 679. However, the classification was criticised by Brownlie as oversimplification of the situation. Brownlie, *supra* note 11, 128. See also Crawford, *supra* note 11, 320–321.

13 Jennings and Watts, *supra* note 11, 679.

14 The traditional paradigm is criticised by some writers. Brownlie, *supra* note 11, 127; Crawford, *supra* note 11, 220; M.N. Shaw, *Title to Territory in Africa: International Legal Issues* (Oxford: Clarendon Press, 1986) 17; Clapham, *supra* note 10, 169; S.P. Sharma, *Territorial Acquisition, Disputes and International Law* (The Hague: Martinus Nijhoff, 1997) 164–173.

15 Brownlie, *supra* note 11, 127.

16 T. Fukamachi, 'Some Reflections on Title to Territory in International Law' (in Japanese) (1994) 61 *Journal of Law and Politics* 67, 83. See also Sookyeon Huh, *The Acquisition of Territory in International Law: The Effectiveness and Legitimacy of Territorial Control* (in Japanese) (Tokyo: Tokyo University Press, 2012) 100.

17 A.L.W. Munkman, 'Adjudication and Adjustment: International Judicial Decision and the Settlement of Territorial and Boundary Disputes' (1972–1973) 46 *BYIL* 1, 94.

18 Shaw, *supra* note 14, 17; Sharma, *supra* note 14, 168–170.

19 Fukamachi, *supra* note 16, 83–84.

20 Emphasis added. *Island of Palmas* case *(The Netherlands v. United States)* (1928) 2 *Reports of International Arbitral Awards (RIAA)* 829, 845.

21 This paradigm is linked to Max Huber's approach to international law. For Max Huber's approach, see J. Delbrück, 'Max Huber's Sociological Approach to International Law Revisited' (2007) 18 *European Journal of International Law* 97–113; J. Klabbers, 'The Sociological Jurisprudence of Max Huber: An Introduction' (1992) 43 *Austrian Journal of Public International Law* 197–213; Sookyeon Huh, *supra* note 16, 142–147.

22 The *Island of Palmas* case, *supra* note 20, 839.

23 Ibid., 839. See also Sookyeon Huh, *supra* note 16, 145.

24 Ibid., 138–141.

25 The *Island of Palmas* case, *supra* note 20, 857.

26 Ibid., 855.

27 Relativity of legal title has more than one meaning, though. See Brownlie, *supra* note 11, 154–156; Sookyeon Huh, *supra* note 16, 140–141.
28 Brownlie, *supra* note 11, 155.
29 See *Legal Status of Eastern Greenland (Denmark v. Norway)*, A/B 53 [1933] *PCIJ Rep.* 22, 46.
30 At the same time, the *dictum* of the *Island of Palmas* arbitration was criticised by some writers. See for instance, Jennings, *supra* note 2, 30–31; Brownlie, *supra* note 11, 125; P.C. Jessup, 'The Palmas Island Arbitration' (1928) 22 *AJIL* 735, 740; Crawford, *supra* note 11, 218. See also Sookyeon Huh, *supra* note 16, 166–169.
31 *Minquiers and Ecrehos (France/United Kingdom)*, Judgment of 17 November 1953 [1953] *ICJ Rep.* 47, 56–57.
32 *The Indo-Pakistan Western Boundary (Rann of Kutch) between India and Pakistan (India v. Pakistan)* (1968) 17 *RIAA* 1, 554.
33 The *Cameroon/Nigeria* case, Judgment, *supra* note 3, 353, para. 68.
34 *Frontier Dispute*, *supra* note 2, 586–587, para. 63.
35 M.G. Kohen, 'La relation titre/effectivités dans le contentieux territorial à la lumière de la jurisprudence récente' (2004) 108 *RGDIP* 561, 563.
36 Sookyeon Huh, *supra* note 16, 231.
37 *Land, Island and Maritime Frontier Dispute* (El Salvador/Honduras: Nicaragua intervening), Judgment of 11 September 1992 [1992] *ICJ Rep.* 351, 398–399, paras 61–62.
38 *Sovereignty over Pulau Ligitan and Pulau Sipadan (Indonesia/Malaysia)* (hereafter the *Indonesia/Malaysia* case), Judgment of 17 December 2002 [2002] *ICJ Rep.* 625, 678, para. 126.
39 *Frontier Dispute* (*Benin/Niger*), Judgment of 12 July 2005 [2005] *ICJ Rep.* 90, 127, para. 77.
40 *Case Concerning Territorial and Maritime Dispute between Nicaragua and Honduras in the Caribbean Sea* (*Nicaragua v. Honduras*), Judgment of 8 October 2007 [2007] *ICJ Rep.* 659, 706, para. 151 *et seq.*
41 *Territorial and Maritime Dispute (Nicaragua v. Colombia)* [2012] *ICJ Rep.* (unreported), paras 39–84.
42 The *Cameroon/Nigeria* case, Judgment, *supra* note 3, 333, para. 37.
43 Ibid., 402, paras 200–201. See also Counter-Memorial of the Federal Republic of Nigeria, Vol. 1, 158–162, paras 8.28–8.40; Rejoinder of the Federal Republic of Nigeria, para. 1.58.
44 The *Island of Palmas* case, *supra* note 20, 858–859.
45 *Western Sahara*, Advisory Opinion of 16 October 1975 [1975] *ICJ Rep.* 12, 39, para. 80. See also Shaw, *supra* note 14, 45.
46 The *Cameroon/Nigeria* case, Judgment, *supra* note 3, 405, para. 205.
47 Ibid., 405–406, paras 206–207.
48 Ibid., 406–407, paras 207–209. See also Mendelson, *supra* note 9, 230–234.
49 Counter-Memorial of Nigeria, *supra* note 43, 109, para. 6.63.
50 Separate Opinion of Judge Al-Khasawneh [2002] *ICJ Rep.* 492, 504, para. 20.
51 Dissenting Opinion of Judge Koroma [2002] *ICJ Rep.* 474, 479–480, para. 15.
52 Emphasis original. Separate Opinion of Judge Mbaye [2002] *ICJ Rep.* 506, 519, para. 67.
53 The *Cameroon/Nigeria* case, Judgment, *supra* note 3, 406, para. 207.
54 Separate Opinion of Judge Al-Khasawneh, *supra* note 50, 499, para. 9.
55 Declaration of Judge Rezek [2002] *ICJ Rep.* 489, 490.
56 Separate Opinion of Judge Al-Khasawneh, *supra* note 50, 504–505, paras 20–21.
57 Dissenting Opinion of Judge Ajibola [2002] *ICJ Rep.* 538, 567–568, para. 88. According to Judge Ajibola, the 1884 Treaty 'is clearly a treaty of protection and no more'. Ibid., 575, para. 115. See also G. Oduntan, *International Law and Boundary Disputes in Africa* (London: Routledge, 2015) 236–237.
58 The *Cameroon/Nigeria* case, Judgment, *supra* note 3, 407, para. 210.
59 Ibid., 409, para. 212.
60 Ibid., 410, para. 213.
61 Ibid., 410–411, para. 214.
62 Ibid., 411, para. 215. For more on oil concessions granted by the parties see the chapter in this book by Mark Osa Igiehon (Chapter 8).
63 Ibid. For Judge Al-Khasawneh, this is the only reason to accept Cameroonian sovereignty over Bakassi. Separate Opinion of Judge Al-Khasawneh, *supra* note 50, 493, para. 1 and 505, para. 22.

64 The *Cameroon/Nigeria* case, Judgment, *supra* note 3, 412, para. 217.
65 Emphasis added. *Fisheries (United Kingdom v. Norway)*, Judgment of 18 December 1951 [1951] *ICJ Rep.* 116, 138.
66 Charles de Visscher, *Theory and Reality in Public International Law* (translated by P.E. Corbett) (Princeton: Princeton University Press 1968) 209. See also D.H.N. Johnson, 'Consolidation as a Root of Title in International Law' (1955) *Cambridge Law Journal* 215–225 (in particular, 222–225).
67 For a critical analysis of the concept of historical consolidation, see Jennings, *supra* note 2, pp. 23–28; Sharma, *supra* note 14, 173–179; M.G. Kohen, *Possession contestée et souveraineté territorial* (Paris: PUF, 1997) 40–45. See also Brownlie, *supra* note 11, 156–158; Crawford, *supra* note 11, 235–236.
68 Charles de Visscher, *supra* note 66, 320; Brownlie, *supra* note 11, 157.
69 The *Cameroon/Nigeria* case, Judgment, *supra* note 3, 349, para. 62. Counter-Memorial of Nigeria, *supra* note 49, 419–433, paras 17.17–17.72.
70 Ibid., 433–437, paras 17.73–17.85; the *Cameroon/Nigeria* case, Judgment, *supra* note 3, 350, para. 62.
71 Ibid., 352, para. 65.
72 The ICJ considered that the frontier in the Lake Chad area was delimited by the Thomson–Marchand Declaration of 1929–1930. Ibid., 341, para. 50. See also 344, para. 55.
73 Ibid., 353, para. 68.
74 Ibid., 354, para. 70.
75 Ibid., 353, para. 68.
76 Counter-Memorial of Nigeria, *supra* note 43, 223, paras 10.25 *et seq.*; CR 2002/9 (Brownlie), 49–65, paras 155–228.
77 The *Cameroon/Nigeria* case, Judgment, *supra* note 3, 414, para. 220.
78 Dissenting Opinion of Judge Koroma, *supra* note 51, 476, para. 8.
79 Dissenting Opinion of Judge Ajibola, *supra* note 57, 585–586, para. 145.
80 Ibid., 581, para. 134.
81 The *Cameroon/Nigeria* case, Judgment, *supra* note 3, 414, para. 222.
82 Ibid., 415, para. 223.
83 The *Frontier Dispute* case, *supra* note 2, 586–587, para. 63.
84 The *Cameroon/Nigeria* case, Judgment, *supra* note 3, 415, para. 223.
85 Ibid., 416, para. 224.
86 Ibid., 416, para. 225.
87 Further, see Y. Tanaka, 'Reflections on Maritime Delimitation in the *Cameroon/Nigeria* Case' (2004) 53 *ICLQ* 369, 402–405. For an analysis of issues on the law of the sea in the *Cameroon/Nigeria* case, see Egede's chapter in this book (Chapter 7). See also Y. Tanaka, *Predictability and Flexibility in the Law of Maritime Delimitation* (Oxford: Hart Publishing, 2006) 257–262; D. Bardonnet, 'Frontières terrestres et frontières maritimes' (1989) 35 *AFDI* 1, 6–22.
88 The *Cameroon/Nigeria* case, Judgment, *supra* note 3, 431, para. 268.
89 The *Cameroon/Nigeria* case, Judgment, *supra* note 3, 416, para. 223, emphasis added. See also Reply of Cameroon, 349–350, para. 7.23.
90 Tanaka, *supra* note 87, 404.
91 *Frontier Dispute*, *supra* note 2, 586, para. 63. For the principle of *uti possidetis*, see, for instance, M.G. Kohen, 'L'uti possidetis revisite: L'arrêt du 11 septembre 1992 dans l'affaire El Salvador/Honduras' (1993) 97 *RGDIP* 939–973; J.-M. Sorel and R. Mehdi, 'L'uti possidetis entre la consécration juridique et la pratique: essai de réactualistion' (1994) 40 *AFDI* 11–40; Kohen, *supra* note 67, 425 *et seq.*; J. Castellino and S. Allen, 'The Doctrine of Uti Possidetis: Crystallization of Modern Post-Colonial Identity' (2000) 43 *German Yearbook of International Law* 205–226; S. Lalonde, 'Uti Possidetis: Its Colonial Past Revisited' (2001) *Revue Belge de droit international* 23–99; S.N. Lalonde, *Determining Boundaries in a Conflict World: The Role of* Uti Possidetis (Montreal: McGill-Queen's University Press, 2002); G. Abi-Saab, 'Le principe de l'*uti possidetis*, son rôle et ses limites dans le contentieux territorial international', in M.G. Kohen (ed.), *Promoting Justice, Human Rights and Conflict Resolution through International Law: Liber Amicorum Lucius Caflisch* (Leiden: Brill, 2007) 657–671; Oduntan, *supra* note 57, 330–349.
92 Sookyeon Huh, *supra* note 16, 297.

93 The *Indonesia/Malaysia* case, *supra* note 38, 643, paras 32–33.
94 *Land, Island and Maritime Frontier Dispute*, *supra* note 37, 399, para. 62. See also 388–389, paras 45.
95 The *Benin/Niger* case, *supra* note 39, 143, para. 127; 148–149, para. 141.
96 The *Nicaragua/Honduras* case, *supra* note 40, 706, para. 154 *et seq.*
97 The *Nicaragua/Colombia* case, *supra* note 41, paras 39–65.
98 *Frontier Dispute*, *supra* note 2, 586, para. 63. See also Sookyeon Huh, *supra* note 16, 254.
99 The *Indonesia/Malaysia* case, *supra* note 38, 685–686, paras 148–149.
100 The *Benin/Niger* case, *supra* note 39, 127–133, paras 76–103.
101 *Land, Island and Maritime Frontier Dispute*, *supra* note 37, 399, para. 62.
102 The *Nicaragua/Honduras* case, *supra* note 40, 710–722, paras 165–208.
103 The Court's approach was criticised by Judge Koroma. See Dissenting Opinion of Judge Koroma, *supra* note 51, 476, para. 8.
104 *Territorial Sovereignty and Scope of the Dispute (Eritrea and Yemen)*, 9 October 1998, 22 *RIAA* 209.
105 *Decision regarding Delimitation of the Border between Eritrea and Ethiopia*, 13 April 2002, 25 *RIAA* 83.
106 The *Eritrea/Yemen* arbitration, *supra* note 104, 312, para. 451.
107 Ibid.
108 The *Eritrea/Ethiopia* decision, supra note 105, 109, para. 3.3.
109 Ibid., 132–138, paras 4.60–4.86.
110 For a criticism concerning the Commission's approach, see M. Kohen, 'The Decision on the Delimitation of the Eritrea/Ethiopia Boundary of 13 April 2002: A Singular Approach to International Law Applicable to Territorial Disputes', in *Promoting Justice*, *supra* note 91, 772; Kohen, *supra* note 35, 571–572.
111 The *Cameroon/Nigeria* case, Judgment, *supra* note 3, 414, para. 221. According to Brownlie, a permanent population of Nigeria living in the Bakassi was 156,000. CR 2002/9 (Brownlie), 65, para. 226.
112 The *Cameroon/Nigeria* case, Judgment, *supra* note 3, 414, para. 221.
113 See also Oduntan, *supra* note 57, 238–239.
114 Limitations of space preclude examining the implementation process of the *Cameroon/Nigeria* judgment. On this issue, see ibid., 227–235.
115 The *Cameroon/Nigeria* case, Judgment, *supra* note 3, 457, para. 325(V)(C).
116 *Sovereignty over Pedra Branca/Pulau Batu Puteh, Middle Rocks and South Ledge (Malaysia/Singapore)*, Judgment of 23 May 2008 [2008] *ICJ Rep.* 12. Because of limitations of spaces, a detailed examination of the *Pedra Branca* case falls outside scope of this chapter. For an overview of this case, see for instance, Y. Tanaka, 'Passing of Sovereignty: The *Malaysia/Singapore* Territorial Dispute before the ICJ' (2008) 3 *Hague Justice Journal* 5–15; C. Bories, 'L'arrêt de la Court internationale de justice du 23 mai 2008 dans l'affaire souveraineté sur Pedra Branca/Pulau Batu Puteh, Middle Rocks et South Ledge (Malaisie/Singapour)' (2008) 54 *AFDI* 227–236; M. Kohen, 'Original Title in the Light of the ICJ Judgment on Sovereignty over Pedra Branca' (2013) 15 *Journal of the History of International Law* 151–171; R Beckman, 'Case between Malaysia and Singapore Concerning Sovereignty over Pedra Branca/Pulau Batu Puteh, Middle Rocks and South Ledge' (2008) 14 *Asian Yearbook of International Law* 275–286; E. David, 'Le différend insulaire Malaisie/Singapour', in *Le procès international: Liber Amicorum Jean-Pierre Cot* (Brussels: Bruylant, 2009) 77–94; S.V. Suarez, 'Sovereignty over Pedra Branca/Pulau Batu Puteh, Middle Rocks and South Ledge Case (Malaysia/Singapore)', in R. Wolfrum (ed.), *Max Planck Encyclopaedia of Public International Law* (online edition).
117 Reply of Singapore, 36–37, paras 3.3–3.7; CR 2007/28 (Pellet), 37–50, paras 1–29.
118 Memorial of Malaysia, Vol. I, 3–6, paras 5–12; Reply of Malaysia, 25–52, paras 54–109; CR 2007/24 (Crawford), 57–66, paras 1–22; CR 2007/25 (Crawford), 12–24, paras 1–34.
119 The *Malaysia/Singapore* case, *supra* note 116, 49, para. 117.
120 Ibid., 50, paras 118–119.
121 Ibid., 80, para. 223; 82, para. 230. See also Separate Opinion of Judge ad hoc Sreenivasa Rao [2008] *ICJ Rep.* 153, 170, para. 35.
122 Judgment, *supra* note 116, 82–95, paras 231–272.
123 Ibid., 96, paras 276–277; 101, para. 300(1).

124 In fact, the ICJ explicitly referred to the *Island of Palmas* case. The *Malaysia/Singapore* case, *supra* note 116, 50, para. 121.
125 Ibid., 65, para. 162.
126 Ibid., 80, para. 224.
127 Ibid., 96, para. 276. It appears that the three terms are used interchangeably in the *Malaysia/Singapore* judgment.
128 Ibid., 96, para. 275.
129 Ibid., 50, para. 121.
130 Ibid., 51, para. 122. See also Joint Dissenting Opinion of Judges Simma and Abraham [2008] *ICJ Rep.* 116, 120, para. 13.

7 *The Land and Maritime Boundary between Cameroon and Nigeria (Cameroon v. Nigeria Equatorial Guinea intervening)* case

Interrogating some ongoing law of the sea challenges

Edwin E. Egede[1]

Introduction

The Land and Maritime Boundary between Cameroon and Nigeria (Cameroon v. Nigeria: Equatorial Guinea intervening) case (hereinafter referred to as the Bakassi case), which was filed on 29 March 1994 before the International Court of Justice (ICJ), was initially limited to the question of sovereignty over the Bakassi Peninsula and the delimitation of the maritime boundary between Cameroon and Nigeria,[2] but the scope of the dispute was expanded by an additional application filed on 6 June 1994 by Cameroon relating to the question of sovereignty over land territory around the Lake Chad area. In the latter application, Cameroon requested the Court to 'specify definitively' 'the frontier between the two States from Lake Chad to the sea' and to examine both the maritime and terrestrial aspects of the Case in a single case.[3] The ICJ identified the important difference between the delimitation of land boundaries on the one hand and maritime ones on the other. It pointed out that 'these are two distinct areas of the law, to which different factors and considerations apply'.[4] On 30 June 1999, Equatorial Guinea filed an application to the ICJ to intervene in the case because its legal rights and interests could be affected by the decision of the Case as regards the maritime boundaries claims by the Parties to the case. The Court agreed that Equatorial Guinea had sufficiently established an interest of a legal nature that could be affected by the decision of the Court and thus by an Order dated 21 October 1999 authorised it to intervene as a non-Party intervener.[5]

Although the Bakassi case dealt with issues beyond the law of the sea, this chapter will address crucial issues of the law of the sea in the Bakassi case and subsequent challenges. For reasons of space, this chapter will focus on the continuing challenges in three specific areas: delimitation of maritime boundaries of the Exclusive Economic Zone (EEZ)/ Continental Shelf, certain domestic littoral implications of the Bakassi case in Nigeria, and the issue of innocent passage by warships in the territorial sea.

Delimitation of maritime boundary

The need to delimit overlapping maritime zones within national jurisdictions between either adjacent or opposite coastal States has become a crucial issue in the law of the sea, which relevant treaties, international cases and academic literature have had to engage with. In this regard, Tanaka pointed out that: '[w]ithout rules on maritime delimitation in spaces where coastal State jurisdictions overlap, coastal States cannot enjoy the legal uses of maritime spaces effectively. Hence the law of maritime delimitation is of paramount importance in the law of the sea.'[6] One of the claims of Cameroon, in its application to the ICJ, was a request that the Court determine the maritime boundary between it and an adjacent coastal State, Nigeria, beyond the line (point G) as indicated by the colonial treaty, the Anglo-German Agreement 1913, and post-independent Agreements, including the Yaoundé II Agreement 1971 and the Maroua Agreement 1975, agreed to by both States.[7] The Court observed that the Bakassi case was 'a classic case of maritime delimitation between States with adjacent coasts',[8] and that the maritime areas to be delimited in the case were beyond the outer limits of the territorial seas of the two disputing States and, as agreed by the States, the delimitation of their respective Continental Shelves and EEZs would be effected by a single delimitation line.[9] It must be noted that the maritime delimitation up to Point G was determined by conventional means as required by Articles 74 and 83 and thus there was a partial delimitation.[10] In the absence of an agreement by the Parties, however, the Court had to delimit the area beyond Point G by applying the principles of international maritime boundary delimitation.

The decision in this regard may be described as a landmark one as this was the first time in the ICJ jurisprudence that the Court adopted the equidistance/relevant circumstances method under Articles 74 and 83 of the UNCLOS 82.[11] Although Articles 74 and 83 did not make reference to a specific method of delimitation but merely require that such delimitation should be effected to 'achieve an equitable solution', the Court, by 'a creative interpretation',[12] incorporated the equidistance/relevant circumstances (in the case of States with opposite coasts median line/relevant circumstances) method into these provisions of the UNCLOS 82.[13] With this methodology, the Court starts from a provisional equidistance line and then makes necessary adjustment if justified by relevant circumstances. The equidistance/relevant circumstances method ('corrective equity' approach) may be contrasted with another approach that gives primacy to achieving an equitable solution rather than insisting on a particular method ('result-oriented equity' approach).[14] This contrast triggered a rather complex debate on whether the rule on delimitation should be based on the equidistance/relevant circumstances method or whether it should merely aim for an equitable solution. A raft of decisions of the international courts and tribunals and academic literature has engaged with this debate.[15] In essence, this debate juxtaposes achieving some level of predictability, with the former method, on the one hand, and a flexibility and unpredictability arising from the latter.[16] The Bakassi case, by applying the equidistance/relevant circumstances method, thus falls squarely in favour of predictability in the delimitation methodology. Recent trends in international jurisprudence appear to have adopted this approach, although some other cases seem to have indicated a preference for flexibility in methodology.

The equidistance/relevant circumstances was initially regarded as a two-stage process, as applied in the Bakassi case, but ever since the case concerning *Maritime Delimitation in the Black Sea (Romania/Ukraine)* the process has been characterised as a three-stage process.[17] With this approach, the delimitation process is divided thus. The first stage involves establishing a provisional equidistance line. Thereafter, the second stage is to explore whether there are relevant circumstances that would justify the adjustment of the equidistance line in order to achieve an equitable result. Then, last, it involves the conducting of a disproportionality test to ensure that such delimitation does not cause any inequality to the relevant Parties. As mentioned by Churchill, what had simply occurred was that the third stage, which had previously been subsumed in the second stage of the previous two-stage process, had now been given prominence as a separate and final stage in the delimitation process.[18] Providing a justification for the three-stage approach, Fietta and Cleverly pointed out that:

> It is done so because the use of the equidistance at the first stage is transparent and objective, while the application of relevant circumstances at the second stage provides necessary flexibility, particularly with reference to the geography of the area, in order to achieve the equitable solution ultimately mandated by UNCLOS. The third stage is treated as a 'final check' of the equitableness of the line.[19]

In the *Territorial and Maritime Dispute Case (Nicaragua/Colombia)*[20] and the *Maritime Dispute Case (Peru/Chile)*,[21] cases involving a dispute between a Party to the UNCLOS 82 and a non-Party, the ICJ progressed on the basis that the provisions of Articles 74(1) and 83(1) of UNCLOS 82 were declaratory of customary international law, and proceeded to apply the equidistance/relevant circumstances method to delimit the respective Continental Shelves and EEZs of the disputing States. In the *Territorial and Maritime Dispute Case (Nicaragua/Columbia)*, although the ICJ pointed out that the equidistance/relevant circumstances should not be applied in a mechanical fashion and recognised that it would not be appropriate in every case to begin with this method,[22] it still applied the three-stage approach.[23] The Court rejected the argument of Nicaragua that it should not apply the three-stage approach in this case, but rather should apply a different methodology.[24] As far as the Court was concerned, the particular case was not one where the construction of the provisional median line was not feasible and it was of the view that the concerns raised by Nicaragua were factors to be considered at the second stage to determine if they were relevant circumstances requiring the adjustment or shifting of the provisional line.[25] It distinguished this case from the earlier case of the *Territorial and Maritime Dispute between Nicaragua and Honduras in the Caribbean Sea (Nicaragua v. Honduras)*.[26] The ICJ in the latter case did not apply the equidistance/relevant circumstances but rather applied the angle-bisector method. The Court, in the *Nicaragua v. Honduras* case, applied the angle-bisector method because geographical factors made the determination of the base points difficult, thus making the equidistance/relevant circumstances method inappropriate to achieve an equitable result.[27] Additionally, both Parties in this case, in contrast with the *Nicaragua/Columbia* case, were agreed that the three-stage methodology would not be the appropriate delimitation method to achieve an equitable result in the particular case.[28] According to the Court in this case:

> The jurisprudence of the Court sets out the reasons why the equidistance method is widely used in the practice of maritime delimitation: it has a certain intrinsic value because of its scientific character and the relative ease with which it can be applied. However, the equidistance method does not automatically have priority over other methods of delimitation and, in particular circumstances, there may be factors which make the application of the equidistance method inappropriate.[29]

It further said:

> [t]he use of a bisector – the line formed by bisecting the angle created by the linear approximations of coastlines – has proved to be a viable substitute method in certain circumstances where equidistance is not possible or appropriate. The justification for

> the application of the bisector method in maritime delimitation lies in the configuration of and relationship between the relevant coastal fronts and the maritime areas to be delimited.[30]

In essence, the Court appeared to indicate that the equidistance/relevant circumstances method was the preferred option for maritime delimitation, but when this would not achieve equitable results other methods may be utilised, with a preference for the angle-bisector method as substitute. In the *Maritime Dispute Case (Peru/Chile)*,[31] the ICJ applied the three-stage approach and described it as the 'usual methodology' for delimitation.[32]

The International Tribunal for the Law of the Sea (ITLOS), in *The Bay of Bengal Case (Bangladesh/Myanmar)*, while applying the three-stage methodology for the single-line delimitation of the Continental Shelves and EEZs of Bangladesh and Myanmar,[33] stated as follows:

> the issue of which method should be followed in drawing the maritime delimitation line should be considered in light of the circumstances of each case. The goal of achieving an equitable result must be the paramount consideration guiding the action of the Tribunal in this connection. Therefore the method to be followed should be one that, under the prevailing geographic realities and the particular circumstances of each case, can lead to an equitable result.[34]

Although Bangladesh proposed that the ITLOS employ the angle-bisector method, the ITLOS was of the view that, in the circumstances of the particular case, this was not an appropriate delimitation method.[35] Although recent jurisprudence appears to lean towards the three-stage methodology in maritime delimitation, Malcolm Evans, after exploring various international cases on international maritime delimitation, warns as follows:

> While it is relatively easy to identify the relevant elements of treaty and customary law concerning maritime boundary delimitation, the application of that law remains complex and perplexing. The oscillation between predictability and flexibility seems set to remain a feature of the jurisprudence … The 'equidistance versus equitable principles' debate has never gone away, nor is it ever likely to.[36]

While the catalogue of relevant circumstances that the international courts and tribunals consider in adjusting the provisional equidistance line are not closed, they include geographical factors, such as configuration of coasts, baselines, presence of islands and third States, geological and geomorphological factors; economic factors, such as the existence of natural resources and the level of the States' dependency on such resources;[37] conduct of the Parties; security, navigational and environmental factors.[38] Thus, in essence the international courts and tribunals do have wide discretion in determining what factors to consider in arriving at an equitable solution. In the Bakassi case, the ICJ applying the equidistance-relevant circumstances, at that time a two-stage process, considered the following relevant circumstances: concavity of the coastline, the presence of islands, the substantial difference in the lengths of the Parties' respective coastlines and the oil practice of the Parties. However, it did not regard these as relevant circumstances, based on the facts of the particular case that would necessitate the adjustment of the equidistance line in order to achieve an equitable solution. The Court pointed out that though in previous cases the concavity of the coastline, the presence of islands and the substantial difference in the lengths of coastlines had been regarded as relevant circumstances, this was not the case in the Bakassi case for the following reasons. First, the concavity of the coastline in this case did not fall within the sectors of the coastline relevant to the delimitation, but fell primarily within the sectors that affected the legal interest of a third State.[39] Second, the presence of an island – Bioko Island – in the presence case did not fall within the sovereignty of the disputing States, but rather within the sovereignty of a third State – Equatorial Guinea.[40] Third, the relevant coastline of Cameroon (the Claimant State) was not longer than that of Nigeria and thus was not an appropriate relevant circumstance that would justify a shift of the equidistance line in favour of Cameroon.[41] Finally, on whether the oil practices of the disputing States was a factor to be taken into consideration for the purposes of delimitation, the Court pointed out that oil concessions and oil wells were not in themselves to be considered as relevant circumstances that would justify the adjustment of the equidistance line. Nonetheless, after examining previous jurisprudence of the ICJ and Arbitral Tribunals, it indicated that the existence of an express or tacit agreement between the Parties on the siting of their oil concessions and oil wells could point to a consensus on the maritime areas they were entitled to.[42] However, the Court took the position that, in the Bakassi case, there was no tacit or express agreement between the Parties regarding oil concessions and oil wells, and thus it was not prepared to take the oil practice of the Parties into consideration in the maritime delimitation.[43]

Another key issue the ICJ delved into in the Bakassi case was the impact of third States on delimitation. Equatorial Guinea had applied under Article 62 of the Statute of the ICJ as a non-Party intervener, an application to which both Parties to the case had no objections.[44] The possibility of the decision of the Court having an impact on third States, namely, Equatorial Guinea (a non-Party intervener) and Sao Tome and Principe (which did not even intervene) obviously had an impact on the precise maritime boundaries the ICJ could delimit.[45] The Court had to refrain from making a decision on parts of the maritime boundary that would have an impact on Equatorial Guinea and Sao Tome and Principe. It would be recalled that Nigeria, as one of its objections in the preliminary stage of the case, had argued that the Court should refuse to carry out in whole or part the maritime delimitation as requested by Cameroon because the delimitation would have an impact on areas claimed by third States, notably Equatorial Guinea and Sao Tome.[46] However, the Court noted that this particular objection did not have 'an exclusively preliminary character' so it had to be deferred to the merit stage of the case.[47] Even though, at the merit stage of the case, the ICJ disagreed that the involvement of the rights of third States could in itself preclude the Court from having jurisdiction over the maritime delimitation, it conceded that it could not rule on the claims of Cameroon in so far as such ruling might affect the rights and legal interests of the third States, namely Equatorial Guinea and Sao Tome and Principe.[48] As far as the Court was concerned, the provision of Article 59 of the Statute of the ICJ would not sufficiently protect the two third States from the effects of a judgment that implicated their legal rights.[49] The core basis of this decision was the notion that the Court's jurisdiction was founded solely on the consent of the States Parties. Since the third States, in this case Equatorial Guinea and Sao Tome and Principe, had not consented to such delimitation, the ICJ was unable to rule on parts of the maritime boundary that would affect the rights of these third States.[50] It is important to emphasise that this position of the ICJ would apply when the third State(s) choose either to intervene as a non-Party intervener or not to intervene.[51] The situation would obviously be different if a third State, on being aware of the decision, chooses to intervene as a Party. In such instances, the jurisdiction of the Court over such third State would have to be founded on the consent of all the States Parties as indicated in Article 36 of the Statute of the ICJ.[52]

The ICJ in the Bakassi case did not accept Cameroon's contention that account should be taken of the coastline that included Cap Lopez in Gabon in the maritime delimitation. Further, the Court held that the base points for construction of the equidistance line could only be determined by reference to points on the coasts of the two disputing States in the case and not of third States. It also insisted that no account would be taken of Bioko Island, a constituent part of Equatorial Guinea, in determining relevant circumstances that would justify adjusting the equidistance line.[53] In addition, it refrained from extending the equidistant line beyond a point where it would affect the rights of Equatorial Guinea.[54] After determining that from point G the delimitation line moved in a westward direction joining point X and from the latter point continued southwards along the equidistance line, the Court decided that it could not extend this equidistance line very far because it might affect the rights of Equatorial Guinea. It was constrained by this to do no more than indicate the general direction of the equidistance line from point X without extending this to areas that may have an impact on Equatorial Guinea.[55] It is interesting to note that before the decision of the ICJ Nigeria entered into two bilateral treaties with Equatorial Guinea and Sao Tome and Principe respectively to seek to delimit its maritime boundary with these States and to enter into Joint Development Agreements (JDAs).[56] Besides, Equatorial Guinea and Sao Tome and Principe are currently having diplomatic talks on the possibility of creating a partnership for oil exploration on their common maritime boundary.[57]

Domestic law of the sea implications of the Bakassi case: reconfiguring Nigerian domestic maritime boundaries

Apart from the obvious law of the sea implications that the Bakassi case has had on nation-states' relations, especially as regard the delimitation of maritime boundaries of Cameroon and Nigeria, it also has had far-reaching implications on domestic maritime boundaries, especially on the Nigerian side. As a background, it is important to note that Nigeria, a Federal State, which is located on the western coast of Africa with a coastline of about 853 kilometres,[58] is made up of the central federal government and 36 States (referred to in this section as sub-States).[59] Initially eight of these sub-States immediately proximate to the coast were regarded as littoral States (hereinafter referred to as 'littoral sub-States').[60] In 2001, a major constitutional case was filed before the Supreme Court of Nigeria by the federal government against all the sub-States of the federation.[61] The case had to determine whether, for the purposes of calculating revenue derived from mineral resources exploited from the territory of a sub-State (popularly known as the derivation formula), as required by the Constitution,[62] the off-shore maritime zones within national jurisdiction (i.e. the Territorial Sea, Continental Shelf and Exclusive Economic Zone) should be regarded as part of the adjacent littoral sub-State for the purposes of the application of the derivation formula. After grappling with law of the sea issues arising by referring to UNCLOS 82, wading through a number of foreign cases dealing with the issue of 'ownership' of the offshore bed as between the central government and the sub-States, as well as reference to certain Colonial Orders in Council, the Supreme Court arrived at the decision that the derivation formula did not apply as regards offshore seabed within national jurisdiction adjacent to littoral sub-States.[63] In an attempt to douse the obvious emotive response to this decision of the Nigerian Supreme Court because of the far-reaching adverse financial implication for littoral sub-States, the federal government decided look towards a 'political solution' on the issue.[64] This eventually led to enactment of the Allocation of Revenue (Abolition of Dichotomy in the Application of the Principle of Derivation) Act, 2004, which states as follows:

> As from the commencement of this Act, the 200 meter water depth isobath contiguous to a State of the Federation shall be deemed to be a part of that State for the purposes of computing the Revenue accruing to the Federation Account from the State pursuant to the provisions of the Constitution of the Federal Republic of Nigeria, 1999 or any other enactment.[65]

This legislation generated a number of cases at the Supreme Court of Nigeria, such as *Attorney-General, Cross Rivers v. Attorney-General of the Federation*,[66] *Attorney-General, Adamawa State & 21 Ors v. Attorney-General of the Federation & 8 Ors* (a case between non-littoral sub-States in Nigeria and the federal government and littoral sub-States);[67] *Attorney-General, Rivers State v. Attorney-General Akwa-Ibom State & Attorney-General of the Federation*;[68] and *Attorney-General, Cross River State v. Attorney-General of the Federation & Attorney-General, Akwa Ibom State*.[69] These decisions were clear that the 2004 legislation applied only to littoral sub-States. According to Uwais CJN, who was then the Chief Justice of Nigeria, the essence of the legislation was that 'the extension deemed to have been given [by the Act] to the seaward boundary of the littoral [sub-States] is specifically for the purposes of computing the revenue … which accrues to the littoral [sub-States] from the Federation'.[70]

An interesting point to note, at this juncture, is that an attempt by counsel in a Nigerian Supreme Court case, *Attorney-General, Rivers State v. Attorney-General, Akwa Ibom State & Anor*,[71] dealing with the delimitation of internal maritime boundaries between littoral sub-States within Nigeria for the purposes of applying the offshore revenue derivation formula, to rely on the principles of international law on delimitation of maritime boundaries between nation-states, was rejected by the Nigerian Court. This is even though there is no specific domestic legislation in Nigeria that identifies a precise method for delimiting such internal maritime boundaries.[72] The Nigerian Supreme Court pointed out that the principles of delimitation of maritime boundaries as enunciated by the UNCLOS 82 and expatiated upon by international jurisprudence was not relevant to the delimitation of Nigerian internal maritime boundaries because the UNCLOS was only applicable to nation-states.[73] According to one of the Justices of the Supreme Court of Nigeria in this case, Onnoghen JSC, reading the lead judgment:

> it follows that all the beautiful submissions of both counsel on the principles/methods of International Law, including the United Nations Convention on the Law of the Sea, 1982 applicable to the delimitation of maritime territorial boundaries of nation States do not apply to the delimitation of the internal maritime boundaries of the littoral States within the Federal Republic of Nigeria, as in this case; be it the Strict Equidistance Line Method, Historical Title Method or any modification of them.[74]

Although the Nigerian Supreme Court was unwilling to accept that principles of international maritime delimitation were binding on it and applicable to the delimitation of internal maritime boundaries, the statement of one of the Justices of the Supreme Court seemed to suggest that she was not averse to using such principles for guidance in internal maritime delimitation cases. For instance, after rejecting the application of UNCLOS 82, she stated: '[t]he broad general principle of every maritime boundary dispute settlement is the achievement of an equitable solution consistent with domestic laws and practices'.[75] In this writer's view, this is a better approach. While the principles of delimitation of international maritime boundaries, in the absence of domestic legislation specifically incorporating this, certainly cannot be binding on the Nigerian courts, it could resort to such principles and international jurisprudence for guidance in seeking to achieve an equitable solution in internal maritime boundaries delimitation. Moreover, if it is accepted that Articles 15(1), 74(1) and 83(1) of UNCLOS are not merely conventional norms but are declaratory of customary international law,[76] since customary international law, in contrast with treaties,[77] applies automatically in Nigeria without the need for domestication by legislation, it could technically be argued that the equidistance/relevant circumstances as a methodology in delimitation of maritime boundaries is actually part of Nigerian law.[78]

The decision of the ICJ also had the significant impact of reducing the number of littoral sub-States in Nigeria, with concomitant impact on revenue sharing among the sub-States. Prior to the decision in the Bakassi case it was clear, as mentioned above, that there were eight littoral sub-States in Nigeria, but with the decision of the ICJ and the implementation of the decision, via the Greentree Agreement, it became unclear if one of such sub-States, Cross Rivers, still retained its status as a littoral sub-State and thus was still able to continue to receive revenue from offshore resources under the derivation formula, in line with the 2004 legislation mentioned above. This issue engaged the attention of the Supreme Court in two key cases, *Attorney-General, Cross Rivers v. Attorney-General of the Federation*,[79] leading to a 2005 decision of the Court, as well as the *Attorney-General, Cross River State v. Attorney-General of the Federation & Attorney-General, Akwa Ibom State*, in which the Court delivered its decision in 2012.[80]

In the 2005 decision, the Supreme Court had decided that the effect of the ICJ decision in the Bakassi case was that Cross Rivers no longer had a seaward boundary within the Nigerian maritime zones.[81] However, before the final handover of the Bakassi Peninsula, Nigeria had sought to negotiate with Cameroon to retain Western Bakassi and the Cross River estuarine, which would have allowed Cross Rivers to remain a littoral sub-State. In 2006 to resolve a dispute between Akwa Ibom, Rivers and Cross River sub-States as regards certain offshore oil wells within the Nigerian maritime zones for the purposes of determining entitlement to revenue, based on the derivation principle and the 2004 legislation, the then President of Nigeria, Olusegun Obasanjo, adopting a 'political' rather than legal solution, entered into an agreement dividing the offshore oil wells between the three sub-States. The allocation of certain offshore oil wells to Cross River was premised on the understanding that the federal government would be successful in its negotiations to retain Western Bakassi Peninsula and the Cross River estuarine, but this was unsuccessful as Cameroon insisted that all parts of the Peninsula remain as Cameroonian territory. Thus, after the final handover of Bakassi to Cameroon, in line with the ICJ decision and the Greentree Agreement, the Nigerian Boundary Commission adopted a 2008 maritime boundary delineation map reflecting that Cross River had ceased to be a littoral sub-State, for the purposes of the application of the derivation principle to offshore natural resources in Nigerian maritime zone in accordance with the 2004 legislation.[82] Cross River therefore filed the action that led to the 2012 decision, arguing that it retained its littoral status and it sought to rely on the 2006 Agreement as between the federal government, on the one hand, and Akwa Ibom, Rivers and Cross Rivers, on the other hand. This Agreement had been endorsed by the Supreme Court in a 2011 decision on *Attorney-General of Rivers State v. the Attorney-General of Akwa Ibom State and the Attorney-General of the Federation* as a valid one. However, in the 2012 decision, the Supreme Court held that the 2006 Agreement had been frustrated as regards Cross River State, which had ceased to be a littoral sub-State, because of the ICJ decision and the final transfer of Bakassi Peninsula, including Western Bakassi Peninsula and the Cross River estuarine, to Cameroon. In the lead judgment of the latter decision, one of the Justices of the Nigerian Supreme Court, Adekeye JSC, defined a littoral sub-State as one that is 'contiguous or abut[s] the sea' and having 'direct access to the sea through its own territory',[83] while another Justice of the Supreme Court, Rhodes-Vivour JSC, defined it as one 'adjacent to the shore, or lying along the shore, adjoining or bordering the shore'.[84] The Supreme Court was unanimous that Cross Rivers, which prior to the Bakassi Decision was a littoral State, had lost such status since the decision of the ICJ, as well as the subsequent implementation of the decision in line with the Greentree Agreement, had effectively transferred the Peninsula and the estuary to Cameroon.[85] According to the lead judgment of the Supreme Court, in this case, the status of Cross Rivers 'was changed irredeemably by the International Court of Justice judgement which found in favour of Cameroon in 2002' and the 'implementation and final execution of the judgement ... between 2006–2008'.[86] Furthermore, the lead judgment stated 'the ICJ judgement wiped off what used to be the estuarine sector of Cross River [sub-State] as a result of which [it] is hemmed in by the International boundary between Nigeria and Cameroon' and thus it 'no longer has any maritime boundary. It is landlocked.'[87] Another Justice of the Supreme Court, Galadima JSC, put it this way, that Cross Rivers 'used to be a Nigerian littoral [sub-State] but that was before [the] ICJ judgement redrew and redefined the maritime boundary between Nigeria and Cameroon'.[88] Furthermore, Rhodes-Vivour JSC, another Justice of the Court, pointed out emphatically that the littoral sub-States in Nigeria after the ICJ judgment are 'Lagos, Ogun, Ondo, Delta, Bayelsa, Rivers and Akwa Ibom', leaving out Cross Rivers.[89] He declared that

> [t]he judgement of the International Court of Justice (ICJ) took away Bakassi Peninsula from Nigeria (i.e. the Southern part of Cross Rivers State) and gave it to Cameroon. Bakassi is now Cameroonian territory. With that judgement, Cross River ... is no longer a littoral [sub-State]. [It] is now hemmed in. It is landlocked. It has no shoreline with the Atlantic Ocean.[90]

Even though this chapter, because of space constraints, does not intend to engage in a detailed discourse on the implications of the Bakassi Decision on the relationship between international law and domestic law, there is no doubt that these Supreme Court decisions on the littoral status of Cross River are far-reaching in a dualist system such as is operated in Nigeria.[91] First, the Supreme Court of Nigeria in these decisions appears to assume that the ICJ decision and the Greentree Agreement, a treaty that had not been domesticated, were automatically binding on it. The basis for this assumption is not clearly set out in the judgments, especially in view of the fact that, under the Nigerian Constitution, the Supreme Court of Nigeria is meant to be the final court in Nigeria and the National Assembly had not enacted the Greentree Agreement, a treaty, as law.[92] This raises the interesting point of whether this endorses a Nigerian state practice that ICJ decisions, especially those involving Nigeria, would be automatically binding in the Nigerian domestic legal system. Further, is this case a backing for the viewpoint that delimitation treaties are an exception to section 12(1) of the Nigerian Constitution and thus not required to be enacted as domestic law to be enforced? It interesting that the Supreme Court in this case was willing to accept that the littoral status of a sub-State in Nigeria had ceased, owing to the decision of the ICJ and its implementation, without an accompanying domestic legislation. Further, a careful perusal of the case appears to show that there was no real clarity on when the Cross River ceased to be a littoral sub-State. Should it have been when the ICJ gave its decision in 2002 or when the decision was fully implemented in 2008? The majority of the Supreme Court Justices appeared to take the view that the appropriate cut-off date when Cross River ceased to be a littoral sub-State was 2008, when the judgment was fully implemented.[93] One of the Justices taking this approach said: 'Cross River [sub-State] used to be a littoral up to 2008 when the ICJ judgment was fully implemented with the ceding of Cross River estuary and the physical handover of the entirety of Bakassi Peninsula by Nigeria to Cameroon.'[94] Surely, it should follow logically that the relevant cut-off date for Cross River losing its status should be 2002, when under international law, as decided by the ICJ, Bakassi legally belonged to Cameroon, and not 2008 when it was finally physically handed over to Cameroon. The only justice who appeared to endorse the 2002 cut-off date said: 'Cross River [sub-State] was qualified until the International Court of Justice judgment on 10/10/2002, but now it is no longer qualified since by that judgment it became a landlocked State.'[95] The reasoning of the majority of the Justices for choosing 2008 as the cut-off date is not convincing as legally the whole of the Bakassi Peninsula ceased to belong to Nigeria from the date of the ICJ judgment. It may only be presumed that their position was more of a policy decision, perhaps in the interest of fairness, that sought to preclude Cross River, which lost its littoral status through no fault of its own, from the burden of having to refund to the federation account the huge amount of revenue it was paid as a littoral sub-State between 2004 (when the derivation legislation was enacted) to 2008.

Territorial sea and innocent passage of warships

Almost immediately after the decision of the ICJ in the Bakassi case, the Nigerian federal government issued a statement with regard to the case.[96] In this statement, the federal government, under the heading 'access to Calabar', stated as follows:

> Whilst the effect of the Court's decision is to grant sovereignty over Bakassi to Cameroon, it does not affect the right of innocent passage enjoyed under international law by all vessels, including Nigerian navy vessels, travelling to and from the sea to the west of Bakassi, whether on the Nigerian or the Cameroonian side of the Maroua line.

This statement claims that the right to innocent passage, as regards what now becomes Cameroonian territorial sea, would apply to Nigerian warships as well. The silence on the issue of the need for prior notification or authorisation to exercise this right would seem to imply that Nigeria, at this point, did not endorse this requirement.[97] This is particularly stimulating since the subsequent Greentree Agreement, which identified that following the transfer of the Bakassi Peninsula (the Zone) there would be a special transitional regime for a non-renewable period of five years, appears to have excluded the innocent passage of Nigerian warships in the territorial sea of the Zone. The Agreement stated, among other things, that Cameroon would: '[a]llow innocent passage in the territorial waters of the Zone to civilian ships sailing under the Nigerian flag, consistent with the provisions of this agreement, to the exclusion of Nigerian warships'.[98] Eventually, the final transfer of authority in the Bakassi Peninsula by Nigeria to Cameroon was completed in August 2008 and the five-year non-renewal special transitional regime ended in August 2013.[99] Hence, this raises the issue of whether subsequent to the transitional regime the right to innocent passage now extends to Nigerian warships as well. Would Nigerian warships enjoy innocent passage in the territorial sea of the Bakassi Peninsula without the need of prior notification or consent of the Cameroonian Government? The question of whether or not warships enjoy the right to innocent passage in the territorial sea is particularly significant as the Nigerian eastern naval command has Calabar in Cross Rivers sub-State as its headquarters, which, as we see from discussions in the previous section, has ceased to have direct access to the sea because of the handing over of Bakassi Peninsula and Cross Rivers Estuary to Cameroon.[100] Thus, the Nigerian navy may have to transit the Cameroonian territorial sea to access certain parts of the Atlantic Ocean.

The issue of whether or not foreign warships enjoy the right to innocent passage in the territorial sea has not been settled in the law of the sea. In 1989, the USA and the former USSR adopted a joint statement on the Uniform Interpretation of Norms of International Law Governing Innocent Passage that insist '[a]ll ships, including warships, regardless of cargo, armament or means of propulsion, enjoy the right of innocent passage through the territorial sea in accordance with international law, for which neither prior notification nor authorization is required'.[101] Furthermore, Martin Tsamenyi and Kwame Mfodwo argue as follows:

> there are strong textual reasons for asserting that a requirement for either authorisation or notification would be inconsistent with the LOSC [Law of the Sea Convention]. A requirement for prior authorisation would be in clear conflict with the prohibition on coastal States imposing requirements that have the effect of 'denying or impairing the right of innocent passage'. Furthermore, articles of both the LOSC and the Convention on the Territorial Sea and Contiguous Zone relate to the navigation of submarines and non-compliance by warships with laws and regulations of coastal States, implying such a right of innocent passage. Indeed, the list of non-innocent passage contained in art. 19(2) clearly indicates that the activities in (a)–(f) are concerned primarily with warships, and would be superfluous if such a right of innocent passage did not exist.[102]

However, in spite of the 1989 statement between the USA and the former USSR (succeeded by Russia) and the arguments of Tsamenyi and Mfodwo, there is uncertainty as regards the actual position under international law. Churchill and Lowe identify that there are inconsistencies in state practices on if foreign warships enjoy the right to innocent passage in the territorial sea of another State and if so, whether they would be required to give prior notice or actually obtain the authorisation of the coastal State to transit through the latter's territorial sea.[103] Dupuy and Vignes point out that '[t]he existence of a right of innocent passage for warships is the most controversial point in the overall issue of innocent passage'.[104] In the UNCLOS 82, for instance, the various declarations made upon signature, ratification, accession or succession, or at a time thereafter, reflect the divergent positions of different States.[105] It is interesting to note that neither Cameroon nor Nigeria filed any declarations to the UNCLOS 82 stating what exactly their state practices are in this regard. The main divergence on the issue appears to be between States, which insist a warship, like any other ship, has the right to innocent passage in the territorial sea without the need for prior authorisation or notification by the flag State to the coastal State, on the one hand, and States insisting on such authorisation or notification, on the other hand. Very few States seem to insist that foreign warships do not enjoy the right of innocent passage in the territorial sea. It is therefore doubtful that Cameroon could continue to insist on entirely excluding Nigerian naval ships from exercising the right to innocent passage in their territorial sea. For one, the Nigerian navy could insist that its warships have an unfettered right to innocent passage in the Cameroonian territorial sea, including those around the Bakassi Peninsula, and protest any attempt by the Cameroonian Government to fetter this right. On the other hand, the Cameroonians could insist that Nigerian naval warships have no right to innocent passage. These two rather extreme options would result in heightened tension between the two States.

The most prominent State that insists that foreign warships require prior approval or authorisation before they are able to enjoy the right to innocent passage in its territorial sea is China.[106] This has inevitably resulted in tensions between China and other States, such as Australia and the USA, which take the view that foreign warships may traverse the territorial sea in exercise of the right of innocent passage without the need of prior authorisation by, or even prior notification of, the coastal State.[107] The issue is thus a critical security issue, which would need to be clarified as between Cameroon and Nigeria, especially with regard the territorial sea of the Bakassi Peninsula. Despite what appears to be posturing by the two States, especially immediately after the judgment in the case, a senior Nigerian naval officer disclosed to this author that the rights of innocent passage in the Bakassi waters by warships of both States 'have always been done in the spirit of good neighbourliness having due regard to the age-old commonalities between the citizens in the region'.[108] Thus, whenever Nigerian warships want to transit Cameroonian territorial sea in exercise of the right of innocent passage, prior notification would be given to the Cameroonian Government through the appropriate diplomatic channels. He insists that the Nigerian state practice, now, is that prior notification, and not necessarily prior consent or authorisation, is required of all warships transiting Nigerian territorial sea.[109] It would appear that there is a growing trend towards States, especially developing States, insisting on prior notification or authorisation before a foreign warship may exercise the right of innocent passage in their territorial seas.[110] Scholars such as Zou Keyuan, however, have argued that rather than to require foreign warships to have prior authorisation or approval of a coastal State before traversing the territorial sea in the exercise of the right to innocent passage, the requirement of mere prior notification may be more consistent with UNCLOS 82.[111] This author agrees with Zou Keyuan: the right of a warship to exercise the right of innocent passage with prior notification is more consistent with the UNCLOS. The core concern of the coastal State is to seek to ensure that security in its territorial sea is guaranteed. Thus, merely requiring the foreign warship to give prior notification would seem to be a reasonable midway standpoint that would avoid unnecessary tension when a warship wishes to transit the territorial sea of another State.

Concluding remarks

The Bakassi case has had significant implications on the law of the sea. Due to the constraint of space, this chapter has specifically focused on three key issues. First, it was a landmark case, in the sense of being the first ICJ decision to apply the relevant provisions of the UNCLOS 82 on the delimitation of the EEZ and Continental Shelf after the treaty came into force. It continued with what appears to be a move towards some level of predictability in international jurisprudence on maritime boundary delimitation by applying the equidistance/relevant circumstances methodology. This trend has continued in some international cases on maritime delimitation. Second, the domino effect of the decision is that it reconfigured the Nigerian maritime boundaries and resulted in a reduction in the number of littoral sub-States within the nation. From having eight littoral sub-States in Nigeria, the ICJ decision led to one of these sub-States, Cross River, losing its littoral status with regard to its right under the Constitution to obtain revenue from offshore exploitation of the nation's natural resources. Third, it has also again brought to the forefront the need to clarify the right of foreign warships to transit in the territorial sea of another State. The issue of whether a foreign warship has the right to innocent passage in the territorial sea of a coastal State, similar to other ships, or whether it needs to obtain the authorisation by the coastal State or give prior notification, is still a contested issue. It would appear that the Nigerian State has shifted from the position taken in a statement it issued immediately after the Bakassi Decision, which gave the impression that it was insistent that its warships had an unfettered right of innocent passage as provided for in the UNCLOS (Table 7.1), to one where it has adopted the state practice of recognising that foreign warships need to give prior notification before exercising the right to innocent passage in the territorial sea of a coastal State.

Table 7.1 Declarations in UNCLOS 82 on innocent passage of foreign warships in territorial sea[112]

Country	*Declaration*
Argentina	Upon ratification on 1 December 1995 stated: 'With regard to those provisions of the Convention which deal with innocent passage through the territorial sea, it is the intention of the Government of the Argentine Republic to continue to apply the regime currently in force to the passage of foreign warships through the Argentine territorial sea, since that regime is totally compatible with the provisions of the Convention.'
Bangladesh	Upon ratification on 27 July 2001 stated: 'The exercise of the right of innocent passage of warships through the territorial sea of other States should also be perceived to be a peaceful one. Effective and speedy means of communication are easily available and make the prior notification of the exercise of the right of innocent passage of warships reasonable and not incompatible with the Convention. Such notification is already required by some States. Bangladesh reserves the right to legislate on this point.'
Cabo Verde	Upon signature on 10 December 1982 and affirmed upon ratification on 19 August 1987 stated: 'This Convention recognizes the right of coastal States to adopt measures to safeguard their security interests, including the right to adopt laws and regulations relating to the innocent passage of foreign warships through their territorial sea or archipelagic waters. This right is in full conformity with articles 19 and 25 of the Convention, as it was clearly stated in the Declaration made by the President of the Third United Nations Conference on the Law of the Sea in the plenary meeting of the Conference on April 26, 1982.'
China	Upon ratification on 7 June 1996 stated: 'The People's Republic of China reaffirms that the provisions of the United Nations Convention on the Law of the Sea concerning innocent passage through the territorial sea shall not prejudice the right of a coastal State to request, in accordance with its laws and regulations, a foreign State to obtain advance approval from or give prior notification to the coastal State for the passage of its warships through the territorial sea of the coastal State.'

continued

Table 7.1 continued

Country	*Declaration*
Croatia	Upon succession on 5 April 1995 stated: 'The Republic of Croatia considers that, in accordance with article 53 of the Vienna Convention on the Law of Treaties of 29 May 1969, there is no peremptory norm of general international law which would forbid a coastal State to request by its laws and regulations foreign warships to notify their intention of innocent passage through its territorial waters, and to limit the number of warships allowed to exercise the right of innocent passage at the same time (articles 17 to 32 of the Convention).'
Ecuador	Upon ratification 24 September 2012 states: 'It declares that States whose warships, naval auxiliaries, or other vessels or aircraft that, subject to prior notification of and authorization by the Ecuadorian State, may pass through the maritime spaces subject to its sovereignty and jurisdiction, are liable for any damage they cause by polluting the marine environment, pursuant to articles 235 and 236 of the Convention.'
Egypt	Upon ratification on 26 August 1983 states 'Warships shall be ensured innocent passage through the territorial sea of Egypt, subject to prior notification.'
Finland	Upon signature on 10 December 1982 stated: 'As regards those parts of the Convention which deal with innocent passage through the territorial sea, it is the intention of the Government of Finland to continue to apply the present régime to the passage of foreign warships and other government-owned vessels used for non-commercial purposes through the Finnish territorial sea, that régime being fully compatible with the Convention.'
Germany	Upon succession stated: 'None of the provisions of the Convention, which in so far [as they] reflect existing international law, can be regarded as entitling the coastal State to make the innocent passage of any specific category of foreign ships dependent on prior consent or notification.'
Iran	Upon signature on 10 December 1982 stated: 'In the light of customary international law, the provisions of article 21, read in association with article 19 (on the Meaning of Innocent Passage) and article 25 (on the Rights of Protection of the Coastal States), recognize (though implicitly) the rights of the Coastal States to take measures to safeguard their security interests including the adoption of laws and regulations regarding, ***inter alia***, the requirements of prior authorization for warships willing to exercise the right of innocent passage through the territorial sea.'
Italy	Upon ratification on 13 January 1995 stated: 'None of the provisions of the Convention, which corresponds on this matter to customary international law, can be regarded as entitling the coastal State to make innocent passage of particular categories of foreign ships dependent on prior consent or notification.'
Malta	Upon ratification on 20 May 1993 stated: 'The exercise of the right of innocent passage of warships through the territorial sea of other States should also be perceived to be a peaceful one. Effective and speedy means of communication are easily available and make the prior notification of the exercise of the right of innocent passage of warships reasonable and not incompatible with the Convention. Such notification is already required by some States. Malta reserves the right to legislate on this point.'
Netherlands	Upon ratification on 28 June 1996 stated: 'The Convention permits innocent passage in the territorial sea for all ships, including foreign warships, nuclear-powered ships and ships carrying nuclear or hazardous waste, without any prior consent or notification, and with due observance of special precautionary measures established for such ships by international agreements.'

Country	*Declaration*
Oman	Upon ratification on 17 August 1989 stated: 'Innocent passage is guaranteed to warships through Omani territorial waters, subject to prior permission. This also applies to submarines, on condition that they navigate on the surface and fly the flag of their home State.'
Romania	Upon signature on 10 December 1982 and confirmed upon ratification on 17 December 1996 stated: 'Romania reaffirms the right of coastal States to adopt measures to safeguard their security interests, including the right to adopt national laws and regulations relating to the passage of foreign warships through their territorial sea.'
Sao Tome and Principe	Upon signature on 13 July 1983 stated: 'The Government of the Democratic Republic of Sao Tome and Principe reserves the right to adopt laws and regulations relating to the innocent passage of foreign warships through its territorial sea or its archipelagic waters and to take any other measures aimed at safeguarding its security.'
Serbia and Montenegro	Upon succession on 12 March 2001 stated: 'Proceeding from the right that States parties have on the basis of article 310 of the United Nations Convention on the Law of the Sea, the Government of the Socialist Federal Republic of Yugoslavia considers that a coastal State may, by its laws and regulations, subject the passage of foreign warships to the requirement of previous notification to the respective coastal State and limit the number of ships simultaneously passing, on the basis of the international customary law and in compliance with the right of innocent passage (articles 17 to 32 of the Convention).'
Sweden	Upon signature on 10 December 1982 stated: 'As regards those parts of the Convention which deal with innocent passage through the territorial sea, it is the intention of the Government of Sweden to continue to apply the present régime for the passage of foreign warships and other government-owned vessels used for non-commercial purposes through the Swedish territorial sea, that régime being fully compatible with the Convention.'
United Kingdom	Upon accession 25 July 1997 stated: 'The United Kingdom considers that declarations and statements not in conformity with articles 309 and 310 include, inter alia, the following: ... those which purport to require any form of notification or permission before warships or other ships exercise the right of innocent passage or freedom of navigation or which otherwise purport to limit navigational rights in ways not permitted by the Convention'.
Yemen	Upon ratification on 21 July 1987 stated: 'The People's Democratic Republic of Yemen will give precedence to its national laws in force which require prior permission for the entry or transit of foreign warships or of submarines or ships operated by nuclear power or carrying radioactive materials.'

Notes

1 The author expresses his special thanks to Prince Emmanuel for his support and inspiration: he is a friend who sticks closer than a brother does. All opinions expressed and any errors, however, are solely the author's. Email: EgedeE@cardiff.ac.uk.

2 Para. 1 of *Land and Maritime Boundary between Cameroon and Nigeria (Cameroon v. Nigeria: Equatorial Guinea intervening)*, Judgment, *ICJ Reports* 2002, p. 303 (hereinafter referred to as the Bakassi Decision on merits). See www.icj-cij.org/docket/files/94/7203.pdf. For discourse on the sovereignty over land territories in this case, see Tanaka's chapter in this book (Chapter 6).

3 Para. 3, ibid.

4 Para. 238 of the Bakassi Decision on merits.
5 *Land and Maritime Boundary between Cameroon and Nigeria*, Application to Intervene, Order of 21 October 1999, *ICJ Reports* 1999, p. 1029; and Para. 18, ibid.
6 Yoshifumi Tanaka, *The International Law of the Sea* (Cambridge: Cambridge University Press, 2015, second edition), at 196.
7 Paras 210, 226, 262–268 of the Bakassi Decision on merits.
8 Para. 269, ibid.
9 Paras 276, 285 and 286, ibid. Maritime boundary delimitation by its very nature cannot be done unilaterally, but necessarily involves two or more States. This was highlighted by the Chamber of the International Court of Justice in the *Delimitation of the Maritime Boundary in the Gulf of Maine Area (Canada v. United States of America)* [1984] *ICJ Rep.*, p. 299 at para. 112, where the Court said: 'No maritime delimitation between States with opposite or adjacent coasts may be effected unilaterally by one of those States.'
10 See para. 268 of the Bakassi Decision on merits. Also see Arts 74(1) and 83(1) of UNCLOS 82 and Yoshifumi Tanaka, 'Reflections on Maritime Delimitation in the Cameroon/Nigeria Case' (2004) 53(2) *International and Comparative Law Quarterly*, p. 369 at 373; and Pieter Bekker, 'Land and Maritime Boundary between Cameroon and Nigeria (Cameroon v. Nigeria: Equatorial Guinea Intervening)' (2003) 97(2) *American Journal of International Law*, p. 387 at 392–394.
11 See paras 285, 288 and 290. Both States – Cameroon and Nigeria – are States Parties to the UNCLOS 82. See Tanaka, ibid., at 369, 371–376, 388–393; and Bekker, ibid., at 394–395.
12 Tanaka, *The International Law of the Sea*, second edition, op. cit., at 205.
13 Tanaka, 'Reflections on Maritime Delimitation in the Cameroon/Nigeria Case', op. cit., at 389.
14 Ibid. at 381–393.
15 See, for example, Prosper Weil, *The Law of Maritime Delimitation: Reflections* (translated from the French by Maureen MacGlashan) (Cambridge: Grotius, 1989); M.D. Evans, *Relevant Circumstances and Maritime Delimitation* (Oxford: Clarendon, 1989); J.L. Charney, 'Progress on International Maritime Boundary Delimitation Law' (1994) 88 *American Journal of International Law*, pp. 227–256; Y. Tanaka, *Predictability and Flexibility in the Law of Maritime Delimitation* (Oxford: Hart Publishing, 2006); and T. Cottier, *Equitable Principles of Maritime Boundary Delimitation: The Quest for Distributive Justice in International Law* (Cambridge: Cambridge University Press, 2015).
16 See Tanaka, *The International Law of the Sea*, second edition, op. cit., at 196–228; and see generally Tanaka, *Predictability and Flexibility*, ibid.
17 *ICJ Reports* 2009, p. 61 at 101–130. See Robin Churchill, 'The Bangladesh/Myanmar Case: Continuity and Novelty in the Law of Maritime Boundary Delimitation' (2012) 1(1) *Cambridge Journal of International and Comparative Law*, p. 137 at 141–146.
18 Churchill, ibid., at 141.
19 Stephen Fietta and Robin Cleverly, *A Practitioner's Guide to Maritime Boundary Delimitation* (Oxford: Oxford University Press, 2016, first edition), Part A, Chapter 2(II). They point out that, interestingly, the international case law so far had not led to further adjustment of the equidistance line with the application of the third stage of the three-stage process.
20 Judgment, *ICJ Reports* 2012, p. 624 at paras 138–139 and 190–194.
21 Judgment, *ICJ Reports* 2014, p. 3 at paras 178–180 and 189.
22 Para. 194.
23 Para. 199.
24 Nicaragua had argued that the Court should apply the so-called enclave methodology; ibid. at paras 185–186 and 194–195.
25 Paras 195–197, ibid.
26 Judgment, *ICJ Reports* 2007, p. 659, at p. 741, para. 271.
27 Paras 265 and 287.
28 Para. 273–275.
29 Para. 272.
30 Para. 276.
31 Supra at note 20.
32 Para. 187.
33 Paras 239 and 240.

34 Para. 235.

35 Paras 236–237.

36 Malcolm D. Evans, 'Maritime Boundary Delimitation', in Donald R. Rothwell, Alex G. Oude Elferink, Karen N. Scott and Tim Stephens (eds), *The Oxford Handbook of the Law of the Sea* (Oxford: Oxford University Press, 2015), Chapter 12, p. 254 at 278. Evans in this chapter suggests that the equidistance vs equitable principles debates tend to obscure other debates that ought to be taking place, such as those on the relationship between inner and outer Continental Shelf and the influence of certain significant factors on delimitation that are not currently regarded as relevant circumstances.

37 It is important to note that, to this date, this factor has not been regarded as a relevant circumstance in the jurisprudence.

38 Tanaka, *The International Law of the Sea*, second edition, op. cit., pp. 209–224. Also, it is crucial to point out that to this date, environmental factor has not been regarded as a relevant circumstance in the jurisprudence.

39 Para. 297.

40 Para. 299.

41 Para. 301.

42 Such as the *Case Concerning the Continental Shelf (Tunisia/Libyan Arab Jamahiriya) ICJ Reports* 1982, p. 18; *Case Concerning Delimitation of the Maritime Boundary in the Gulf of Maine Area (Canada/United States of America) ICJ Reports* 1984, p. 310; *Case Concerning the Continental Shelf (Libyan Arab Jamahiriya/Malta) ICJ Reports* 1985, p. 13; *Guinea/Guinea Bissau* case, *ILM* Vol. 25 (1986), p. 281, para. 63; and *Case Concerning Delimitation of Maritime Areas between Canada and the French Republic (St Pierre et Miquelon) ILM*, Vol. 31 (1992), pp. 1174–1175, paras 89–91.

43 Para. 304.

44 *Case Concerning the Land and Maritime Boundary between Cameroon and Nigeria (Cameroon v. Nigeria)*, Application by Equatorial Guinea for Permission to Intervene, Order of 21 October 1999, www.icj-cij.org/docket/files/94/7449.pdf.

45 See summary of Equatorial Guinea arguments as a non-Party intervener at para. 284 of the Bakassi Decision on merits.

46 Paras 226–236 of case on merits and paras 115–117 of *Land and Maritime Boundary between Cameroon and Nigeria*, Preliminary Objections, Judgment, *ICJ Reports* 1998, p. 275.

47 Para. 237 of merits case.

48 Paras 231 and 238, ibid.

49 Para. 238, ibid.

50 Ibid.

51 In this case, Equatorial Guinea chose to intervene as a non-Party intervener while Sao Tome and Principe did not intervene at all. See, however, the *Case Concerning the Continental Shelf (Tunisia/Libyan Arab Jamahiriya)*, Application by Malta for Permission to Intervene, ICJ Judgment of 14 April 1981, paras 33 to 36; the ICJ refused to allow Malta to intervene in the case because the interest of a legal nature it invoked was not considered to be one 'which may be affected by the decision in the case within the meaning of Article 62 of the Statute of the ICJ', and also the Court was not convinced that the direct yet limited form of participation for which Malta sought permission fell within the terms of intervention under Article 62. Contrast this with paras 103–105, *Case Concerning the Land, Island and Maritime Frontier Dispute (El Salvador/Honduras)*, Application by Nicaragua for Permission to Intervene, ICJ Judgment of 13 September 1990.

52 Paras 93–101 *Case Concerning the Land, Island and Maritime Frontier Dispute (El Salvador/Honduras)*, Application by Nicaragua for Permission to Intervene, ICJ Judgment of 13 September 1990.

53 Paras 290–291 and 299.

54 Para. 292.

55 Para. 307.

56 See Treaty between the Federal Republic of Nigeria and the Republic of Equatorial Guinea concerning their maritime boundary, 23 September 2000 (entry into force: 3 April 2002) and the Protocol on implementation of Article 6.2 of the Treaty between the Federal Republic of Nigeria and the Republic of Equatorial Guinea concerning their maritime boundary, 2 April 2002 (entry into force: 29 June 2002). The 2000 treaty states *inter alia* as follows:

> The purpose of this Treaty is to establish the partial maritime boundary between the Federal Republic of Nigeria and the Republic of Equatorial Guinea described in Article 2, and provide for the remainder of the maritime boundary in accordance with Article 3.
>
> (Art. 1)
>
> Northwards and eastwards from Point (i) identified in Article 2 the maritime boundary shall be established by the Contracting Parties, and recorded in a Protocol to this *Treaty*, following completion of the maritime aspects of the case before the International Court of Justice between the Federal Republic of Nigeria and the Republic of Cameroon, concerning the land and maritime frontier between them.
>
> (Art. 3)
>
> (1) Should the maritime boundary established by this *Treaty* run through any field of hydrocarbon deposits so that part of the field lies on the Nigerian side of the boundary and part lies on the Equatorial Guinea side, the Contracting Parties shall seek to reach appropriate unitisation arrangements for each such field. (2) In implementing paragraph 1 of this Article within the area formed by straight lines connecting points (ii), (iii), (iv) and (v) set forth in Article 2, the Contracting Parties shall authorise the relevant government entities in association with the relevant concession holders to establish appropriate unitisation and other arrangements to enable this area to be developed in a commercially feasible manner. Such arrangements shall not be effective until the entry into force of this Treaty.
>
> (Art.6)

Also the Treaty between the Federal Republic of Nigeria and the Democratic Republic of Sao Tome and Principe on the Joint Development of Petroleum and other Resources, in respect of Areas of the Exclusive Economic Zone of the Two States, 21 February 2001, which states, *inter alia*:

> The Zone is hereby established as an area of joint development by the States Parties in accordance with, and for the purposes set out in, this Treaty.
>
> (Art. 2.1)
>
> (4.1) Nothing contained in this Treaty shall be interpreted as a renunciation of any right or claim relating to the whole or any part of the Zone by either State Party or as recognition of the other State Party's position with regard to any right or claim to the Zone or any part thereof. (4.2) No act or activities taking place as a consequence of this Treaty or its operation, and no law operating in the Zone by virtue of this Treaty, may be relied on as a basis for asserting, supporting or denying the position of either State Party with regard to rights or claims over the Zone or any part thereof.
>
> (Art. 4)

On Cameroon's negotiations with these third States on maritime delimitations see Nkwelle Ekaney's chapter in this book (Chapter 4) and for more on JDAs see Chapter 9 of this book.

57 See 'Equatorial Guinea Proposes Oil Exploration Partnership with Sao Tome and Principe', 19 October 2015, http://macauhub.com.mo/2015/10/19/equatorial-guinea-proposes-oil-exploration-partnership-with-sao-tome-and-principe/; and 'São Tomé and Equatorial Guinea Reactivate Partnership for Oil Exploration', 26 October 2016, http://macauhub.com.mo/2016/10/26/sao-tome-and-equatorial-guinea-reactivate-partnership-for-oil-exploration/.

58 See CIA, *The World Factbook 2017*, www.cia.gov/library/publications/the-world-factbook/geos/ni.html.

59 See sections 2 and 3 of the 1999 Constitution of the Federal Republic of Nigeria.

60 Akwa-Ibom, Bayelsa, Cross River, Delta, Lagos, Ogun, Ondo and Rivers.

61 *Attorney-General of the Federation v. Attorney-General of Abia State & 35 Ors* [2002] 6 *NWLR* (part 764), 542.

62 Section 162(2) of the 1999 Constitution states:

> The President, upon the receipt of advice from the Revenue Mobilisation Allocation and Fiscal Commission, shall table before the National Assembly proposals for revenue allocation from the Federation Account, and in determining the formula, the National Assembly shall take into account, the allocation principles especially those of population, equality of States, internal revenue generation, land mass, terrain as well as population density. Provided that

> the principle of derivation shall be constantly reflected in any approved formula as being not less than thirteen per cent of the revenue accruing to the Federation Account directly from any natural resources.

For an analysis of historical background of the derivation principle, See K. Ebeku, 'Nigerian Supreme Court and Ownership of Offshore Oil' (2003) 27 *Natural Resources Forum*, pp. 291–299.

63 See this author's article criticising the decision, Edwin Egede, 'Who Owns the Nigerian Offshore Seabed: Federal or States? An Examination of the *Attorney General of the Federation v. Attorney General of Abia State & 35 Ors* Case' (2005) 49 *Journal of African Law*, pp. 73–93.

64 Ibid. at 91–93.

65 Section 1(1). Professor Patrick Vrancken is of the view that this wording is somewhat problematical. He points out that an isobath is a line and there seems to be little purpose in proclaiming that a line is part of a State. He suggests that this provision would perhaps be clearer if it reads something like: 'the seabed and its subsoil up to the 200 meter water depth isobath ... shall be deemed a part of that State'. The communication in this regard of Professor Vrancken is on file with the author.

66 [2005] 15 *NWLR* (Part 947), 71.

67 [2005] 18 *NWLR* (Part 958), 581.

68 [2011] 8 *NWLR* (Part 1248), 31.

69 [2012] 16 *NWLR* (Part 1327), 425.

70 [2005] 18 *NWLR* (Part 958), 581 at 637.

71 [2011] 8 *NWLR* (Part 1248), 31.

72 The only Nigerian legislation that deals with delimitation of maritime boundaries is the Nigerian Exclusive Economic Zone Act no. 28 of 1978, which focuses on the delimitation of the Nigerian EEZ with neighbouring nation-states, states that

> Notwithstanding subsection (1) of this section but subject to the provisions of any treaty or other written agreement between Nigeria and any neighbouring littoral State, the delimitation of the Exclusive Zone between Nigeria and any such State shall be the median or equidistance line.
>
> (Section 1[2])

It goes on to state:

> For the purposes of this section, 'the median or equidistance line' means the line every point of which is equidistant from the nearest points of the baselines from which the breadth of the territorial waters of Nigeria and the State concerned are measured.
>
> (Section 1[3])

73 Ibid. at p. 104.

74 Ibid. at 105. Justice Onnoghen has since been appointed as the Chief Justice of the Supreme Court of Nigeria. See also Fabiyi JSC at 155 and Adekeye JSC at 176.

75 Ibid. at 182. Per Adekeye JSC. This appears to be in line with Articles 74(1) and 83(1) of UNCLOS 82. Article 74(1), which is similar to Article 83(1) applicable to the Continental Shelf, states:

> [t]he delimitation of the exclusive economic zone between States with opposite or adjacent coasts shall be effected by agreement on the basis of international law, as referred to in Article 38 of the Statute of the International Court of Justice, in order to achieve an equitable solution.

76 See *Case Concerning Maritime Delimitation and Territorial Questions between Qatar and Bahrain (Qatar/Bahrain)* [2001] *ICJ Rep.*, p. 40 at paras 174–177 (Art. 15 of UNCLOS 82) and the *Territorial and Maritime Dispute Case (Nicaragua/Colombia)*, op. cit., and *Maritime Dispute Case (Peru/Chile)*, op. cit. (Arts 74 and 83 of UNCLOS 82). (See notes 20 and 21 above.)

77 See section 12(1) of the Nigerian 1999 Constitution, which states: 'No treaty between the federation and any other country shall have the force of law except to the extent to which any such treaty has been enacted into law by the National Assembly.'

78 In an earlier Supreme Court of Nigeria case of *Ibidapo v. Lufthansa Airlines*, Wali JSC had explained, 'Nigeria, like any other Commonwealth country, inherited the English common law

rules governing the municipal application of international law.' Also see the English cases of *Buvot v. Babuit* (1737) cases t. Talbot 281; *Triquet v. Bath* (1764) 3 Burr. 1478; *Trendtex Trading Corporation v. Central Bank of Nigeria* [1977] 2 *WLR* 356; *R v. Bow Street Magistrate*, Ex parte Pinochet (No 3) [1999] 2 *WLR* 827 HL (E). See Edwin Egede, 'Bringing Human Rights Home: An Examination of the Domestication of Human Rights Treaties in Nigeria' (2007) 51(2) *Journal of African Law*, p. 249 at 250–251 and 276–278.

79 [2005] 15 *NWLR* (Part 947), 71.

80 [2012]16 *NWLR* (Part 1327), 425.

81 (2005)15 *NWLR* (Part 947), 77.

82 One of the functions of the Nigeria Boundary Commission is to 'define, and delimitate boundaries between States, Local Government Areas or communities in the Federation and between Nigeria and her neighbours in accordance with delimitation instrument or document established for that purpose'. See section 7(c) of the National Boundary Commission Act 2006, http://lawnigeria.com/LawsoftheFederation/National-Boundary-Commission-(Establishment)-Act,-2006.html.

83 [2012] *supra* at 475. See also Musdapher JSC, [2012] 16 *NWLR* (Part 1327) at 481.

84 Ibid. at 511.

85 Ibid. at 469 and 479.

86 Ibid. at 476.

87 Ibid.

88 Ibid. at 505.

89 Ibid. at 514.

90 Ibid. at 512.

91 Section 12(1) of the Nigerian 1999 Constitution (see note 77). See Edwin Egede, 'Bringing Human Rights Home: An Examination of the Domestication of Human Rights Treaties in Nigeria' op. cit. pp. 249–284 for an analysis of this section of the Nigerian Constitution in relation to human rights treaties.

92 The Supreme Court of Nigeria is the ultimate court in Nigeria under the Nigerian Constitution. See Chapter VII of the 1999 Nigerian Constitution.

93 [2012] *supra*, Adekeye JSC, who read the lead judgment, at pp. 473 and 479; Musdapher JSC at p. 482; Mohammed JSC at pp. 484–485; Fabiyi JSC at p. 490; Galadima JSC at p. 510 and Ngwuta JSC at pp. 517–518 (appeared to regard the cut-off point when Cross River ceased to be a littoral sub-State as 2008 when the decision was fully implemented). However, Rhodes Vivour JSC at 514 appeared to take the cut-off point as 2002 when the ICJ delivered its judgment.

94 Adekeye JSC, at p. 473.

95 Rhodes JSC, at p. 514.

96 Statement of the Federal Government of Nigeria on the Judgement of The International Court of Justice at The Hague (*Cameroon v. Nigeria with Equatorial Guinea Intervening*), Abuja, 24 October 2002.

97 Edwin Egede, 'The Nigerian Territorial Waters Legislation and the 1982 Law of the Sea Convention' (2004) 19(2) *International Journal of Marine and Coastal Law*, pp. 151 at 166–168, where the author, referring to the Statement of the Nigerian Government, arrives at this conclusion since there is no specific legislation that gives an indication of Nigerian state practice on this.

98 See Annex 1 of the Greentree Agreement entered into on 12 June 2006, para. 4(d).

99 The Final Authority transferring Bakassi Peninsula to Cameroon was done on 14 August 2008, www.un.org/press/en/2008/sgsm11745.doc.htm.

100 The Nigerian navy has five commands headed by Flag Officers Commanding (FOCs) and five autonomous units. The commands are made up of three operational commands, namely: Western, Eastern and Central Naval Commands (WNC, ENC and CNC) which are responsible for the protection and policing of the nation's maritime environment; a Naval Training Command (NAVTRAC); and a Logistics Command (LOG COMD). The autonomous units are the Nigerian Naval Dockyard (NND), Nigerian Naval Shipyard (NNSY), the Naval Ordnance Depot (NOD), Nigerian Navy Holdings Limited (NNHL) and Naval Doctrine and Assessment Centre (NDAC). See www.navy.mil.ng/Commands#ENC.

101 Para. 2 of 1989 USA–USSR: Joint Statement with Attached Uniform Interpretation of Rules of International Law Governing Innocent Passage, adopted at Wyoming, USA, on 23 September

1989, See Office of Ocean Affairs and the Law of the Sea, *Law of the Sea Bulletin* No. 14 of December 1989, www.un.org/depts/los/doalos_publications/LOSBulletins/bulletinpdf/bulE14.pdf.

102 Martin Tsamenyi and Kwame Mfodwo, 'Analysis of Contemporary and Emerging Navigational Issues in the Law of the Sea', Royal Australian Navy Sea Power Centre and Centre for Maritime Policy, Working Paper No. 8, November 2001, at pp. 20–22, www.navy.gov.au/sites/default/files/documents/Working_Paper_8.pdf.

103 R.R. Churchill and A.V. Lowe, *The Law of the Sea* (Dartmouth: Manchester University Press, 1999), pp. 88–92. Also see Gamaliel Rodriguez Ballester, 'The Right of Innocent Passage of Warships: A Debated Issue' (2014–2015) 54 *Revista De Derecho Puertorriqueno*, pp. 87–118.

104 Rene-Jean Dupuy and Daniel Vignes, *A Handbook on the New Law of the Sea, Vol. 2* (Dordrecht: Martinus Nijhoff, 1991), p. 929.

105 See Appendix 7.1 to this chapter for declarations of States Parties to the UNCLOS 82 on the innocent passage of warships.

106 See Zou Keyuan, 'Innocent Passage for Warships: The Chinese Doctrine and Practice' (1998) 29 *Ocean Development and International Law*, pp. 195–223; Erik Franckx, 'American and Chinese Views on Navigational Rights of Warships' (2011) 10 *Chinese Journal of International Law*, pp. 187–206; and Anh Duc Ton, 'Innocent Passage of Warships' (2016) 1 *Asia-Pacific Journal of Ocean Law and Policy*, pp. 210–243.

107 Anh Duc Ton, ibid., at 220–221.

108 The communication in this regard with the senior Nigerian naval officer is on file with the author.

109 Ibid.

110 See Appendix 7.1 and Anh Duc Ton, op. cit., at pp. 216–236. See also Republic of Latvia Procedures, by which Foreign Warships shall Enter and Stay in the Territorial Sea, Inland Waters, and Ports of the Republic of Latvia and Leave Them, Cabinet Regulation No. 08 Adopted 23 February 2016, www.vvc.gov.lv/export/sites/default/docs/LRTA/Citi/Cab._Reg._No._108_-_Foreign_Warships_shall_Enter_and_Stay_in_the_Territorial_Sea.pdf.

111 Keyuan, 'Innocent Passage for Warships', op. cit., at 205.

112 See https://treaties.un.org/Pages/ViewDetailsIII.aspx?src=TREATY&mtdsg_no=XXI-6&chapter=21&Temp=mtdsg3&clang=_en.

8 The ICJ Bakassi Decision

Prospects and implications for the exploitation of petroleum resources in contested waters

Mark Osa Igiehon[1]

Introduction

Among the many border disputes that Cameroon and Nigeria have had in the years since independence, the dispute over the Bakassi Peninsula stands out very clearly as the most serious dispute of all. That portion of the disputed border between Cameroon and Nigeria increased in attention particularly as it became apparent that the Bakassi area was very rich in oil and natural gas.

Geographically speaking, the entire area forms part of the Delta of the River Niger, which is blessed with prodigious oil and gas reservoirs. Nigeria was first in exploring and exploiting the resources of its section of the Niger Delta while Cameroon and Equatorial Guinea came later. As at 1997, it was estimated that 96 per cent of the geographic Niger Delta's recoverable petroleum (oil and gas) was in Nigeria, with 3.5 per cent in Cameroon and 0.5 per cent in Equatorial Guinea.[2]

The contest between Nigeria and Cameroon has lasted decades and from time to time degenerated to a show of arms and military conflict, which left many dead and wounded on both sides. From time to time, clashes occurred on the lands adjacent the peninsula, on the peninsula itself and on the sea.[3] The immediate focus that faced both nations was sovereignty and entitlement to the mineral-rich peninsula.[4] Both countries exercised forms of occupations, although Nigeria's occupation was most effective.[5]

The conflict was itself, in part, a legacy of both the imperialist European colonial division rule era and the neo-colonial regimes in Africa. European colonial powers like Portugal, Germany, France and Britain deployed economic, political and strategic calculations in the nineteenth century, in their quest to divide up Africa and access its resources. In doing so, there was arguably near complete disregard for the power and cultural structures of pre-colonial states. The colonial scramble for and division of Africa, and the ensuing colonial era administration, largely established the foundation for future conflict across post-colonial Africa. The foundation for dysfunction and conflict within Africa was perhaps inadvertently prepared through practices such as the divide-and-rule system of administration; and the partitioning of African States and her peoples without regard for pre-colonial arrangements; and lack of regard for the damage caused and the destructive impact on the peoples' language, institutions, socio-political life, cultural connections and ancestral lineage. The behaviour of the arguably self-seeking European colonial powers at that time divided ethnic groups into territories controlled by the colonial powers and in many cases without any regard for history, culture and homogeneity. Thus was the foundation set for much of the dysfunction and conflicts across Africa today.[6]

In this chapter, we examine the implications of the ICJ's Bakassi Decision for exploitation of oil and gas in disputed waters; we also examine a number of other maritime boundary disputes which like the Bakassi Dispute, carry one common feature – the presence of rich petroleum reserves in contested waters. We consider both the positive implications for other disputes as well as the complications emanating from the ICJ Decision.

Toxic mix of maritime boundary disputes and contest for access to petroleum resources

It would appear and the author contends that long-simmering maritime boundary disputes become toxified when mixed with the presence of rich petroleum and mineral resources in the disputed areas. The Bakassi Peninsula dispute, though with long historical origins, in later years became even more protracted as a contest between Cameroon and Nigeria for access to the rich petroleum reserves of the Bakassi waters. Oil became the main driving force underlying the dispute over the Bakassi Peninsula.[7] By the time the matter was referred to the ICJ, there were already US, Swiss and French oil companies eyeing the deposits and keenly awaiting the decision of the International Court of Justice.[8]

It is also to be noted that long before the discovery of oil in Bakassi, Cameroonians and Nigerians in the region lived in harmony despite a few minor disagreements from time to time. Both nations for a long time viewed the Bakassi area as remote and their governments largely ignored the Bakassi people and region. When oil and other natural resources were discovered in the peninsula and it became apparent that the area could potentially yield large economic gains, attention from both nations and their colonial connections was ignited, resulting in tension, arguments and, in some cases, violent military clashes. One could therefore argue that if oil had never been discovered in the region, both nations may not have clashed so violently and perhaps the dispute would not have been sent to the ICJ.[9] Similar arguments could be made about the pending Kenya and Somalia dispute.

As with the dispute between Cameroon and Nigeria for access to the oil-rich Bakassi waters, some of the oil-bearing nations of Africa have, at some point, become involved in maritime boundary disputes with their neighbours.

Dispute between Somalia and Kenya over the oil-rich East African coast

Presently there is a long-running maritime boundary dispute between Kenya and Somalia over entitlement to the potentially oil-rich reserves off their East African coasts. The maritime dispute is pitched over the respective entitlement to territorial sea and continental shelf. In 2009, Kenya and Somalia reached agreement by means of a Memorandum of Agreement (2009 MOU). They agreed to demarcate the disputed waters by negotiated means. However, Somalia, which at the time lacked an effective government, through its parliament rejected the 2009 MOU reached with Kenya.

A significant but understated complicating factor of the dispute is the fact that the waters are potentially rich in petroleum resources, especially as East Africa has become an attractive and newly emerging petroleum province. Although the Somalia and Kenya maritime boundary delimitation dispute goes as far back as 1972, it would appear that the trend noted earlier of East Africa becoming the newest petroleum-rich province, mixed with the strong interest of international oil companies (IOCs) to secure oil blocks off the coasts of East African States, has transformed a long-simmering boundary argument into a toxic dispute with clear and present pressure on Kenya to access the resources of the disrupted waters.

Following the MOU with Somalia, Kenya was disposed to proceeding on the basis of the 2009 MOU. It went forward to create oil blocks and issued exploitation licences to a number of multinationals, including licences over the particular maritime area which is the core of the dispute between the two States.

In 2015, Somalia filed action before the ICJ asking for maritime delimitation of the territorial sea and continental shelf with Kenya. Kenya has attempted to have the dispute resolved by arbitration but Somalia has insisted on pursuing delimitation through the ICJ. Kenya formally objected to the ICJ's jurisdiction on the principal basis that the 2009 MOU constituted an exclusive agreement by Somalia and Kenya to settle the maritime boundary dispute by negotiation, after the Commission on the Limits of the Continental Shelf (CLCS) had reverted on the respective claims of both States. Kenya therefore argued that the 2009 MOU excluded recourse to the ICJ for maritime boundary delimitation. By its February 2017 judgment, the ICJ rejected Kenya's preliminary objections and assumed jurisdiction of the maritime boundary dispute on the principal basis that though the MOU expressed the expectation of both States as to one method (CLCS, then negotiation) to reach agreement on the delimitation of their continental shelf, the MOU did not constitute an agreement that imposed an exclusive obligation on the parties to delimit their maritime boundary by only one method, and therefore that recourse to the jurisdiction of the ICJ was not precluded.[10]

Dispute between Ghana and Côte d'Ivoire over oil-rich waters

The sudden transformation of the long-standing maritime boundary disagreement between Ghana and Côte d'Ivoire into a toxic dispute bears similarities with the evolution of the Kenya and Somalia maritime boundary dispute. Ghana's sudden transformation into a significant petroleum-producing State would appear to have converted the long-simmering maritime boundary delimitation dispute with Côte d'Ivoire, into a toxic conflict, with each State seeking an early resolution to its own benefit in order that it could access the rich petroleum reserves of the waters in dispute.

In September 2014, Ghana formally filed action against Côte d'Ivoire before the International Tribunal for the Law of the Sea (ITLOS). Côte d'Ivoire responded and requested in February 2015 that the ITLOS issue provisional measures to stop Ghana's petroleum exploration and construction activities in the disputed maritime waters. It particularly requested the ITLOS to order Ghana: first, to suspend all ongoing petroleum exploration and exploitation operations in the disputed area; second, to desist from granting new petroleum exploration and exploitation permits for the disputed area; third, to take all steps to prevent information resulting from exploration activities conducted by or on behalf of Ghana, from being used in any way detrimental to Côte d'Ivoire; fourth, for Ghana to take all necessary steps to preserve the continental shelf; and fifth, for Ghana to refrain from any unilateral action that may prejudice the rights of Côte d'Ivoire or aggravate the dispute.[11] Côte d'Ivoire based its request for provisional measures on its allegations that Ghana's petroleum operations in the disputed area had raised significant environmental pollution concerns and that Ghana's petroleum licensing legislative framework was out of step with international standards. Ghana on her part rejected the Côte d'Ivoire requests and allegations. Ghana contended before the ITLOS, among others, that Côte d'Ivoire was attempting to completely shut down its offshore petroleum operations; there had been no pollution incident reaching shore; and in any event, loss, if any, could be compensated to Côte d'Ivoire by financial measures. Ghana argued that its petroleum operations 'are being operated in a transparent manner, in full accordance with contractual commitments, best industry practice, and the highest international standards, including the environmental and social standards of the World Bank's International Finance Corporation (IFC)'.[12]

The ITLOS, by its April 2015 decision, held that where there is a real and imminent risk of prejudice to the rights of one party, it could order provisional measures well ahead of final determination of the substantive case. However, it declined to order a complete halt of Ghana's petroleum operations in the disputed area but instead, among other measures, ordered Ghana to ensure that no new drilling takes place in the disputed area; and for Ghana to conduct continuous monitoring to avoid serious harm to the environment.[13]

The decided Bakassi Dispute and the pending disputes of Somalia/Kenya and Ghana/Côte d'Ivoire, are strong illustrations of maritime boundary disputes that could also be equally characterised as disputes for access to the petroleum resources of the disputed maritime areas. These are also evidence to support the contention that long-simmering maritime border conflicts become toxified when mixed with contest for the petroleum riches of the disputed waters.

Implications of maritime boundary disputes for petroleum exploration investments in contested waters

Industry's changing appetite for investment in contested waters

The question arises as to what effect these disputes have on the prospects for foreign investment, at least from the perspective of international oil companies. A logical view would be that disputes between States over entitlement to contested maritime areas would surely stifle investment. Security of investment can be seen as a principal requirement of any investor looking to access new business prospects, and even more so given the scale: very high value, very high technical risks of long-term foreign technical and financial investments that the industry needs to explore and exploit petroleum reserves. Do the risks associated with maritime boundary disputes translate the totality of investment risks into unacceptable levels for international oil companies?

If we take North Sea Oil as an example,

> Barzel suggested that oil companies would not have invested in oil exploration there unless they expected their ownership of what they might find to be secure. Barzel pointed to the significance of a multilateral agreement signed in 1958, which clearly delineated the mineral resources among the states bordering the North Sea and thus significantly reduced the likelihood of boundary disputes.[14]

Framework agreements like the 1958 North Sea agreement have ensured that countries such as the United Kingdom and Norway were able to amicably explore, drill for and share straddling resources between them, which resulted in a more appealing investment opportunity for IOCs.

Boundary experts were therefore historically of the view that foreign investors, particularly oil companies, are extremely reluctant to invest in disputed territories.[15] There is, however, late evidence (of which the Ghana/Côte d'Ivoire and Kenya/Somalia disputes are recent examples) which suggests that there is a changing attitude to the risks presented by maritime boundary disputes. The willingness of IOCs to secure licences from the Kenyan Government in the face of the active dispute with Somalia is remarkable and suggestive of the changing appetite for risk-taking by IOCs, perhaps attributable in part, to the maturity of most of the globally well known oil-rich provinces and the end of so-called 'easy oil'.

Despite the severity of the Nigeria/Cameroon controversy case, oil companies were still prepared to operate in and around the Bakassi Peninsula throughout the duration of the dispute. A number of oil companies carried out oil exploration on the Nigerian side of the disputed Bakassi Peninsula as well as on the Cameroonian side of the disputed border. Elf-Aquitaine (Total Group) invested in oil operations there amid the troubles between the two nations.[16] Further evidence shows that, in September 1996, the US oil company Mobil started oil production from the Zafiro Oil Field in the offshore area between Equatorial Guinea, Nigeria and Cameroon, under an agreement with the Government of Equatorial Guinea. Mobil expanded its investment in the region near the area in dispute.[17] We can therefore conclude, in agreement with Frynas, that

> oil resources were the chief cause of the boundary dispute or they escalated the dispute. Therefore, not only are oil companies willing to make investments despite insecure legal titles, but they also operate in an industry which appears to be inherently prone to rouse conflicts.[18]

Is the Gulf of Guinea moving from disputes to cooperation and joint development?

Africa as a whole has never been issue-free because of external drivers, which attempt to stifle progression of its resource sector. Cases ranging from the Bakassi Peninsular dispute to the Niger Delta oil spills highlight the problematic nature of extracting resources from this continent but, despite this, IOCs continue to develop and progress activities in the region. Each new case of maritime boundary dispute would initially unsettle the outlook of governments and the petroleum industry. However, over time, the maritime boundary dispute cases arguably strengthen the sector, as they lead to the continued development of the law which governs inter-boundary disputes, and final resolution is reached on disputes, many of which are the hangover of colonialism. Thus the overall situation can be viewed to be improving as time moves on.

For example, because of the improved security environment in the Gulf of Guinea/West Africa sub-region, joint exploration efforts are now possible, as illustrated by the joint development between São Tomé and Nigeria in the Atlantic Ocean that overlaps their respective continental shelves and exclusive economic zones.[19] A view can also be taken of the fact that throughout the Bakassi controversy, oil and gas operations were never truly halted by the process of the dispute. Then again, the argument can be made that if Nigeria and Cameroon had adopted such an efficient approach as joint development to their delimitation issues, and aimed for early and amicable resolution of such matters, the two nations may perhaps be at a place of mutual advantage compared to where they stand today. Thus one could consider that nations which stall the delimitation process only fall behind and waste time in a world which progressively yearns for higher quantities of the hydrocarbon resources, year on year.

The significance of oil concessions and licences over contested waters in maritime boundary delimitation

It is worth noting that in many maritime boundary disputes which tangle with the toxifying presence of petroleum resources, the award of oil licences or concessions by one or both disputing States is a frequent escalating factor, as was the case in the Somalia/Kenya and Ghana/Côte d'Ivoire pending disputes discussed earlier.

Oil concessions granted over disputed Bakassi waters

In the Bakassi case before the ICJ, the question arose as to what significance to give to oil concessions granted over the disputed maritime areas. Should oil concessions be treated as act of state practice and thus strengthen the case for entitlement by the State which granted licences over the disputed area? The issue is topical to many maritime boundary disputes involving areas bearing significant mineral resources. We would recall the earlier discussion as to the Kenya and Somalia dispute, where Kenya has created and awarded oil blocks over areas disputed by Somalia. This was a significant issue in the Bakassi case before the ICJ and the ICJ's decision on the issue deserves forensic examination.

In the Bakassi case, Nigeria contended that grant of oil concessions over the disputed area is state practice within the understanding of public international law. Nigeria therefore argued that its grant of oil concessions over the disputed Bakassi waters amounted to a decisive factor, which the ICJ should take into account in establishing the boundaries. Nigeria further argued that the ICJ could not by the principles of international law delimit the maritime boundary in such a way as to redistribute the oil licences and concessions already granted by Nigeria to IOCs.[20]

For her part, Cameroon argued that the granting of oil licences and concessions over the disputed area by one of the disputing States does not, under the principles of international law, have any major significance or value in the exercise of delimiting maritime boundary.[21]

The ICJ's attempt to settle the role of oil practice in maritime delimitation

In response to the diametrically opposed contentions by Nigeria and Cameroon as to the role and value to attribute to the granting of oil concessions over disputed maritime areas, the ICJ in the Bakassi case took the opportunity to undertake a comprehensive review and restate the principles of international law as ascertainable from previous ICJ judgments, as well as arbitral decisions, as to state practice in maritime boundary delimitation.

The first case where the role of oil practice in maritime delimitation dispute arose was in the case of *Continental Shelf (Tunisia/Libyan Arab Jamahiriya)*, where the ICJ refused to take into account the boundaries of the Libyan petroleum zones in one area, but with reference to another area it held that the concessions of the parties showed and confirmed the existence of a modus vivendi. In the case of *Maritime Boundary in the Gulf of Maine Area (Canada/United States of America)*, the ICJ held that, on the facts of the case, there did not exist any modus vivendi, distinguishing the circumstances as totally different from the Tunisia/Libya case. In the Guinea/Guinea Bissau case, the Arbitral Tribunal declined to take into consideration an oil concession granted by Portugal. The Arbitral Tribunal in the *Delimitation of Maritime Areas between Canada and the French Republic (St Pierre et Miquelon)* accorded no importance to the oil concessions granted by the parties.

Following a review of previous decisions on the subject, the ICJ in the Bakassi case concluded:

> Overall, it follows from the jurisprudence that, although the existence of an express or tacit agreement between the Parties on the siting of their respective oil concessions may indicate a consensus on the maritime areas to which they are entitled, oil concessions and oil wells are not in themselves to be considered as relevant circumstances justifying the adjustment or shifting of the provisional delimitation line. Only if they are based on express or tacit agreement between the Parties may they be taken into account. In the present case there is no agreement between the Parties regarding oil concessions. The Court is therefore of the opinion that the oil practice of the Parties is not a factor to be taken into account in … maritime delimitation.[22]

Inherent contradictions and complications of ICJ's decision on the grant of petroleum concessions over disputed waters

In sum, the ICJ decided, following review of previous ICJ decisions and arbitral determinations, that the granting of oil concessions over the disputed areas by one of the disputing States would not be given significance or considered as a significant circumstance in the formal maritime boundary delimitation, unless there was express agreement by the disputing States to one party's grant of licences. However, and in apparent contradiction to its restated international law principles, the ICJ itself, in the actual delimitation exercise of the maritime boundary between Cameroon and Nigeria, would appear to have gone on to attribute a role and significance to the oil concessions granted by Cameroon without Nigeria's consent when the Court held that:

> In the view of the Court, this common understanding of the Parties is also reflected by the geographic pattern of the oil concessions granted by the two Parties up to 1991. While no precise offshore delimitation lines were adhered to in the grants made, their underlying assumption was that Cameroon had the right to the resources in those waters that depended on the land boundary in Bakassi as fixed in the Anglo-German Agreement of 11 March 1913. It is true, as Nigeria insists, that oil licensing 'is certainly not a cession of territory'. The Court finds, however, that the geographic pattern of the licensing is consistent with the understanding of the Parties, evidenced elsewhere, as to pre-existing Cameroon title in Bakassi. Nor can this striking consistency (save for a very few exceptions) be explained by the contention that the Parties simply chose to deal with matters of oil exploitation in a manner wholly unrelated to territorial title.[23]

In the face of the apparent contradiction between the principles restated by the ICJ itself in the case, on the one hand, and the manner it applied the principles in the actual delimitation, where it gave credence to Cameroon's licensing, one is left in some confusion as to which part of the ICJ Decision should be taken as paramount – the stated principles or the principles deducible from its actual boundary delimitation. It would therefore appear that, though the ICJ sought in the Bakassi Decision to restate the principles on the role and significance of oil concessions as state practice in maritime boundary delimitation, its actual delimitation exercise has left the subject in some confusion. Considering the many other cases of maritime boundary disputes where oil concessions have been granted by one of the disputing States, the ICJ contradictory approach in the Bakassi case could be argued to have made the work of jurists, oil and gas lawyers, States and IOCs more difficult, as to how to predict how the ICJ and arbitral tribunals would treat oil concessions in boundary disputes.[24] The inherent contradiction in the ICJ's Bakassi Decision has made it more difficult to ascertain, with exactitude, the international law role and significance of unilateral oil concessions in later delimitation exercises.

ITLOS vs ICJ approaches to maritime boundary delimitation – Bangladesh v. Myanmar (dispute in the Bay of Bengal) case study

The Bay of Bengal is an area within the Indian Ocean which is believed to be rich in natural resource deposits such as oil and gas. The maritime delimitation of this area was the long-running dispute between three States which shared in the coastline of the Bay – India, Bangladesh and Myanmar. Because of the energy shortfalls and rising prices of natural resources, exploration of the maritime areas of the Bay of Bengal has become imperative for the States involved.[25] An interesting feature of this case presents itself where Bangladesh had to establish a maritime boundary not only with India but also with Myanmar, as Bangladesh straddles both India and Myanmar.

Reference to the International Tribunal on the Law of the Sea (ITLOS)

The two States had started negotiations to resolve their maritime boundaries in 1974, yet the boundary had still to be settled by 2009 when Bangladesh initiated formal proceedings. Myanmar had authorised exploration within a contested area following the discovery of natural resource deposits in 2008. Although Bangladesh sent warships to the contested area, armed conflict was avoided at that time through efficient negotiations between the two States.[26] Bangladesh and Myanmar took their maritime boundary delimitation dispute to the ITLOS, which in March 2012 delivered its judgment.[27]

The landmark ITLOS judgment

The ITLOS judgment became a landmark in many respects. The decision by the tribunal established the boundary of the territorial sea, exclusive economic zone and the continental shelf between the two States. Second, the case was the first to be decided in the Bay of Bengal and marked the beginning of exploitation of natural resources in the area, thus opening the prospect for other countries in the region to approach the ITLOS to resolve their maritime boundary disputes. Third, the judgment was the first time the ITLOS was called upon to delimit the maritime boundary between two States as, until then, maritime delimitation cases had been decided primary by the ICJ and, on occasions, by ad hoc arbitral tribunals. It had been feared by many that bringing a new court (the ITLOS) into this field would lead to fragmentation of the law.[28] The ITLOS delimitation procedure appeared to have been applied equitably and efficiently, well taking into consideration past case law in this field.

Remarkably, both Bangladesh and Myanmar were pleased with the outcome. They both claimed victory and quickly went on to compete to offer the most attractive terms to international oil companies interested in accessing the gas reserves in the Bay of Bengal.[29] It is for this reason and the foregoing that the author commends the legal, practical and pragmatic approach of the ITLOS to maritime boundary delimitation. The specialist and dedicated ITLOS may become the better and preferred forum for countries with long-standing maritime boundary disputes, particularly when mixed with contest for petroleum resources.

The increasing prominence of the ITLOS in resolving maritime boundary delimitation (especially when mixed with contest for maritime resources), coupled with its opening and well-received decision in the Bangladesh v. Myanmar case, demonstrates that it could become a sound alternative to ICJ delimitation. One wonders if the ITLOS would have given such significance to the pre-colonial treaties as the ICJ did in the Bakassi case (see discussion below). The author would argue that the ITLOS, as a specialist tribunal which uses legal rules in a practical and pragmatic manner, may in the longer term become the forum of choice for disputing States.

Peaceful implementation of ICJ's Bakassi Decision as 'good practice' in resolving maritime boundary disputes?

As with any maritime delimitation case, the ideal end point for the courts and nations involved in maritime boundary disputes is to come to a fair, equitable and sustainable resolution, which furthers the interests of both sides party to the dispute. As can be seen from the Bakassi case, a resolution was achieved once matters had reached an extreme position entailing violence and death. However, the Bakassi case is an exception and not a standard. If anything, the Bakassi case highlights how extremely difficult a maritime delimitation case can become and still achieve resolution. It therefore in itself stands as a precedent for disputing nations to follow. The Bakassi dispute and case is one within a number of maritime delimitation cases which have a past and future presence in the international field of law. Collectively they help mould the law and shape it towards a more structured template, but this area of international law is very much still in development.

Further to the earlier discussion of the disputes between Somalia/Kenya, and Ghana/Côte d'Ivoire, the following case demonstrates the intractability surrounding international boundary delimitation when mixed with the presence of rich oil and gas resources. This case study involves a delimitation case, which has contested oil and gas resources as a 'toxifying' factor in the maritime boundary dispute. Could the progress of the Bakassi case convince the long-contending States in the case study to seek for a resolution? Could the eagerness of African States to approach the ITLOS (Ghana v. Côte d'Ivoire) and the ICJ (Somalia v. Kenya) convince other States with long-simmering disputes to seek some resolution with the ITLOS, if not the ICJ?

Greece/Turkey delimitation dispute

The relations between the Mediterranean States of Greece and Turkey, similarly to Nigeria and Cameroon, have been historically marked by periods of mutual hostility and reconciliation ever since Greece's independence from the Ottoman Empire in 1821.[30] Since this period the two countries have faced each other in four major wars. The conflict no longer relates to war or indeed the breach of security between the States, considering that the last major war ended in 1922. Rather, the conflict now appears to centre around the question as to which of the two contending States is entitled to the natural resources in the Aegean continental shelf shared between the two States.

The Greek/Turkish dispute over the continental shelf was triggered around 1973, when the Turkish Government Gazette published the Turkish Government's decision to grant the Turkish national petroleum company permits to conduct research in the Greek continental shelf, west of the Greek islands in the Aegean Sea.[31] This incident led to friction between the States, leading to Turkey's many attempts at violating Greece's sovereign rights over the continental shelf. Greece, on its part, strongly contends that the sovereign rights to the continental shelf are exclusive, in the sense that if Greece chooses not to explore the continental shelf or exploit its natural resources, then no one may undertake these activities without the express consent of Greece.[32]

In 1976, Greece unilaterally filed a claim before the International Court of Justice in the Hague.[33] Turkey, however, objected to the jurisdiction of the ICJ by simple letter and refused to appear before the Court. The ICJ heard arguments by Greece and considered the contents of Turkey's letter. The ICJ thereafter declined jurisdiction by the Aegean Sea Continental Shelf Case (Jurisdiction of the Court) judgment[34] and held that the relevant Treaty in force between Greece and Turkey had by Turkey's reservation excluded issues regarding the territorial status of Greece (and extended to the subject of delimitation of the continental shelf).[35]

Greece and Turkey together with the two neighbouring Cypriot States are constantly at edge over the unresolved maritime boundary dispute and access to the vast hydrocarbon reserves in the Aegean Sea. One would hope that both Turkey and Greece could consider the option of arbitration before the ITLOS even if they cannot agree on delimitation before the ICJ. The unresolved dispute locks out all the parties to the petroleum reserves as well as keeping the region on the edge of instability.

Maritime delimitation in the Black Sea – Romania/Ukraine

In September 2004, Romania submitted a case to the ICJ against Ukraine in order to establish a single maritime boundary between the two States in the Black Sea, thereby delimiting the continental shelf and the exclusive economic zones (EEZ) relating to them.[36] Romania requested that the Court draw the boundary in accordance with international law and, more specifically, criteria which had been laid down in a previous additional agreement to a Treaty between Romania and Ukraine,[37] which had entered into force in October 2007.

Interestingly, the dispute was as much a maritime boundary controversy as a contest for access to the petroleum resources of the disputed area, and the significance, or not, of petroleum concessions granted by Ukraine, was in issue.[38]

The ICJ in its judgment observed that it would apply the relevant provisions held within UNCLOS[39] in accordance with the 1969 Vienna Convention on the law of treaties and, using various methods to draw an equidistance line in consideration of proportionality, came to a decision. The verdict handed down by the Court means Romania now exploits 80 per cent of the 100 billion cubic metres of gas and 15 million tonnes of crude oil[40] in the disputed zone. This leaves the remaining deposits to Ukraine and creates a situation where Romania possesses a larger area to exploit these inherent natural resources than Ukraine. Despite this, the Black Sea itself had finally seen resolution as, before the ICJ Decision, the dispute had prevented either side from organising tenders for interested companies to extract the natural resources held in the seabed. With this decision finally resolving the dispute and setting the boundary, the States could move forward and help each other exploit and develop the full productive capabilities of the area.

Gulf of Guinea Commission and West Africa's evolving practice of peaceful resolution

As we have examined earlier, some States in West Africa and East Africa have actively sought to definitively settle their maritime contest by submitting to the ICJ or the International Tribunal on the Law of the Sea (ITLOS). The trend suggests that best practice is now heading in a direction which aims to amicably resolve these issues without recourse to violence and forceful actions. In addition to this, the Gulf of Guinea Commission was established with the aim to facilitate peaceful relations between mineral States in West Central Africa and again highlights the peaceful direction in which these disputes are now headed. Together these legal mechanisms are acting as a framework in progress, which will ultimately strengthen not just the nations who are party to them but their inherent relationships as a whole. As each case further defines the law, it will continue to work alongside these mechanisms to develop a standard which is not only to be followed in Africa but worldwide. Progress is being made, but it must be allowed time to develop.

The Gulf of Guinea States have formalised the evolving practice of peaceful resolution by establishing the Gulf of Guinea Commission (GGC), with a secretariat based in Angola.[41] The objectives of the GGC are clearly declared to address the twin factors – maritime boundary dispute and contest for natural resources in the contested waters – that have the effect of toxifying boundary disputes. Thus the Treaty Establishing the Gulf of Guinea declares the objective of the GGC to be the establishment of a

> framework of consultation among the countries of the Gulf of Guinea for cooperation and development, as well as for the prevention, management and resolution of conflicts that may arise from the delimitation of borders and the economic and commercial exploitation of natural resources within the territorial boundaries, particularly in the overlapping Exclusive Economic Zones (EEZ) of our States.[42]

The objectives are declared to arise from the underlying understanding:

> of the need to put the natural resources of our countries at the service of economic development and social progress of our peoples; ... CONVINCED in this regard that our common and concerted action is the sure guarantee for a harmonious, rational and peaceful exploitation of our natural resources; RECOGNISING that the Gulf of Guinea is replete with natural resources, which could contribute to the economic development of all the coastal states and to the general well-being of our peoples; DESIROUS to tap these resources to ensure the economic development of our States and the well-being of our peoples; ... ANXIOUS to settle our disputes by peaceful means; CONVINCED that dialogue and negotiation remain the best ways of resolving permanently any dispute in accordance with the provisions of the Charters of the United Nations and the Organisation of African Unity/African Union; CONSCIOUS of the need to put in place an appropriate dialogue and consultation mechanism for the prevention, management and resolution of conflicts connected to the delimitation of borders, to the economic and commercial exploitation of the natural resources within the territorial boundaries, particularly in the overlapping Exclusive Economic Zones (EEZ) of our States.[43]

Case management of maritime boundary disputes with underlying battle for petroleum resources: Nigerian–Bakassi case study

Considering the earlier conclusion that the Bakassi case (as with the case of Ghana/Côte d'Ivoire) was as much a boundary dispute as a contest for access to hugely valuable oil and gas resources, one would assume that States would take the highest care and attention to take clearly intentioned and pre-emptive steps to manage their dispute so as to reach the most favourable outcome possible. Some scholars suggest that Nigeria could have better managed the maritime boundary dispute, when it is considered that access to significant and hugely valuable petroleum resources was also in play.

Boundary settlements which are mutually satisfactory, favourable and sustainable

Although the Bakassi case is a signal example of an international boundary dispute finally decided by the ICJ between two States, there are still many open issues arising from the Bakassi Decision and its implementation that creates the climate or potential for future instability of the Bakassi Peninsula, post transfer to Cameroonian control. The two States ought to ensure that the deep upset of the peoples of Bakassi, and their separated communities on the Nigerian side, does not create the climate for conflict and possible self-determination away from both Cameroon and Nigeria. Therefore, there are valuable lessons for other States to learn in order that they can make the best decisions to produce the most amicable, favourable and sustainable outcomes in resolving their maritime boundary disputes, and thereby enhance the long-term sustainability of their petroleum extraction activities.

The ICJ Bakassi Decision when compared, for example, with the ITLOS Decision in Bangladesh v. Myanmar, is uniquely an unhappy decision for one of the two contesting States. So one would contend that the non-mutually satisfying ICJ Bakassi Decision is in itself a signal lesson for other States contemplating maritime boundary delimitation mixed with contest for petroleum resources. Such States should aim and manage the resolution of their conflict to reach mutually satisfying outcomes. For example, it is arguable that Cameroon and Nigeria would have been better off reaching the most mutually satisfying outcome by negotiating a joint development agreement (JDA)[44] over the contested area rather than the post-ICJ Decision implementation outcome, which has foisted the unwilling Bakassi people on Cameroon when in reality the best (uncomplicated) benefit to Cameroon was to have access to the petroleum riches of the Bakassi waters. On Nigeria's part, the transfer of Bakassi lands and her peoples remains a constant and troubling subject which is revisited by every new government.

In view of the vast petroleum resources of Nigeria's Niger Delta, access to the resources of the Bakassi waters means more to Cameroon than Nigeria. An amicably reached and mutually satisfying outcome could have left the status of the Bakassi peoples unchanged but given Cameroon access to the petroleum resources of the Bakassi waters. It is perhaps partly for this reason that it is argued in another chapter that both Cameroon and Nigeria, even as matters presently stand, should consider and pursue Joint Development Agreements.

ICJ's biased judgment or Nigeria's middling case management?

While many scholars questioned and concluded that the ICJ was biased in its judgment for its disregard of the pre-colonial treaties, others disagree. First, there is a sense that the

Nigerian State misguided itself almost throughout the length of the Bakassi dispute, from the beginning to the commencement of ICJ proceedings by Cameroon, with the mishandling of its first response to the case filed by Cameroon before the ICJ case, poor case management of the ICJ litigation, poor outcomes from the agreements reached post the ICJ Decision, unclear objectives in the course of implementation of the agreements, and dithering over whether to approach the ICJ for revision of its decision before expiry of the ten-year window. LeFebvre concluded, for example, that pre and during the ICJ litigation:

> Unfortunately, Nigeria's argument was weakened by the lack of seriousness displayed by the Nigerian leadership over time, as they failed to protest the 1913 treaty and then signed agreements during the pre-coup regimes of the 1970s that they later claimed to be invalid.[45]

It has been argued that some eminent Nigerian legal experts with historical consciousness had advised the Nigerian Government not to go to or allowed itself to be dragged before the ICJ for claim of ownership over Bakassi, on the considered view that ICJ jurisprudence, which disregards pre-colonial treaties with pre-colonial African States and crowns, did not favour Nigeria's case. The then Attorney-General of Nigeria, Dr Teslim Elias,[46] who later became President of the ICJ, had advised the Gowon administration in Nigeria (1966–1976), perhaps on the basis of the post-colonial agreements, that Nigeria had no legal basis for contesting the Bakassi Peninsula before the International Court of Justice. He predicted that Nigeria would not win the Bakassi case in the ICJ, should Nigeria initiate any legal action against Cameroon or ever allow itself to be dragged to the Court over the Bakassi issue. Was Elias's position based in awareness that ICJ jurisprudence did not give effect to treaties between European colonial powers and African pre-colonial Kingdoms and Empires, which was the basis of Nigeria's claim to Bakassi?

Although the Nigerian Government did not reject the ICJ Bakassi Decision openly yet it felt that could be challenged. They called for an agreement that would provide 'peace with honour, with the interest and welfare of our people'.[47] The outcome of the controversy was a de facto Nigerian refusal to withdraw its troops from Bakassi and transfer sovereignty. That led to a protracted situation, which eventually led to a negotiated implementation and transfer of territory from Nigeria to Cameroon.

It has been said that '[t]he process of transferring the peninsula to Cameroon was not without its problems, including the ongoing issue of resettling Nigerians displaced by the transfer and the dissatisfaction of those who remained but were now under Cameroonian rule'.[48] On 12 June 2006, the two parties concluded the Greentree Agreement, negotiated by the Cameroon–Nigeria Mixed Commission established by the UN. In November 2007, Nigeria's Senate voted to void the agreement that had ceded the Bakassi Peninsula to Cameroon. The Nigerian Senate by resolution called for a referendum to be held in the Bakassi Peninsula for the inhabitants to decide whether to stay with Nigeria or transfer to Cameroon. However, this action did not affect the actual status of the peninsula, and a ceremony held on 14 August 2008 marked the completion of the peninsula's transfer from Nigeria to Cameroon. According to the terms of the Greentree Agreement, Nigerians in the area could choose either to return to Nigeria or stay in Bakassi. Those who chose to stay could maintain their Nigerian citizenship or naturalise as Cameroonians. In either case, the accord requires that Cameroon respect the fundamental rights of Nigerians there.[49] This is important as an unstable population might have led to a Nigerian migrant community uprising in the peninsula, which might have had a negative effect on oil development and other economic activities.

Could the Bakassi peoples by referendum have overruled the ICJ's decision that the Bakassi Peninsula should be transferred by Nigeria to Cameroon?

The great outcry in the Nigerian media and among the Bakassi peoples particularly, and the southeastern Nigeria region generally, would appear to have prompted the Nigeria's Senate in November 2007 to seek to void the Greentree Agreement that had ceded the Bakassi Peninsula to Cameroon, and the Senate by resolution called for a referendum to be held in the Bakassi Peninsula for the inhabitants to decide whether to stay with Nigeria or transfer to Cameroon. If the Nigerian State had followed its Senate's proposal to organise a referendum, what would have been the status in international law of the referendum? As the area was safely left alone until discovery of mineral resources, it is the author's opinion that the Nigerian Senate also had an immediate vested economic interest in the area and therefore provided motivation for the Senate's proposal. However, would such a referendum be contrary to the ICJ Decision and thus international law? What if the referendum had led to the Bakassi peoples' decision to remain with Nigeria: would such a referendum decision suffice to override the ICJ Decision which mandated the transfer of Bakassi to Cameroon? It is safe to assume that the people of Bakassi would have overwhelmingly voted to remain part of Nigeria, insofar as 90 per cent of the population considered themselves Nigerians.

These questions are analogous to the Russian State's annexation of the internationally recognised Ukrainian territory of Crimea which was annexed by the Russian Federation in March 2014. The Russian State formally annexed the territory on 18 March 2014 and since then Russia has de facto administered the territory as two federal subjects – the Republic of Crimea and the city of Sevastopol – within the Crimean Federal District.[50] The annexation was preceded by Russian military occupation, which was not repulsed by Ukraine. That was followed by a referendum, held on 16 March 2014, on the status of Crimea, which was called for and nominally organised by the legislature of the Crimea as well as the local government of Sevastopol, both subdivisions of Ukraine. The referendum asked the people of Crimea to decide whether to become a federal unit of the Russian State or retain Crimea's status as part of Ukraine. The ballot was fixed ten days before it was held. Most countries including the European Union States, the United States and Canada regarded the Crimean referendum as largely illegitimate. The United Nations Security Council considered a resolution to declare the referendum invalid. The resolution was vetoed by Russia, with China abstaining. On 27 March 2014, the UN General Assembly (by 100 votes in favour and 11 against, with 58 abstentions) approved a resolution which declared the Crimean referendum leading to annexation of Crimea by Russia as illegal and affirmed Crimea as Ukrainian territory.[51] Presently Crimea is de facto a part of the Russian State.

What would have been the position if post the ICJ Decision, the Nigerian State had allowed the Bakassi peoples to decide by referendum whether to remain part of the Nigerian State or to join the Cameroonian State? If the Bakassi peoples had voted to remain Nigerian, what would be the status of the Bakassi territory within Nigeria? While a full examination of the subject is worthy of further research and investigation, such is beyond the remit of this analysis. One can at least conclude that the status of Bakassi remaining in Nigeria after the ICJ Decision but pursuant to a referendum would have been somewhat controversial, and thus a disincentive to oil and gas companies seeking licence and title to explore and exploit the resources of the Bakassi Peninsula.

Conclusion

In this chapter, we have investigated the positive implications and the unresolved complications arising from the ICJ's Bakassi judgment (Cameroon v. Nigeria), as generally applicable to the oil and gas law, the petroleum sector and the search for petroleum riches in contested waters. There are many lessons which are commended to other States yet to resolve their maritime boundary disputes, especially where such involve contest for petroleum riches in the disputed waters.

Notwithstanding the post-ICJ Decision implementation challenges and the negative complications and contradictions, there is one clear and significant outcome from the Bakassi case which is worth commending to other disputing States – there is some resolution of a long-standing boundary dispute which had on several occasions degenerated to violent military clashes. The Bakassi case stands as arguably the most important boundary dispute case from Africa in recent times and thus an example of how a protracted dispute can reach its zenith and yet be on its way to final resolution. That demonstrates the power of international law in this area. States such as Greece/Turkey and Japan/China which are yet to resolve such delimitation issues may choose to view the Bakassi case as a precedent to one day leading to peaceful resolution of their own internal disputes.

States involved in disputes for maritime boundary delimitation with mixed petroleum reserves should also learn from the debate as to whether Nigeria could have done better in managing the outcome of its long dispute with Cameroon. States should establish long-term objectives in relation to the contested waters as well as a long-term strategy to achieve those objectives. The objectives should include the early possibility of amicably negotiating and reaching amicable and most mutually satisfying outcomes States would do well to avoid, to the maximum extent possible, resort to judicial resolution. Judicial resolution should not be sought without having first exhausted all amicable arrangements such as by negotiating Joint Development Agreements. If all else fails, contesting States should be careful in choosing the forum for judicial resolution. With the positive and landmark entrance of the ITLOS (discussed above) as an attractive alternative to the ICJ for maritime boundary delimitation, States should be strategic in choosing the forum that will best understand and apply the principle of international law in a practical and pragmatic way. If the ITLOS were to continue to reach decisions (such as the judgment in Bangladesh v. Myanmar), which are soundly legal and yet pragmatic, one could foresee the ITLOS becoming the forum of preference for disputing States who have tried but failed to reach amicable arrangements. This is especially the case for African States that have to contend with the unsatisfactory legal legacies of the colonial era and the ICJ's disputed jurisprudence on the subject, which remains one of the most challenged outcomes of the ICJ's Bakassi Decision

The ICJ's jurisprudence on the status of pre-colonial treaties entered into by European colonial powers and the pre-colonial African Kings and States, and their impact of Africa's post-colonial borders, is one subject which the Bakassi case has worsened rather than resolved, at least from the perspective of African States. The rather unexpected and controversial Bakassi Decision on pre-colonial treaties has further heightened the confusion as to whether the agreements reached with the African pre-colonial authorities are respected by the European States and Western jurisprudence. The ICJ Decision on the point has made the exercise of predicting the outcomes of disputes even more difficult for scholars, lawyers and analysts. African States would have to consider how to deal with the issue into the future. Should there be an African Court of Justice (ACJ), which could develop the jurisprudence on such matters and provide a judicial forum of international standing which would give right recognition to the pre-colonial treaties and other unsatisfactory legacies of the colonial era?[52]

The foregoing is another reason that the author argues that maritime States involved in boundary delimitation disputes would do well to proactively push for mutually beneficial and long-lasting resolution of their disputes. Arrangements such as Joint Development Agreements would have served both Cameroon and Nigeria better than the outcome of the ICJ judgment.[53] If States have to resort to international judicial resolution, the ITLOS may well emerge as the preferred forum for resolving maritime boundary disputes mixed with contest for the petroleum resources of the disputed waters.

Notes

1 I am grateful for the research support of Dulkith Samaraweera, analyst at OMFG.

2 The Niger Delta Petroleum System:

> Exploration of the small portions of the Niger Delta in Cameroon and Equatorial Guinea began much later than in Nigeria. Recoverable oil and gas (produced plus proved reserves) are much smaller than in Nigeria. In 1997, 96% of the Niger Delta recoverable petroleum was in Nigeria, 3.5% in Cameroon, and 0.5% in Equatorial Guinea.
>
> (http://pubs.usgs.gov/of/1999/ofr-99-0050/OF99-50H/ChapterA.html)

3 Mbuh, M. (2004) 'The Bakassi Peninsula Dispute, Justice. International Law and Conflicts, Resolving Border and Sovereignty Disputes in Africa', www.postwatchmagazine.com.

4 Price, F. (2005) ICE Case Studies, 'The Bakassi Peninsula – The Border Dispute between Nigeria and Cameroon', www.american.edu/ted/ice/nigeria-cameroon.htm.

5

> The military struggle between the two nations resulted in some form of partition of the islands. Given the disadvantage that Cameroon's population is about one-tenth that of Nigeria (roughly 12 million to 120 million), it was no surprise that Cameroon naturally resorted to accusing Nigeria for using its population advantage to populate the Bakassi Peninsula – a tactic of claiming ownership. From the Nigerian end, it is common to hear accusations of Cameroon Gendarmes and their tax-drive assaults on Nigerians living in the area. Thus Cameroon initially claimed it had to exercise its sovereignty and protect its territorial integrity by taxing those who live on its soil, and Nigeria, while not relinquishing its claims of sovereignty over the peninsula had to send in troops to protect its citizens from Cameroon aggression.
>
> (www.american.edu/ted/ice/nigeria-cameroon.htm)

6 Tarlebbea, N.K. and Baroni, S. (2010) 'The Cameroon and Nigeria Negotiation Process over the Contested Oil Rich Bakassi Peninsula', *Journal of Alternative Perspectives in the Social Sciences*, Vol. 2, No. 1, pp. 198–210, at p. 201.

7 Tarlebbea, N.K. and Baroni, S. (2010) 'The Cameroon and Nigeria Negotiation Process over the Contested Oil Rich Bakassi Peninsula', *Journal of Alternative Perspectives in the Social Sciences*, Vol. 2, No. 1, p. 203.

8 Kalumba, K.M. (2007) 'Border Dispute Settlements in Africa and their Impact on Human Rights of Indigenous Occupants of Disputed Territories', Ch 3.2.1, p. 35. Unpublished thesis accessible via University of Zambia Institutional Repository: http://dspace.unza.zm:8080/xmlui/handle/123456789/18/discover?query=kalumba&submit=.

9 Tarlebbea, N.K. and Baroni, S. (2010) 'The Cameroon and Nigeria Negotiation Process over the Contested Oil Rich Bakassi Peninsula', *Journal of Alternative Perspectives in the Social Sciences*, Vol. 2,.No. 1, p. 203. See also Klabbers, J. *International Law* (Cambridge: Cambridge University Press, 2017, second edition) at p. 9, who points out:

> For much of the second part of the twentieth century, the cases that would reach the ICJ tended to be those involving the precise limits of territorial ownership, either on land or, more commonly, at sea. And they often found their cause in the discovery of oil and natural gas deposits; whereas states were not all that interested in establishing the precise boundaries of their jurisdiction earlier, they became a lot keener when they realized that they might be sitting on huge oil reserves.

10 The ICJ in its 2 February 2017 judgment on Kenya's Preliminary Objections held that

> the MOU reflected the expectation of the Parties that, in light of Article 83, paragraph 1, of UNCLOS, they would negotiate their maritime boundary in the area of the continental shelf after receipt of the CLCS's recommendations, keeping the two processes of delimitation and delineation distinct. As between States Parties to UNCLOS, such negotiations are the first step in undertaking delimitation of the continental shelf. The Court does not, however, consider that the text of the sixth paragraph, viewed in light of the text of the MOU as a whole, the object and purpose of the MOU, and in its context, could have been intended to establish a method of dispute settlement in relation to the delimitation of the maritime boundary between the Parties. It neither binds the Parties to wait for the outcome of the CLCS process before attempting to reach agreement on their maritime boundary, nor does it impose an obligation on the Parties to settle their maritime boundary dispute through a particular method of settlement.
>
> (See para. 98, Maritime Delimitation in the Indian Ocean (Somalia vs Kenya), Judgment of 2 Feb 2017: www.icj-cij.org/docket/files/161/19330.pdf)

11 Dispute Concerning the Delimitation of the Maritime Boundary Between Ghana and Côte d'Ivoire in the Atlantic Ocean (Ghana/Côte d'Ivoire), Order on Provisional Measures of 25 April 2015: www.itlos.org/fileadmin/itlos/documents/cases/case_no.23_prov_meas/C23_Order_prov.measures_25.04.2015_orig_Eng.pdf. See paras 36–70.

12 Ibid., at para. 56.

13 Ibid., paragraphs 70 to 108.

14 Frynas, J.G. (2000) 'Foreign Investment and International Boundary Disputes in Africa: Evidence from the Oil Industry', African Studies Centre Paper No. 9, p. 3.

15 Ibid.

16 Ibid., p. 7.

17 Ibid., p. 8.

18 Ibid.

19 Khan, F., *Geopolitics of Cameroon and Nigeria Boarder [sic] Crises: Energy Impact of the International Court of Justice Decision on Production of Oil in the Gulf of Guinea* (Pakistan: F. Khan, 2009), Section 2.4, p. 34.

20 See ICJ Decision, op cit., at para. 282:

> Nigeria further argues that the Parties' conduct in respect of the granting and exploitation of oil concessions, leading to the establishment of de facto lines, plays a very important role in establishing maritime boundaries. It contends that, within the area to be delimited, the Court cannot redistribute the oil concessions established by the practice of Nigeria, Equatorial Guinea and Cameroon, and that it must respect the configuration of the concessions in its determination of the course of the maritime boundary. In Nigeria's view, international jurisprudence has never disregarded such practice in order to redistribute oil concessions, and this restrained approach is all the more understandable because the change in long-standing rights and oil concessions resulting from such a redistribution would create major difficulties and would not be in keeping with the equitable considerations which must be taken into account in delimitation.
>
> According to Nigeria, Cameroon's line of delimitation completely disregards the substantial, long-standing practice, followed by Nigeria as well as by Cameroon, in respect of oil exploration and exploitation activity on the continental shelf, and would result in allotting to Cameroon a large number of concessions belonging to Nigeria or Equatorial Guinea, in which billions of dollars in infrastructure have been invested. Nigeria states that its oil concession practice is long established, contending that, contrary to what Cameroon claims ... it dates back to well before 1970, when, according to Cameroon, its maritime delimitation

dispute with Nigeria arose. The existence of any areas of overlapping licences is moreover considered by Nigeria to be without effect on the evidentiary weight of oil practice. Nigeria states that its operations within the maritime areas now claimed by Cameroon have always been particularly significant and completely open; Cameroon never disputed them and lodged no protest until the date on which these proceedings were instituted. Nigeria concludes that its oil practice in the area was public, open and of long duration, and is therefore a basis for acquiescence and the establishment of vested rights. It denies that it failed in an obligation to inform Cameroon of this practice, and states that the information was in any event publicly available.

21 See ICJ Decision, op cit., at para. 283:

> In reply to Nigeria's argument on the oil practice, Cameroon, for its part, maintains that the existence and limits of oil concessions have been given only limited significance in matters of maritime delimitation in international case law. This limited significance is said to accord with the essential nature of the concept of the continental shelf, over which coastal States have an inherent right which 'does not depend on its being exercised' (North Sea Continental Shelf, Judgment…). Cameroon argues that the granting of oil concessions is a unilateral fait accompli, and not a legal fact that is opposable to another State.
>
> In the area immediately south of point G, Cameroon claims that there are in fact areas of overlap of the concessions granted by Cameroon, Equatorial Guinea and Nigeria, and that, because of this, it cannot be said that there is any consensual line of oil practices forming a de facto line which could serve as a basis for delimitation.

In the area further south of point G, Cameroon argues that there can be no question of a de facto line, since Cameroon refrained from granting any concessions there, because of the negotiations between the Parties and the present proceedings. According to Cameroon, Nigeria, by granting concessions in this area, has sought to present the Court with a fait accompli.

Moreover, Cameroon claims that Nigeria's description of the state practice in terms of oil concessions and the conclusions it draws therefrom are erroneous. Cameroon insists that, contrary to Nigeria's claim, the concessions cited by Nigeria are all (with the exception of concession OML 67) subsequent to 1990, well after the maritime delimitation dispute arose at the end of the 1970s, while three of them were even granted after the Application instituting proceedings was filed and therefore are of no relevance for purposes of settling the present dispute.

Further, Cameroon states that nothing can be inferred from its silence with regard to Nigerian concessions, since the Nigerian authorities never informed Cameroon, as they had promised to do, of new concessions and Nigeria itself has remained silent with respect to Cameroonian concessions, even when these encroached on zones which Nigeria appears to consider as its own.

22 Cameroon v. Nigeria, ICJ Decision, op cit., para. 302.

23 See ICJ Decision, para. 215.

24 The grant of oil concessions is directly in issue in the Kenya/Somali dispute (before the ICJ) and the Ghana/Côte d'Ivoire dispute (arbitration).

25 Rashid, H. (2012) 'Maritime Boundary with India: Arbitration or Bilateral Negotiations', *The Daily Star*, 28 March 2012, www.thedailystar.net/newDesign/news-details.php?nid=227962.

26 Blog of the *European Journal of International Law*, 'From the North Sea to the Bay of Bengal: Maritime Delimitation of the International Tribunal for the Law of the Sea', 23 March 2012, www.ejiltalk.org/from-the-north-sea-to-the-bay-of-bengal-maritime-delimitation-at-the-international-tribunal-for-the-law-of-the-sea/.

27 Dispute concerning Delimitation of the Maritime Boundary between Bangladesh and Myanmar in the Bay of Bengal (Bangladesh/Myanmar), ITLOS Judgement of 14 March 2012, www.itlos.org/fileadmin/itlos/documents/cases/case_no_16/published/C16_Judgment.pdf.

28 Blog of the *European Journal of International Law*, 'From the North Sea to the Bay of Bengal: Maritime Delimitation of the International Tribunal for the Law of the Sea', 23 March 2012, www.ejiltalk.org/from-the-north-sea-to-the-bay-of-bengal-maritime-delimitation-at-the-international-tribunal-for-the-law-of-the-sea/.

29 Watson, S., 'The Bangladesh/Myanmar Maritime Dispute: Lessons for Peaceful Resolution', October 2015, Asia Maritime Transparency Initiative, https://amti.csis.org/the-bangladeshmyanmar-maritime-dispute-lessons-for-peaceful-resolution/.

30 CNN World, 'Greece and Turkey: History of Hate', http://articles.cnn.com/2001-09-06/world/turkey.greece_1_greece-and-turkey-greek-people-greek-islands?_s=PM:WORLD.
31 Hellenic Republic, Ministry of Foreign Affairs, 'Greek–Turkish Dispute over the Delimitation of the Continental Shelf', www.mfa.gr/en/issues-of-greek-turkish-relations/relevant-documents/delimitation-of-the-continental-shelf.html.
32 Tanaka, Y., *The International Law of the Sea* (Cambridge: Cambridge University Press, 2012), p. 138. Also see Article 77 of the Law of the Sea Convention (LOSC) 1982.
33 Hellenic Republic, Ministry of Foreign Affairs, 'Greek–Turkish Dispute over the Delimitation of the Continental Shelf', www.mfa.gr/en/issues-of-greek-turkish-relations/relevant-documents/delimitation-of-the-continental-shelf.html.
34 ICJ Judgment of 19 December 1978, *ICJ Reports*, www.icj-cij.org/docket/files/62/6245.pdf.
35 Ibid. para. 90.
36 The Hague Justice Portal – Maritime Delimitation in the Black Sea (Romania v. Ukraine), www.haguejusticeportal.net/index.php?id=6185.
37 Additional Agreement to the Treaty on Good Neighbourliness and Co-operation, Turkey/Ukraine [2007].
38 Romania v. Ukraine, ICJ Judgment, paras 190–203.
39 Ibid.
40 Euobserver.com, 'EU's Black Sea Border Set in Stone', 3 February 2009, http://euobserver.com/foreign/27525.
41 For more on the Gulf of Guinea Commission, see their webpages, http://cggrps.org/en/.
42 Article 2 of the Treaty Establishing the Gulf of Guinea Commission, of 3 July 2001, accessible on GGC webpages, http://cggrps.org/wp-content/uploads/Tratado-EN1.pdf.
43 See preamble of the Treaty Establishing the Gulf of Guinea Commission, http://cggrps.org/wp-content/uploads/Tratado-EN1.pdf.
44 Nigeria had talks with Sao Tome and Principe, during the pendency of the ICJ Bakassi case. The mutual negotiations led to the Nigeria–São Tomé Joint Development Treaty of 2001; see www.juristep.com/legis/jdz_treaty.pdf.
45 LeFebvre, K.R. (2014) 'Interests and Identities in Peace Negotiations: Nigeria, Cameroon and the Bakassi Peninsula', *African Social Science Review*, Vol. 6, No. 1.
46 Ibid.
47 Hamilton, A. and Kirk-Greene, M. 'Federal Republic of Nigeria', in *Encyclopedia Britannica*, www.britannica.com/EBchecked/topic/414840/Nigeria/259740/Return-to-civilian-rule.
48 'Nigeria Hands over Control of Bakassi Peninsula' (2008), www.haguejusticeportal.net/index.php?id=9635.
49 Chimtom, N.K., 'Nigerians Uncertain of Future in Bakassi Peninsula', ipsnews.net, www.ipsnews.net/2013/09/nigerians-uncertain-of-future-in-bakassi-peninsula/.
50 'Putin Signs Laws on Reunification of Republic of Crimea and Sevastopol with Russia' (2014), http://tass.ru/en/russia/724785.
51 'General Assembly Adopts Resolution Calling upon States Not to Recognize Changes in Status of Crimea Region' (2014), www.un.org/press/en/2014/ga11493.doc.htm.
52 See Egede, E.E. (2016), 'Institutional Gaps in the 2050 African Integrated Maritime Strategy', *Journal of Ocean Law and Governance in Africa*, pp. 1–22 at 10–15, where the author proposes that the merged African Court of Justice and African Court on Human and Peoples' Rights should have jurisdiction over international law of the sea cases, including maritime boundary disputes.
53 See Chapter 9 in this book on JDA.

9 The role of a Joint Development Agreement (JDA) in resolving the conflicts and uncertainties over maritime boundary delimitation

A missed opportunity in the Bakassi case[1]

Eddy Lenusira Wifa, Mark Amakoromo and Ibiateli Johnson-Ogbo

Introduction

The potential or actual presence of significant hydrocarbon resources in disputed maritime areas may have the effect of making it more difficult to settle maritime boundary disputes[2] and could lead to conflict in some situations. Where there are overlapping claims over maritime boundaries and the parties involved have reached a deadlock in their maritime boundary delimitation negotiations, the alternative of a shared management regime rather than a unilateral one may prove attractive.[3] Joint Development Agreements (JDAs) have been utilised in different parts of the world as a provisional measure in situations where two or more States independently claim ownership of resources in an overlapping maritime zone. The use of JDAs does not necessarily mean that the parties have settled their maritime boundary disputes; rather, JDAs encourage joint exploitation of the disputed maritime areas pending final delimitation of the parties' respective maritime boundaries.

According to Shihata and Onaroto, the JDA is a

> procedure under which boundary disputes are set aside, without prejudice to the validity of the conflicting claims, and the interested states agree, instead, to jointly explore and exploit and to share any hydrocarbons found in the area subject to overlapping claims.[4]

JDA has also been defined as

> the common exercise of sovereign rights and jurisdiction based on an international agreement between governments or two or more concerned states for the purpose of exploitation and apportionment of a potential natural resource in an overlapping area of territorial dispute pending final delimitation.[5]

To achieve the purposes of the JDA, the parties involved would identify a Joint Development Zone (JDZ), which will be explored and exploited for the benefit of the parties pending the final delimitation of their respective maritime boundaries.[6]

The importance of a JDA was well captured by Anderson thus:

> The solution of a joint area may be second best to an agreed boundary; but a joint area may well be better than seeing a dispute remain unresolved and possibly grow

> more serious. The governments may prefer a compromise to a defeat in litigation. An effective treaty providing for joint development may allow the industry to work and produce benefit for many years in an area which would otherwise have remained blighted by dispute over jurisdiction. 'Half a loaf is better than no bread', as the saying goes.[7]

There are three different types of JDA models, which can be adopted, depending on the circumstances of any particular case and upon the agreement of the parties. The first is the single-state model where one State manages the resources in the interest of both countries. The Bahrain–Saudi Arabia agreement of 1958, which is managed by Saudi Arabia, is an example of this model of JDA.[8] The second is the two-country JDA model where each State nominates its contractor to enter into a joint venture with the contractor of the other State. Countries that have adopted this model of JDA include the UK and the Netherlands; France and Spain in the Bay of Biscay; the UK and Norway; Japan and South Korea; and Nigeria and Equatorial Guinea (Ekanga/Zafiro field), among others.[9] The third is the Joint Authority Model, where both States delegate power to a single body that becomes responsible for the overall supervision of petroleum activities in the Zone. Countries that have adopted this Joint Authority Model include Saudi Arabia and Sudan in 1994;[10] Australia and Indonesia in 1989; Malaysia and Thailand in 1979/1990; and Nigeria and Sao Tome and Principe in 2001, among others.

If one of the core reasons for conflict over international maritime boundaries is the quest for control of the hydrocarbon resources which are found in the disputed maritime area,[11] then it would be better for States to engage in provisional arrangements such as the JDA pending the final delimitation of their maritime boundaries. Where this happens, conflicts and uncertainties that come with maritime boundary disputes could likely be averted and the countries involved will be able to reap the economic benefits that will flow from the exploration and exploitation of the natural resources in the disputed maritime area.

This chapter holds the view that JDAs can be used as an effective tool in curbing the conflicts and uncertainties that arise as a result of maritime boundary disputes. The Nigeria–Sao Tome and Principe JDA will serve as a classic case study to show the benefits in the use of a JDA, while the Nigeria–Cameroon conflict will serve as a warning on the potential dangers that may arise where a JDA is not utilised.

International legal framework for maritime boundary delimitation

The primary international law governing the delimitation of maritime boundaries is the United Nations Convention on the Law of the Sea (UNCLOS) 1982. Article 3 of UNCLOS 1982 gives every State the right to establish the breadth of its territorial sea up to a limit not exceeding 12 nautical miles, measured from baselines in accordance with UNCLOS 1982. On the delimitation of the territorial sea between States with opposite or adjacent coasts, the UNCLOS provides that:

> Where the coasts of two States are opposite or adjacent to each other, neither of the two States is entitled, failing agreement between them to the contrary, to extend its territorial sea beyond the median line every point of which is equidistant from the nearest points on the baselines from which the breadth of the territorial seas of each of the two States is measured.[12]

With respect to the exclusive economic zone (EEZ), this has been defined as the area beyond and adjacent to the territorial sea under which the rights and jurisdiction of the coastal State and the rights and freedoms of other States are governed by the relevant provisions of the UNCLOS.[13] The UNCLOS grants sovereign rights to the coastal State with respect to its EEZ 'for the purpose of exploring and exploiting, conserving and managing the natural resources' as well as 'with regard to other activities for the economic exploitation and exploration of the zone'.[14] It is worth noting that the EEZ shall not extend beyond 200 nautical miles from the baselines from which the breadth of the territorial sea is measured.[15]

As regards the continental shelf (CS), it is the area comprising:

> the seabed and subsoil of the submarine areas that extend beyond its territorial sea throughout the natural prolongation of the land territory to the outer edge of the continental margin, or to a distance of 200 nautical miles from the baselines from which the breadth of the territorial sea is measured where the outer edge of the continental margin does not extend to that distance.[16]

As with the EEZ, the UNCLOS confers sovereign rights on the coastal State for the purpose of exploring and exploiting the natural resources in its CS.[17] It is worth noting that while as a general rule both the CS and the EEZ are not to extend beyond 200 nautical miles, the UNCLOS makes it possible for a claim to be made for a distance not exceeding 350 nautical miles with respect to the CS alone.[18]

The UNCLOS 1982 makes similar provisions for the delimitation of both the EEZ[19] and the CS[20] between States with opposite or adjacent coasts. The delimitation shall be effected by agreement on the basis of international law, as referred to in Article 38 of the Statute of the International Court of Justice (ICJ), in order to achieve an equitable solution. The problem with maritime delimitation usually arises when the distance between two opposite littoral States is less than 24 nautical miles (nm) and 400 nm. This makes it impossible for each State to claim its full entitlement of 12 nm and 200 nm for their territorial sea and continental shelf respectively.[21] It is this inability to agree that usually leads to different States approaching the ICJ and, lately, the ITLOS (International Tribunal for the Law of the Sea) to make their respective claims and, in some instances, such disputes may lead to conflicts between the States.

Dispute resolution with respect to international maritime boundaries

Where two or more States have a dispute with respect to their international maritime boundaries, several steps have to be taken to resolve them in accordance with international law. Thus, different States have approached notably the ICJ to settle their disputes over maritime boundaries with the Court using its powers to effect the delimitation of maritime boundaries. However, according to geographers, about 400 unresolved boundary issues potentially exist.[22] This underscores the importance of continuous discussions about maritime boundary disputes and how such disputes may be peacefully resolved. According to Ighiehon:

> [T]hough the United Nations Law of the Sea Convention 1982 (UNCLOS) tried to settle the limits and entitlement of littoral states to relevant maritime zones ... the number of delimitation disputes between states pending before the International Court of Justice is but evidence that the matter is yet to be fully settled.[23]

Article 15 of the United Nations Convention on the Law of the Sea (UNCLOS) 1982 provides that where the same continental shelf is adjacent to the territories of States which are adjacent or opposite to each other, the boundary of the CS shall be determined based on the agreement between the parties. In the absence of such agreement, and unless the boundary line is justified by special circumstances, the boundary shall be determined by the application of the equidistance principle.[24] It therefore appears that delimitation of the territorial sea, the continental shelf and the exclusive economic zone will follow three principles, i.e. agreement, the equidistance/median line principle and special circumstances, with priority being given to agreements. For ease of understanding, 'equidistance' refers to 'the line every point of which is equidistant from the nearest points of the baselines from which the breadth of the territorial sea of each of the two States is measured'.[25] It should be noted that the UN Convention on the Continental Shelf (UNCOCS) 1958 contains a similar definition 'but employs the term "median line" for an equidistant line between opposite States and refers only to a boundary determined by application of the principle of equidistance in the case of adjacent States'.[26]

Some judicial authorities on delimitation

Delimiting or demarcating the continental shelf is an issue that could pose significant challenges, and when parties are unable to agree among themselves they turn to the International dispute settlement. The first delimitation of the continental shelf cases was brought before the ICJ in the 1969 judgment of the North Sea Continental Shelf cases between Germany and Denmark on the one hand and Germany and the Netherlands on the other.[27] The Court in these cases rejected the submissions of both Denmark and the Netherlands that delimitation should be consistent with the equidistance principle; rather, it held that the continental shelf was a natural prolongation of the State's land territory, and therefore the principle behind the Truman declaration was applicable.[28] The Court maintained that the equidistance principle was not binding on the parties as it was just a method of delimitation and not a principle of customary international law.[29]

Again, in the 1984 Gulf of Maine Case[30] between Canada and the United States of America, the ICJ was asked to draw a single line to delimit the area of dispute. The Court maintained that delimitation ought to be by agreement or the application of equitable criteria as well as practical methods to achieve equal results.[31] The ICJ, as in the North Sea cases, rejected applying the median–special circumstances method in the delimitation of the maritime boundary.[32] This principle was also applied in the 1985 Libya v. Malta[33] case where the Court refused to accept the median line principle but departed from the ruling in the North Sea cases, and thus failed to accept the argument that the continental shelf is a natural prolongation of the land and thereby belonged to the State. The Court maintained that the median principle was not a principle of customary international law and therefore not the only permissible method of delimitation.[34]

It was not until the 1993 ICJ ruling in the Denmark v. Norway[35] case that the Court held that for the purpose of delimitation of the CS and EEZ, it would be appropriate to begin with a median line while taking into consideration any relevant circumstances.[36] Also relevant is the maritime delimitation in the Black Sea case between Romania and Ukraine[37] where the parties submitted the matter to the ICJ for determination after several attempts to reach an agreement failed. In that case, the Court maintained that the appropriate starting point in any delimitation exercise would be by applying the equidistance principle and then considering any relevant circumstances which may warrant a shift in that line.[38] It took into consideration the Serpents Island as a relevant circumstance, thus shifting the line in favour of Ukraine.[39] This position was then re-emphasised in the Qatar v. Bahrain[40] case where the ICJ held that:

> even if it were appropriate to apply ... customary law concerning the continental shelf as developed in the decided cases, it is in accordance with precedents to begin with median line as a provisional line and then ask whether 'special circumstances' require any adjustment or shifting of that line.[41]

While what amounts to special circumstance remains a fluid concept devoid of precise definition, the Court in the above case stated that special circumstance includes islands, historical factors or those 'circumstances which might modify the result produced by an unqualified application of the equidistance principle'.[42] From the foregoing, it can be said that the equidistance–special circumstances principle is the established legal formula for the delimitation of the maritime boundary in the absence of any previous agreement.

Legal basis for the adoption of a JDA

The legal basis for JDAs can be traced to Articles 74 (3) and 83 (3) UNCLOS which contain provisions relating to the delimitation of the EEZ and CS respectively. These identical sections provide that:

> the States concerned, in a spirit of understanding and cooperation, shall make every effort to enter into provisional arrangements of a practical nature and, during this transitional period, not to jeopardize or hamper the reaching of the final agreement. Such arrangements shall be without prejudice to the final delimitation.

The justification for this was summarised by Lagoni, who stated that 'the principal object and purpose of paragraph 3 is to further the provisional utilisation of the area to be delimited',[43] by offering practical solution which allows development to proceed even where there is a boundary dispute between the parties[44] which may take a long time to finalise. Although the above provisions did not specifically mention a JDA, Yusuf opines that

> a closer examination of these articles and the relevant practices of states reveal that the creation of a joint development zone, pending boundary delimitation, to develop offshore petroleum resources certainly qualifies as an example of a 'provisional arrangement'.[45]

The Joint Development Agreement has received judicial support. For instance, in the North Sea Continental Shelf cases, the ICJ stated that:

> If ... the delimitation leaves to the Parties areas that overlap, these are to be divided between them in agreed proportions or, failing agreement, equally, unless they decide on a regime of joint jurisdiction, user, or exploitation for the zones of overlap or any part of them.[46]

In his separate opinion, Judge Jessup further opined that the rationale for joint exploitation is appropriate in cases involving the preservation of the unity of deposit as it offers a complete example of full cooperation in both exploitation and profit sharing.[47] Furthermore, the Arbitral Tribunal in the case of Eritrea and Yemen, while encouraging the parties to adopt a joint exploitation arrangement, stated that 'The body of state practice in the exploitation of resources that straddle maritime boundaries import that Eritrea and Yemen should give every consideration to the shared or joint or unitised exploitation of any such resources.'[48]

More recently, in the case of Guyana v. Suriname, the Arbitral Tribunal gave strong judicial support for the JDA when it held that from the provisions of Articles 74(3) and 83(3) of UNCLOS, there is an obligation on disputing parties to 'make every effort to enter into provisional arrangements of a practical nature and not jeopardise or hamper the reaching of a final delimitation agreement'.[49] According to the Tribunal, the obligation of entering into a provisional arrangement was designed 'to promote interim regimes and practical measures that could pave the way for provisional utilization of disputed areas pending delimitation'[50] while negotiating in good faith to achieve such objectives.

The Nigerian–Cameroon land maritime boundary dispute over the oil-rich Bakassi Peninsula

Background of Nigeria and Cameroon oil and gas industry

Oil in commercial quantities was first discovered in Nigeria in 1956 at Olobiri in the current Bayelsa State, with the first export taking place in 1958.[51] Over the years, the oil and gas in Nigeria has earned the status of the key revenue earner for the Nigerian economy. The Nigerian oil and gas sector accounts for more than half of the country's GDP, about 85 per cent of government revenues, and over 90 per cent of exports.[52] Oil output increased from about 5,100 barrels per day (bpd) to about 2.68 million bpd between 1960 and 2012, with government revenue rising from N66 million (naira) in 1970 to over N10 billion in 1980.[53] Nigeria operates a largely monocultural economy and still currently relies heavily on the revenues from its oil and gas sector. This is in spite of the sharp drop in oil prices in recent times and the bombing of oil production facilities by militant activities in the Niger Delta region which have had adverse consequences on daily production.[54] Regarding natural gas, Nigeria ranks in the top ten of natural gas endowment countries with an estimate of 180 trillion cubic feet (Tcf) of natural gas.[55] Unfortunately, it has failed to maximise its gas resources and, rather, flares a significant amount of it.[56] The amount of gas flared could fetch Nigeria approximately US$2.5 billion annually.[57] On the other hand, Cameroon commenced its first oil and gas exploration in 1947 by the French Office of Oil Research. It was in 1972 that oil was first found in commercial quantities in the Betika Oil Field.[58] In 2012, Cameroon had 200 million barrels of proven oil reserves; a drop from its peak of 555 million barrels in 1986.[59] A comparison of proven oil reserves between Nigeria and Cameroon easily reveals that Nigeria is more endowed with this natural resource.

From the above statistics, it would appear that the oil-rich Bakassi region could potentially contribute immensely to the Cameroonian oil reserves and thus lead to greater economic development. Similarly, despite Nigeria's significant oil reserves, it still had strong desires to increase same to satisfy domestic as well as international demands. In addition to the role of pre-colonial and colonial treaties as contributory factors, the conflict of interest and desire to control the oil-rich Bakassi and its hydrocarbon resources led to severe conflict between the two nations.

The Bakassi conflict

In 1913, when Nigeria was a British colony and Cameroon a colony of Germany (and later France after the First World War),[60] Britain and Germany entered into the Anglo-German Treaty where they addressed the issue of the territorial sea and ceded the Bakassi Peninsula, which was a part of the old Calabar Kingdom (Nigeria) to Germany (Cameroon).[61] This secession is evidenced by the Anglo-German Treaty, the Anglo-German Protocol of 12 April 1913 and several correspondences between Britain and Germany.[62] Furthermore, in 1975, the Presidents of both Nigeria and Cameroon signed an agreement, popularly referred to as the Maroua Declaration, which delineated the maritime boundary in favour of Cameroon.[63] After then President Yakubu Gowon of Nigeria, who signed the agreement, was overthrown by a military coup, the Nigerian Government repudiated the agreement, declaring it as invalid, while the Cameroonian Government regarded it as valid and sought to claim sovereignty over the Bakassi.[64]

The area of dispute between Cameroon and Nigeria, which extends from Lake Chad to the sea, has been the subject of dispute between both States from the days they obtained independence in 1960.[65] In the words of President Murtala Muhammed, who succeeded Gowon: 'Nigeria would rather go to war than accept the 'new' border.'[66] Successive governments maintained this and renounced the agreement as being inconsequential, while Cameroon, on the other hand, argued that the 1975 agreement gave it sovereignty over a group of islands on the border of both States, including the Bakassi region.[67]

Cameroon first accused Nigeria of using its population advantage to populate the Bakassi region as a tactic of claiming ownership, thereby scaring the Cameroonians away.[68] On the other hand, Nigeria claimed Cameroon was taxing and assaulting its citizens living in the area, which Cameroon claimed it had the right to do.[69] It was not long after this that Nigeria sent military troops to the region with the aim of protecting its citizens from Cameroonian aggression.[70] The situation worsened on 16 May 1981, when it was reported that Nigerian troops violated Cameroon's territory by entering into the Bakassi region and firing at the Cameroonian navy. In retaliation for this, the Cameroonian troops returned fire, killing five Nigerian soldiers.[71] This act called into question the sovereignty of the Bakassi area, which both countries had refused to address specifically. The armed conflict between Nigeria and Cameroon continued and heightened between 1992 and 1994, when the Cameroonian Government resorted to open oppression in which some Nigerian civilians in Cameroon were killed; in return, Nigeria deployed thousands of military personnel to the Bakassi region, where fighting intensified.[72] It was after this series of fighting that the Cameroonian Government decided to take the matter to the ICJ and deposited an application on 29 March 1994.

The resolution of the conflict

The Cameroonian Government applied to the ICJ seeking a declaration that Cameroon was the owner of the Bakassi and that Nigeria had violated international obligations by occupying the area, hence demanding an order for Nigeria to withdraw its troops from the area and pay reparation.[73] Also, the Court was asked to determine and delimit the maritime boundary area beyond the area fixed by the 1975 agreement, which Nigeria declared as invalid while also contesting the jurisdiction of the Court in its preliminary objections.

According to Cameroon, the delimitation between it and Nigeria was divided into two sections: the territorial sea leading up to point G and the CS/EEZ area beyond point G.[74]

Cameroon argued that the delimitation of the territorial sea up to point G (including the Bakassi area) should be governed by previous agreements such as the Anglo-German Agreement of 11 March 1913, the Cameroon–Nigeria Agreement of 4 April 1971 and the Maroua Declaration of 1 June 1975.[75] Nigeria, on the other hand, argued that these agreements were not binding because the National Assembly did not ratify them and the National Assembly had in particular repudiated the 1975 agreement.[76] Nigeria also argued that since it had occupied the region for a long time, the region belonged to it.[77] It further argued that any delimitation carried out by the ICJ would affect the rights of third-party States and that there was a requirement of prior negotiations which had not been satisfied.[78] The Court rejected these arguments and ruled by a vote of 13 to 3 that the agreements between Nigeria and Cameroon were valid and subsisting, which meant that the oil-rich Bakassi region belonged to Cameroon.[79]

In arriving at this conclusion, the Court started by considering the status and effect of the treaties and agreements.[80] The Court observed that some treaties were for purposes of protection while others were created for acquiring territorial title, which the Nigeria-Cameroon treaties, notably the 1884 Treaty sought to give, and it did give the title of the Bakassi region to Cameroon.[81] Therefore, the Court in its judgment of Thursday 10 October 2002 ruled in favour of Cameroon and declared Bakassi as a part of Cameroon.

With the intervention of the then Secretary-General of the United Nations, Kofi Anan, including several bilateral meetings between the Presidents of both countries, Nigeria was able to hand over the Bakassi region to the Cameroonian Government by signing the Greentree Agreement on 12 June 2006.[82] This was achieved under the watchful eyes of UN envoy Kieran Prendergast and representatives of the UK, France, Germany and the USA, who were present as Nigeria's Minister of Justice Bayo Ojo and his Cameroonian counterpart Maurice Kamto signed the official documents which transferred sovereignty of the Bakassi region to Cameroon.[83] As will be seen in the subsequent segment, this simple act of signing did not automatically lead to an end of the conflict and uncertainties.

Disputes and uncertainties post-ICJ judgment

While many saw the ICJ judgment and the subsequent signing of the Greentree Agreement as an end to the crisis, this was not the view shared by indigenes of the Bakassi region. Professor Boniface Egboka, an indigene of the area, opined that the ICJ judgment was a 'great tragedy of unimaginable magnitude and dimension for the Bakassi people'.[84] It appears this opinion is shared by the vast majority of the 150,000–300,000 inhabitants of the Bakassi who condemned Nigeria's decision to cede their ancestral home to Cameroon.[85] This led to pockets of conflict between some indigenes of the Bakassi who were willing to join Cameroon and those who were not.[86]

The situation also took a somewhat unanticipated turn with the quest of the indigenes of the Bakassi region to become an autonomous, independent State. A group called the Bakassi Self-Determination Movement (BSDM) declared, on behalf of the Bakassi people, its strong desire to be independent of Cameroon and Nigeria in November 2006.[87] According to the leader of the group, 'we insist on our natural right to determine our future ... If Nigeria does not want us, we choose to go it alone and not with Cameroon.' In line with this desire, a new flag was designed for the purpose. To this end, the indigenes of Bakassi consider the ICJ judgment as irrelevant and appear to have completely disregarded the ruling. The question is, if the ICJ has ruled that the Bakassi region belongs to Cameroon, does that also include the people in it? Also, if the indigenes of the area refuse to vacate their land according to the decision of the ICJ, what else can be done? These are grave uncertainties that remain unresolved.

Still on the disputes and uncertainties, in 2007 the Nigerian Senate attempted to repudiate the 2006 Greentree Agreement, declaring it as illegal because it was not brought to the Senate for ratification.[88] This act showed the unwillingness of the Nigerian Government to hand over the Bakassi region and thereby lose 76 oil wells to Cameroon, despite the ICJ ruling. Another incident was the November 2007 killing of 21 Cameroonian soldiers in the Bakassi region as a result of boundary conflicts.[89] At some point, the then Nigerian President ordered that Nigeria return to the ICJ for a review of its decision.[90] It is also worth noting that the indigenes of the disputed Bakassi area sued the Nigerian Federal Government at the Abuja Federal High Court, asking the Court for an order voiding the Greentree Agreement that Nigeria signed with Cameroon in 2006.[91]

The disputes and uncertainties which occurred in the aftermath of the ICJ judgment lend credence to the argument that utilising a JDA would have been a more effective tool at the early stages of the dispute between Nigeria and Cameroon. On a positive note, the maritime boundary between Nigeria and Cameroon has been delimited and agreed upon by the parties. Also, the relationship between the countries has improved significantly, due largely to the efforts of the Cameroon–Nigeria Mixed Commission (CNMC) which was established for the purpose of implementing the 2002 ICJ judgment. The CNMC has also approved the recommendations of the Working Group on the Maritime Boundary, which include provisions relating to cross-border cooperation on hydrocarbon deposits straddling the maritime boundary.[92] Thus both countries have agreed in principle for the exploration of any oil and gas deposits straddling their maritime boundaries since the ICJ decision did not make any provisions for such trans-boundary offshore resources.[93] It has also been reported that both countries have drawn up an agreement for joint management of oil resources in the Bakassi area.[94] Despite these efforts and the recommendation of the CNMC, it is important to note that, at the time of this research, no JDA has been implemented between Nigeria and Cameroon. Nevertheless, efforts have been tailored towards the withdrawal and peaceful transfer of authority from Nigeria to Cameroon. The current Nigerian President, Muhammadu Buhari, has further given an assurance that he will ensure the faithful implementation of the Greentree Agreement, which regulates the ceding of Bakassi to Cameroon.[95] Thus, even though there remains a high level of discontent among the indigenes of the Bakassi region as a result of the ICJ's decision, progress is being made in bringing peace to both countries.

The joint development agreement between Nigeria and Sao Tome and Principe (STP)

The quest of maximising hydrocarbon resources has been the motivation for most maritime boundary conflicts/Joint Development Agreement, and the Nigeria– Sao Tome and STP experience is no exception. This is particularly as the Gulf of Guinea region is one that is significantly enriched with hydrocarbon resources, and both countries, as well as multinational oil companies, are eager to get their fair share.[96] It is suggested that the pressures from the multinational companies and the adverse experiences of the Nigeria–Cameroon conflict significantly contributed to the speedy and smooth negotiation process.[97] Having analysed the failure of both the Nigeria and Cameroonian Governments to adopt a JDA as a provisional measure amid maritime boundary conflicts and the consequences thereof, the Nigeria–Sao Tome and Principe case study is used in this chapter to illustrate the benefits of joint cooperation through the adoption of a JDA in the face of maritime boundary conflicts and uncertainties.

Like most JDAs, the Nigeria–STP JDA began with maritime boundary disagreement. Sao Tome and Principe unilaterally claimed an equidistance line boundary with Nigeria while, on the other hand, Nigeria noted that its much longer coastline warranted a substantial adjustment in its favour of the claimed equidistance line and therefore was not prepared to accept the 100 nm line.[98] Although STP was anxious to reach an agreement, it was unwilling to do so on Nigeria's terms. Finally, the Heads of State of both countries met on 29 November 1999 and gave instructions which led to a series of negotiations.[99] After several meetings and deliberations, it was resolved that the issue of boundary delimitation should be forgone. Therefore, in the interest of cooperation between both parties and having regard to the unresolved differences in their positions, they agreed it would be beneficial to create a JDZ in the area of overlapping claims.[100] It can be argued that this was a relatively smooth process from the 1990 start of negotiations to the formal signing of the treaty in 2001 and the establishment of the Joint Ministerial/Technical Committee in 2002.[101] Perhaps the lessons from the then ongoing Nigeria–Cameroon conflict and external influence from the multinational oil companies contributed to this.

The JDA Treaty contains an appendix and an MOU, and runs to 53 articles.[102] Only sections relevant to the establishment and operation of the joint development agreement will be discussed. For instance, Article 2.1 establishes the JDZ by the state parties for the purpose of joint exploration. Article 3.1 sets out the principles of the joint development. It states that:

> Within the Zone, there shall be joint control by the state parties of the exploration for an exploitation of resources, aimed at achieving optimum commercial utilisation. The state parties shall share, in the proportions Nigeria 60 per cent, Sao Tome and Princ-ipe 40 per cent, all benefits and obligations arising from development activities carried out in the Zone in accordance with this Treaty.[103]

The Treaty or JDA further sets out three guiding principles: the principles of due respect in Article 3.2 and 3.3; the principles of efficient exploitation of resources in Article 3.3; and finally, the principle of diligent implementation of the treaty.[104] In a 'spirit of understanding and cooperation', these principles demonstrate the level of commitment and political will to ensure a hitch-free JDA. It is evident that the treaty is a fulfilment of the requirement of paragraph 3 of Articles 74 and 83 to 'make every effort to enter into a provisional agreement of a practical nature'.[105]

The JDA is structured to contain a single article on definition, which is contained in the preliminary section. Technical terms like 'contract area', 'installations', 'development contract' and 'operating agreement' are defined. The issues of impartiality and conflict of interest are contained in Article 15, while the confidentiality clause is contained in Article 16. While the Joint Ministerial Council has overall responsibility for all matters relating to the exploration and exploitation of the joint development area, the Joint Authority is established to manage the activities relating to the exploration and exploitation of the resources in the JDZ.[106] Regarding finance, Article 17 provides that 'the Authority shall be financed from revenues collected as a result of its activities'.[107]

The JDZ which covers an area of 34,540 square kilometres has provided several oil blocks for exploration. So far, eight wells have been drilled in four blocks in the JDZ region. The most recent development in the region is the Obo-1, which had its production-sharing contract signed on 9 June 2015.[108]

Although the negotiations towards the actualisation of the JDZ were relatively smooth and the focus of this chapter has been on the utilisation of the JDA model in the face of maritime boundary conflicts and uncertainties, it is pertinent to note there could be some challenges in the operation and management of the JDZ. For instance, the Nigeria–Sao Tome and Principe JDA was faced with some significant operational and managerial setbacks. In July 2013, TOTAL withdrew after drilling two wells because 'the find was too limited to justify further investment'.[109] Also, two other companies, Sinopec and Addax, also withdrew from blocks 2–4 for the same reasons. Furthermore, according to the 2014 Extractive Industries Transparency Initiative (EITI) Report, while Nigeria was entitled to US$56.6 million in 2005, only about US$7.1 million was paid. This was because the bank (Hallmark Bank) that was responsible for the payment went bankrupt.[110] Unfortunately, the management of the JDZ has been accused of corruption,[111] and the EITI Report reveals that about US$99.9 million cannot be confirmed as payments to the JDA.[112] Despite these challenges, all stakeholders are optimistic about the future of the JDA and the economic benefits for both countries.

JDA as an alternative in maritime boundary disputes

The advantages of a JDA to disputing coastal States cannot be emphasised enough. This is because it ensures harmonious exploration and exploitation of trans-boundary resources in the interest of disputing States pending final delimitation. It is important to stress that the adoption of a JDA is typically a provisional measure and, as such, it does not prevent a country from pursuing its case for maritime delimitation at the ICJ. We believe that if adopted at the early stages of the dispute, a JDA would have fostered economic development for the Bakassi region, increasing revenue for both disputing countries while encouraging increased trade between Nigeria and Cameroon.[113] This would have further promoted peaceful co-existence among inhabitants and strengthened the bilateral relationship between Nigeria and Cameroon, while helping to build and consolidate the lost and historic bridges between both countries.[114]

It is conceded that a JDA does not automatically constitute a permanent solution to maritime boundary disputes. Its underlying notion, however, is to promote cooperation and peaceful co-existence among disputing countries. Where the JDA is adopted as a provisional measure, it serves as an alternative to a moratorium or confrontation and conflict.[115] In this way, disputing countries can gain benefits from the disputed area pending the final determination of their boundaries, and in some cases it could also serve as 'final measure' where the parties decide to completely put aside the issue of boundary delimitation. Insofar as the maritime boundary dispute between the countries was largely because of the potential resources in the Bakassi region, joint development would have been a wiser option. It is submitted that adoption of a JDA in the early stages of the maritime boundary dispute between Nigeria and Cameroon would have had a significant effect in curbing and possibly preventing the violence that ensued both before and after the ICJ's decision.

It is worth noting that the joint development option still exists between Nigeria and Cameroon, but only for those areas where the hydrocarbon resources are straddling the maritime boundary line agreed to between the countries. Although the CNMC had approved the recommendations of the Working Group on the Maritime Boundary, which suggested cross-border cooperation on hydrocarbon deposits straddling the maritime boundary of both States, unfortunately this suggestion has not led to the adoption of a

JDA.[116] The fact that joint development is still on the cards in the aftermath of the maritime delimitation shows that its utilisation prior to the escalation of conflict would have been in order. Unfortunately, an opportunity was missed to prevent the escalation of hostilities between the two countries with the non-adoption of cooperation building arrangements like the JDA at the early stages of the international maritime boundary dispute.

As stated earlier, the Nigeria–Sao Tome and Principe case study is used in this chapter to illustrate the benefits of joint cooperation through the adoption of a JDA in the face of maritime boundary conflicts and uncertainties. While Nigeria was unable to reach an agreement with Sao Tome and Principe on their maritime boundary, both countries had to establish a JDZ and enter into a JDA which was shared 60:40 in favour of Nigeria.[117] This JDZ has helped to resolve the conflicts and uncertainties which would otherwise have arisen if both counties had not come together in a spirit of cooperation to agree on the JDA as a provisional measure. While the JDA is not perfect, it represents an effective tool in reducing conflicts and uncertainties over the delimitation of maritime boundaries between States.

Conclusion

There is a need for other countries to learn from the mistakes of the Nigeria–Cameroon conflict and promote the use of JDAs in the right circumstances as a conflict prevention and avoidance tool. While admitting the contributions of international law such as UNCLOS and judgments of the international courts and Arbitral Tribunal in resolving maritime boundary disputes, it is clear that certain cases require not just the laws but the necessary political will on the part of the disputing States. This enables them to consider the overall interest of the citizenry as well as the greater economic benefits before engaging in such prolonged and avoidable armed conflict in a bid to resolve their maritime boundary disputes. Approaching the ICJ first without making use of recommended provisional measures such as JDAs could, as was seen in the Nigeria–Cameroon situation, lead to greater conflict and uncertainty.

The Nigeria–Cameroon dispute highlights the case of two coastal States which were eager to control the mineral resources believed to be within their respective jurisdictions and which would stop at nothing until that goal was achieved. Unfortunately, some of the measures adopted led to severe loss of lives and property which would have been avoided had the parties taken a more harmonious means of joint resource management. It is hoped that this chapter will prove to be instructive to other disputing States, such as China and Japan,[118] to consider provisional options like the JDA rather than resort to armed conflict.

The relevance of peace in any country, both developed and developing, cannot be emphasised enough. While it ensures the protection of lives and property, it also enhances economic development and stability. It is for these reasons and more that countries should avoid conflicts, either domestic or otherwise. The question is, could the Nigeria–Cameroon dispute over the oil-rich Bakassi region have been avoided? The answer to this is in the affirmative, primarily because it has been established that the cause of the conflict was principally the management of the potential hydrocarbon resources in the region. Therefore, rather than fight and displace indigenes of the region, a JDA would have been a more economic means of maximisation and management of the resources for the economic good of both countries. With a JDA, it is highly possible that there would have been no reason to visit the ICJ in the first instance. Even if such a visit to the ICJ was contemplated after adopting a JDA, at least the incidences of violence would most likely have been averted.

In light of the above, it can be seen that there is a need for disputing countries to work together towards adopting JDAs at the early stages of maritime boundary disputes. The JDA between Nigeria and Sao Tome and Principe represents a classic example of the benefits of cooperation between States with respect to their maritime boundary disputes. JDAs are believed to be relevant instruments in ensuring a peaceful resolution of trans-boundary conflicts while 'providing a legal mechanism for the development of offshore petroleum resources, thereby ensuring a "win–win" situation for the states involved'.[119]

From the above discussion, it has been established that, despite the presence of a robust international law regime about maritime boundary issues, conflicts and uncertainties persist occasioned by the sensitivity and peculiarity of certain cases such as the Nigeria–Cameroon dispute. From the above case study, it is further revealed that certain maritime disputes cannot be automatically resolved by a decision of the ICJ, hence the need for a more cooperative approach to encourage joint exploration of hydrocarbons in the interest of disputing States, as with the JDZ established between Nigeria and Sao Tome and Principe. The JDA embodies this cooperative approach and acts as a provisional measure before delimitation with the possibility of being converted to a permanent arrangement post-delimitation. There is, therefore, the call for disputing countries to engage in sincere and meaningful negotiations to resolve their differences and encourage the use of a JDA as a useful tool in promoting joint development of the resources and preventing possible armed conflict. Such an adopted JDA will simply serve as an agreement between two states to develop, so as to share jointly in agreed proportions... the offshore oil and gas in a designated zone of the seabed and subsoil of the continental shelf to which either or both of the participating States may be entitled in international law.

Notes

1 This chapter is an extended version of an article published by Eddy Lenusira Wifa, Mark Amakoromo and Ibiateli Johnson-Ogbo titled 'Turning Towards A Joint Development Agreement in the Midst of Disputes and Uncertainties over International Maritime Boundaries: Nigeria–Cameroon Dispute as a Case Study', *Oil, Gas and Energy Law (OGEL) Journal* (2017) 1, online at www.ogel.org/article.asp?key=3675. While the said article only focuses on the Nigeria–Cameroon conflict and how the situation could have possibly been avoided if a JDA was adopted, this chapter presents a more robust discussion on the issue. It extends the discussion to the Nigeria– Sao Tome and Principe maritime boundary conflict and the role a JDA played in resolving it. Eddy Lenusira Wifa, the corresponding author, can be contacted by email at wifa.eddy14@abdn.ac.uk.

2 Junaidu Bello Marshall, 'Joint Development of Offshore Oil and Gas in the Gulf of Guinea: A Case of Energy Security for Nigeria and Cameroon' (2014) 32 *Journal of Law, Policy and Globalization* 138.

3 Clive Schofield, 'Defining Areas for Joint Development in Disputed Waters', in S. Wu and N. Hong (eds), *Recent Developments in the South China Sea Dispute: The Prospect of a Joint Development Regime* (London: Routledge, 2014) 78–98.

4 Ibrahim F. Shihata and William T. Onarato, 'Joint Development of International Petroleum Resources in Undefined Disputed Areas', in Gerald Blake, Chia Lin Sien, Carl Grundy-Warr, Martin Pratt and Clive Schofield (eds), *Boundaries and Energy: Problems and Prospects* (London: Kluwer Law International, 1998) 433.

5 Z. Gao, 'The Legal Concept and Aspects of Joint Development in International Law' (1998) 13 *Oxford Year Book* 112.

6 R. Lagoni, *Report on Joint Development of Non-Living Resources in the Exclusive Economic Zone* (Warsaw Conference of the International Committee on the Exclusive Economic Zone, International Law Association 1988) 2.
7 D.H. Anderson, 'Strategies for Dispute Resolution: Negotiating Joint Agreements', in Gerald Blake, Chia Lin Sien, Carl Grundy-Warr, Martin Pratt and Clive Schofield (eds), *Boundaries and Energy: Problems and Prospects* (London: Kluwer Law International, 1998) 475.
8 R.R. Churchill, M. Nordquist and S.H. Lay (eds) *New Directions in the Law of the Sea, Vol. V* (New York: Oceana, 1976) 207; UN Doc. No. ST/LEG/SER.B/161,409. See also Bureau of Intelligence and Research, Department of State, United States of America, 'Limits of the Sea: Continental Shelf Boundary Bahrain–Saudi Arabia' (10 March 1970), online at www.state.gov/documents/organization/62003.pdf. Others include the Qatar and United Arab Emirates Agreement, Iran and Sharjah Agreement.
9 J.G. Merrills and Malcolm D. Evans, 'The Land and Maritime Boundary Case (Cameroon v. Nigeria): The Interventions by Equatorial Guinea' (2000) 49 *ICLQ* 720–723. See Treaty between the Federal Republic of Nigeria and the Republic of Equatorial Guinea concerning their maritime boundary (23 September 2000), online at www.un.org/depts/los/LEGISLATIONANDTREATIES/PDFFILES/TREATIES/NGA-GNQ2000MB.PDF, accessed 4 April 2017; Agreement Concerning Joint Development of Southern Part of the Continental Shelf Adjacent to the Two Countries, Signed Seoul on 30 January 1974, online at www.un.org/depts/los/LEGISLATIONANDTREATIES/PDFFILES/TREATIES/jap-kor1974south.pdf, accessed 4 April 2017.
10 Ana Bastida, S. Mahmud, T. Walde and A. Okoye, 'Cross-Border Unitization and Joint Development Agreements: An International Law Perspective' (2006–2007) 29 *HJIL* 335, 401.
11 Oladipo Sholanke, 'Delimiting the Territorial Sea between Nigeria and Cameroon: A Rational Approach' (1993) 42 *ICLQ* 398–411.
12 UNCLOS 1982, art. 15.
13 UNCLOS 1982, art. 55.
14 UNCLOS 1982, art. 56.
15 UNCLOS 1982, art. 57.
16 UNCLOS 1982, art. 76.
17 UNCLOS 1982, art. 77 (1).
18 UNCLOS 1982, art. 76 (5).
19 UNCLOS 1982, art. 74.
20 UNCLOS 1982, art. 83.
21 Y. Tanaka, *The International Law of the Sea* (Cambridge: Cambridge University Press, 2012).
22 Mark Osa Igiehon, 'Present International Law on Delimitation of the Continental Shelf' (2006) 18 *IELTR* 208–215.
23 Ibid.
24 UNCLOS 1982, art. 15. It must be noted that similar provisions are contained in articles 74 and 83 regarding the continental shelf and exclusive economic zones respectively.
25 UNCLOS 1982b art. 15.
26 Nugzar Dundua, 'Delimitation of Maritime Boundaries between the Adjacent States' (2006–2007) United Nations – The Nippon Foundation, p. 15; UNCOCS 1958, art. 6.
27 North Sea Continental Shelf Cases, Judgment of 20 February 1969, www.icj-cij.org/docket/index.php?sum=295&code=cs2&p1=3&p2=3&case=52&k=cc&p3=5, 31 March 2017.
28 Ibid.
29 Ibid.
30 Case Concerning Delimitation of the Maritime Boundary in the Gulf of Maine Area, Judgment of 12 October 1984, www.icj-cij.org/docket/index.php?sum=346&p1=3&p2=3&case=67&p3=5, accessed 31 March 2017.
31 Ibid.
32 Y. Tanaka, *The International Law of the Sea* (Cambridge: Cambridge University Press, 2012).
33 Case Concerning the Continental Shelf (Libyan Arab Jamahiriya/Malta), Judgment of 3 June 1985, www.icj-cij.org/docket/index.php?sum=353&p1=3&p2=3&case=68&p3=5, accessed 31 March 2017.
34 Ibid. See also Mark Osa Igiehon, 'Present International law on Delimitation of the Continental Shelf' (2006) 18 *IELTR* 208–215.

35 Case Concerning Maritime Delimitation in the Area between Greenland and Jan Mayen (Denmark v. Norway), Judgment of 14 June 1993, www.icj-cij.org/docket/index.php?sum=401&p1=3&p2=3&case=78&p3=5, accessed 31 March 2017.
36 Ibid.
37 Case Concerning Maritime Delimitation in the Black Sea (Romania v. Ukraine), Judgment of 3 February 2009, documents available at www.haguejusticeportal.net/eCache/DEF/6/185.html, accessed 31 March 2017.
38 Ibid.
39 Ibid.
40 Maritime Delimitation and Territorial Questions between Qatar and Bahrain (Qatar v. Bahrain), Summary of the Judgment of 16 March 2001, www.icj-cij.org/docket/index.php?sum=443&p1=3&p2=3&case=87&p3=5, accessed 31 March 2017.
41 Ibid. at [51].
42 Ibid. at [55].
43 Rainer Lagoni, 'Interim Measures Pending Maritime Delimitation Agreements' (1984) 78 *AJIL* 354.
44 Yusuf M. Yusuf, 'Is Joint Development a Panacea for Maritime Boundary Dispute and for the Exploitation of Offshore Transboundary Petroleum Deposits?' (2009) 4 *IELR* 130–137, 134.
45 Ibid. at 135.
46 North Sea Continental Shelf Cases, 1969 *ICJ Rep.* 3, at page 53, para. 101(C)(2).
47 The Agreement Concerning the Delimitation of the Continental Shelf in the Persian Gulf between Bahrain and Saudi Arabia, 22 February 1958, reproduced in R.R. Churchill, M. Nordquist and S.H. Lay (eds) *New Directions in the Law of the Sea, Vol. V* (New York: Oceana, 1976) at page 207.
48 *Territorial Sovereignty and Scope of the Dispute (Eritrea and Yemen)*, 9 October 1998, 22 *RIAA* 209, Eritrea–Yemen Arbitration Award Phase II, para. 86.
49 Award, ICGJ 370 (PCA 2007), 17th September 2007, Permanent Court of Arbitration [PCA] at para. 465. See generally paras. 459–486.
50 Para. 460, ibid.
51 History of the Nigerian Petroleum Industry, online at www.nnpcgroup.com/NNPCBusiness/Businessinformation/OilGasinNigeria/IndustryHistory.aspx, accessed 31 March 2017.
52 Alex Gboyega, Tina Soreide, Tuan Minh Le and G.P. Shukla, 'Political Economy of the Petroleum Sector in Nigeria' (2011) World Bank Policy Research Working Paper No. 5779, 7.
53 Uwafiokun Idemudia, 'The Resource Curse and the Decentralization of Oil Revenue: The Case of Nigeria' (2012) 35 *Journal of Cleaner Production* 183–193.
54 Freedom C. Onuoha, 'The Resurgence of Militancy in Nigeria's Oil-Rich Niger Delta and the Dangers of Militarisation' (8 June 2016), Aljazeera Centre for Studies, online at http://studies.aljazeera.net/en/reports/2016/06/resurgence-militancy-nigerias-oil-rich-niger-delta-dangers-militarisation-160608065729726.html, accessed 31 March 2017.
55 Nigerian National Petroleum Corporation, 'Development of Nigeria's Oil Industry', online at www.nnpcgroup.com/nnpcbusiness/businessinformation/oilgasinnigeria/developmentoftheindustry.aspx, accessed 31 March 2017.
56 US Energy Information Administration, 'Country Analysis Brief: Nigeria' (6 May 2016), p. 12, online at www.marcon.com/library/country_briefs/Nigeria/nigeria.pdf, accessed 31 March 2017.
57 Green Deal Nigeria, 'Nigeria's Gas: Wealth for All?' online at https://ng.boell.org/sites/default/files/uploads/2014/11/facts_about_nigerias_gas.pdf, accessed 31 March 2017.
58 Freshfields Brackhaus Deringer, 'Cameroon', online at www.freshfields.com/uploadedFiles/SiteWide/News_Room/Insight/Africa_ENR/Cameroon/Cameroon%20oil%20and%20gas.pdf, 31 March 2017.
59 KPMG, 'Oil and Gas in Africa: Africa's Reserves Potential and Prospects', online at www.kpmg.com/Africa/en/IssuesAndInsights/Articles-Publications/Documents/Oil%20and%20Gas%20in%20Africa.pdf, 31 March 2017.
60 Felicia Price, 'The Bakassi Peninsula: The Border Dispute between Nigeria and Cameroon', ICE Case Studies No. 163 (November 2005), online at www1.american.edu/ted/ice/nigeria-cameroon.htm, 31 March 2017.
61 Justice M. Mbuh, 'The Bakassi Peninsula Dispute', in Justice M. Mbuh, *International Law and Conflict: Resolving Border and Sovereignty Disputes in Africa*' (Los Angeles: Universe, 2004).
62 Ibid.

63 Ibid.
64 Oladipo Sholanke, 'Delimiting the Territorial Sea between Nigeria and Cameroon: A Rational Approach' (1993) 42 *ICLQ* 398–411.
65 J.G. Merrills and Malcolm D. Evans, 'The Land and Maritime Boundary Case (Cameroon v. Nigeria): The Interventions by Equatorial Guinea' (2000) 49 *ICLQ* 720–723, 721.
66 *Sunday Punch* (Nigerian newspaper), 24 May 1981.
67 Oladipo Sholanke, 'Delimiting the Territorial Sea between Nigeria and Cameroon: A Rational Approach' (1993) 42 *ICLQ* 398–411.
68 Paragraph 1.67 of Cameroon's Memorial of 16 March 1995.
69 Ibid.
70 Justice M. Mbuh, 'The Bakassi Peninsula Dispute' in Justice M. Mbuh, *International Law and Conflict: Resolving Border and Sovereignty Disputes in Africa* (Los Angeles: Universe, 2004).
71 Ibid.
72 'Nigeria/Cameroon: Blundering into Battle' (16 April 1994) 35(8) *Africa Confidential* 6.
73 Ibid.
74 Nuno Sergio Marques Antunes, 'The Pending Maritime Delimitation in the Cameroon v. Nigeria Case: A Piece in the Jigsaw Puzzle of the Gulf of Guinea' (2000) 15 *IJMCL* 163–192.
75 Ibid.
76 Yoshifumi Tanaka, 'Reflections on the Maritime Delimitation in the Cameroon/Nigeria Case' (2004) 53 *ICLQ* 369–406.
77 Ibid.
78 J.G. Merrills and Malcolm D. Evans, 'The Land and Maritime Boundary Case (Cameroon v. Nigeria): The Interventions by Equatorial Guinea' (2000) 49 *ICLQ* 720–723.
79 Alberto Alvarez-Jimenez, 'Boundary Agreement in the International Court of Justice's Case Law, 2000–2010' (2012) 23 *EJIL* 495–515.
80 Ibid.
81 J.G. Merrills and Malcolm D. Evans, 'The Land and Maritime Boundary Case (Cameroon v. Nigeria): The Interventions by Equatorial Guinea' (2000) 49 *ICLQ* 720–723.
82 'Agreement Between the Republic of Cameroon and the Federal Republic of Nigeria Concerning the Modalities of Withdrawal and Transfer of Authority in the Bakassi Peninsula', online at www.peaceau.org/uploads/cn-agreement-12-06-2006.pdf, 31 March 2017.
83 Molem Christopher Sama and Debora Johnson-Ross, 'Reclaiming the Bakassi Kingdom: The Anglophone Cameroon–Nigeria Border' (2005–2006) 13/14 *Afrika Zamani*, online at www.codesria.org/IMG/pdf/06_Sama_Ross.pdf, 31 March 2017. For more details, see, in this book, Chapter 3 by Bayo Ojo on preventive diplomacy and also Chapter 4 by Nkwelle Ekaney on a Cameroonian perspective.
84 Ibid.
85 Ibid.
86 Ibid.
87 Ibid.
88 'Nigeria: Senate Rejects ICJ Ruling on Bakassi, Urges FG to Appeal Judgment', online at http://allafrica.com/stories/201209270105.html, accessed 31 March 2017.
89 Molem Christopher Sama and Debora Johnson-Ross, 'Reclaiming the Bakassi Kingdom: The Anglophone Cameroon–Nigeria Border' (2005–2006) *Afrika Zamani*, online at www.codesria.org/IMG/pdf/06_Sama_Ross.pdf, accessed 31 March 2017.
90 Ibid.
91 Channels Television, 'Bakassi Indigenes Sue FG, Seek Annulment of Green Tree Agreement', online at www.channelstv.com/2012/10/05/bakassi-indigenes-sue-fg-seek-annulment-of-green-tree-agreement/, accessed 31 March 2017.
92 United Nations Office for West Africa, Cameroon–Nigeria Mixed Commission, online at http://unowa.missions.org/Default.aspx?tabid=804, accessed 31 March 2017.
93 Junaidu Bello Marshall, 'Joint Development of Offshore Oil and Gas in the Gulf of Guinea: A Case of Energy Security for Nigeria and Cameroon' (2014) 32 *Journal of Law, Policy and Globalization* 146.
94 'Cameroon–Nigeria Border Settlement Faces Tough Development Challenges', *Guardian*, 16 February 2014, online at www.theguardian.com/globaldevelopment/2014/feb/16/cameroon-nigeria-border-settlement-development-challenges, accessed 31 March 2017.

95 *Premium Times*, 'Buhari: "No Plan to Challenge Cameroon's Ownership of Bakassi Peninsula"', 29 July 2015, online at www.premiumtimes.com/news/headlines/187462-buhari-no-plan-to-challenge-cameroons-ownership-of-bakassi-peninsula.html, accessed 31 March 2017.

96 Huang Wen-bo, 'Analysis of the Nigeria–Sao Tome and Principe Joint Development Agreement and Suggestions for China' (2015) 4(3) *International Journal for Energy and Power Engineering* 123–128.

97 Tanga J. Biang, 'The Joint Development Zone Between Nigeria and Sao Tome and Principe: A Case of Provisional Arrangement in the Gulf of Guinea International Law, State Practice and Prospects for Regional Integration', online at www.un.org/depts/los/nippon/unnff_programme_home/fellows_pages/fellows_papers/tanga_0910_cameroon.pdf, accessed 31 March 2017.

98 Ibid. at p. 26.

99 Ibid.

100 Ibid.

101 Huang Wen-bo, 'Analysis of the Nigeria–Sao Tome and Principe Joint Development Agreement and Suggestions for China' (2015) 4(3) *International Journal for Energy and Power Engineering* 123–128.

102 Treaty Between the Federal Republic of Nigeria and the Democratic Republic of Sao Tome and Principe on the Joint Development of Petroleum and Other Resources, in Respect of Areas of the Exclusive Economic Zone of the Two States, 21 February 2001, online at www.un.org/depts/los/LEGISLATION ANDTREATIES/PDFFILES/TREATIES/STP-NGA2001.PDF, accessed 31 March 2017.

103 Ibid.

104 Ibid.

105 UNCLOS, Article 74 (3) and Article 84 (3).

106 Article 9.

107 Article 17.

108 Nigeria–Sao Tome and Principe Joint Development Authority, 'New JDZ Block-1 Productions Sharing Contract (PSC)', online at www.nstpjda.com/new-jdz-block-1-production-sharing-contractor-psc/, accessed 31 March 2017.

109 PricewaterhouseCoopers & Associados, 'Nigeria Sao Tome and Principe, Joint Development Zone First EITI Report 2003–2013', p. 7, online at www.min-financas.st/phocadownloadpap/ITIE/publicacao/First%20Report%20%202003–2013%20(Nigeria-Sao%20Tome%20and%20Principe).pdf, accessed 31 March 2017.

110 Ibid.

111 *Thisday* (Nigerian newspaper), 5 July 2016, 'Addressing the Nigeria–Sao Tome JDA Imbroglio', online at www.thisdaylive.com/index.php/2016/07/05/addressing-the-nigeria-sao-tome-jda-imbroglio/, accessed 31 March 2017. See also US Department of State, '2013 Investment Climate Statement – Sao Tome and Principe Report', online at www.state.gov/e/eb/rls/othr/ics/2013/204725.htm, accessed 31 March 2017.

112 PricewaterhouseCoopers & Associados, 'Nigeria Sao Tome and Principe, Joint Development Zone First EITI Report 2003–2013', p. 7, online at www.min-financas.st/phocadownloadpap/ITIE/publicacao/First%20Report%20%202003-2013%20(Nigeria-Sao%20Tome%20and%20Principe).pdf, accessed 31 March 2017.

113 Ibid.

114 Ibid.

115 M.J. Valencia and M. Miyoshi, 'Southeast Asian Seas: Joint Development of Hydrocarbons in Overlapping Claim Areas' (1986) 16 *Ocean Development and International Law* 211 at 247.

116 United Nations Office for West Africa, Cameroon–Nigeria Mixed Commission, online at http://unowa.missions.org/Default.aspx?tabid=804, accessed 15 August 2016.

117 J. Tanga Biang, 'The Joint Development Zone between Nigeria and Sao Tome and Principe: A Case of Provisional Arrangement in the Gulf of Guinea International Law, State Practice and Prospects for Regional Integration' (2010), online at www.un.org/depts/los/nippon/unnff_programme_home/fellows_pages/fellows_papers/tanga_0910_cameroon.pdf, accessed 12 August 2016.

118 The East China Sea dispute between China and Japan is one that remains unresolved and is capable of escalating into armed conflict as Japan is currently carrying out military drills and China is issuing military threats; see generally Gao Jianjun, 'Development in the East China Sea: Not an Easier Challenge than Delimitation' (2008) 23 *IJMCL* 39–75.

119 Ibid.

Index

Page numbers in *italics* denote tables.

FSC
www.fsc.org
MIX
Papier | Fördert gute Waldnutzung
FSC® C083411

Kolibri 360 GmbH
Ferdinand-Jühlke-Straße 7
99095 Erfurt, Deutschland
produktsicherheit@kolibri360.de